Growing up and going out

Manchester University Press

STUDIES IN POPULAR CULTURE

General editor: Professor Jeffrey Richards

There has in recent years been an explosion of interest in culture and cultural studies. The impetus has come from two directions and out of two different traditions. On the one hand, cultural history has grown out of social history to become a distinct and identifiable school of historical investigation. On the other hand, cultural studies has grown out of English literature and has concerned itself to a large extent with contemporary issues. Nevertheless, there is a shared project, its aim, to elucidate the meanings and values implicit and explicit in the art, literature, learning, institutions and everyday behaviour within a given society. Both the cultural historian and the cultural studies scholar seek to explore the ways in which a culture is imagined, represented and received, how it interacts with social processes, how it contributes to individual and collective identities and world views, to stability and change, to social, political and economic activities and programmes. This series aims to provide an arena for the cross-fertilisation of the discipline, so that the work of the cultural historian can take advantage of the most useful and illuminating of the theoretical developments and the cultural studies scholars can extend the purely historical underpinnings of their investigations. The ultimate objective of the series is to provide a range of books which will explain in a readable and accessible way where we are now socially and culturally and how we got to where we are. This should enable people to be better informed, promote an interdisciplinary approach to cultural issues and encourage deeper thought about the issues, attitudes and institutions of popular culture.

To buy or to find out more about the books currently available in this series, please go to: https://manchesteruniversitypress.co.uk/series/studies-in-popular-culture/

Growing up and going out

Youth culture, commerce, and leisure space in post-war Britain

Sarah Kenny

MANCHESTER UNIVERSITY PRESS

Copyright © Sarah Kenny 2025

The right of Sarah Kenny to be identified as the author of this work has been asserted in accordance with the Copyright, Designs and Patents Act 1988.

Published by Manchester University Press
Oxford Road, Manchester M13 9PL

www.manchesteruniversitypress.co.uk

British Library Cataloguing-in-Publication Data
A catalogue record for this book is available from the British Library

ISBN 978 1 5261 5264 0 hardback

First published 2025

The publisher has no responsibility for the persistence or accuracy of URLs for any external or third-party internet websites referred to in this book, and does not guarantee that any content on such websites is, or will remain, accurate or appropriate.

Typeset
by Deanta Global Publishing Services, Chennai, India

Contents

List of figures	*page* vi
Series editor's foreword	vii
Acknowledgements	viii
Introduction	1

Part I: Youth and the changing urban environment

1 Out in the city	31
2 The business of leisure	65
3 Regulating youth after dark	96

Part II: Youth, lived experience, and identity

4 Gymslip drinkers	137
5 Leisure, consumption, and identity	174
Conclusion	206
Appendix	215
Bibliography	221
Index	242

Figures

1.1   Cover image for 'Sheffield: City on the Move' campaign, 1970. © Sheffield City Council and Picture Sheffield.   *page* 36

1.2   Exterior of the King Mojo Club, Pitsmoor, Sheffield, 1966. © Sheffield Newspapers Ltd and Picture Sheffield.   52

2.1   Advert placed in the local press for Mecca's 'New Bristol Centre', 20 May 1966. © Reach PLC and Mirrorpix.   72

2.2   Couple dancing the twist, Majestic Ballroom, Newcastle, 1962. © NCJ Archive and Mirrorpix.   80

3.1   Sunday afternoon 'jazz for lunch' session at the Leadmill, Sheffield, 26 January 1986. © Damon Fairclough.   116

3.2   Tiffany's nightclub, formerly the Locarno Ballroom, London Road, Sheffield, 1977. © Sheffield Newspapers Ltd and Picture Sheffield.   126

4.1   Entrance to Shades nightclub, Ecclesall Road, Sheffield, est. 1968. © Ray Brightman and Picture Sheffield.   152

4.2   Promotional image for the opening of the Stone House, Sheffield, 1971. © Sheffield Newspapers Ltd and Picture Sheffield.   161

5.1   Entrance to the Limit, West Street, Sheffield, 1981. © Sheffield Newspapers Ltd and Picture Sheffield.   191

Series editor's foreword

Sarah Kenny argues in her excellent new book that historians of youth culture have overlooked the special dynamics of music consumption, the rise of club cultures, and the development of 'authentic' spaces in post-war Britain as the city centre after dark became a place dedicated to the hedonistic pleasure of the young. She sets out to analyse the spaces of youth leisure to demonstrate how space and place shaped the youthful experience and what young people understood about the places and spaces they frequented. The post-war leisure boom was fuelled by a growing affluence encapsulated in the celebrated dictum of Prime Minister Harold Macmillan: 'Most of our people have never had it so good.' While for the older generation the spread of television ownership, gardening and DIY provided their leisure opportunities, their focus was on the home. For the young, 'going out' was the objective of their leisure. Youth culture evolved rapidly, and the phenomenon of the 'teenage consumer' was identified in 1959 by the sociologist Mark Abrams. Teenagers were well placed to take advantage of the growth of the commercial leisure industry, spawning alongside the traditional gathering place, the pub, new youth-focused venues such as coffee bars, beat clubs, bars, night clubs, dance halls and discotheques. In this context, Sarah Kenny charts in particular the development of a distinct culture of youth drinking. She also traces the attempts of the authorities to regulate the youth market. For memories of the lived experience of teenagers, she draws on over twenty oral interviews conducted with people growing up in Sheffield from the 1960s to the 1990s. This study can usefully be read alongside Laura Harrison's *Dangerous Amusements: Leisure, the Young Working Class and Urban Space in Britain 1870–1939*, published in the series in 2022.

Jeffrey Richards

Acknowledgements

This book has been a long time in the making, and it is a pleasure to be able to thank those who have helped make this possible. My first thanks go to Adrian Bingham for his kind and patient mentorship over the course of many years. His support has provided a model of academic generosity that I try to take forward in my own work. I also extend my thanks to Julie Gottlieb, who supported the project in its early stages with advice and helpful critique.

Undertaking the research for this book would not have been possible without the guidance and expertise of a great number of people who offered their time and knowledge willingly. In particular I would like to thank the staff at Sheffield City Archives, who have provided advice on their collections and suggested materials to consult. Staff at the National Archives, British Library, and Cadbury Research Library have also been generous with their time and insights. I am also indebted to the students, academics, and professional services staff at the University of Sheffield who have worked on the Witness Oral History project to preserve the history of the city. Finally, I owe a significant debt to those people who agreed to be interviewed for this project. Thank you for sharing your stories, photographs, scrapbooks, and time with me. These conversations offered me some of the most joyful moments of research on this project.

A great many friends and colleagues have supported me during the research and writing of this book, and I am grateful for their insights, support, and, when needed, distraction. At the University of Birmingham, colleagues past and present have been generous with their time and expertise. Particular thanks go to Ben Jackson, Zoë Thomas, Matthew Francis, Matt Houlbrook, Sadiah Qureshi, Chris Moores, Mo Moulton, James Pugh, Karen Harvey, and Gavin Schaffer, who have read chapters, drafts, and provided invaluable advice. Thanks also go to Hannah Elizabeth, Liz Goodwin, Laura Harrison, Jenny Crane, Patrick Glen, Matt Worley, David Beckingham, Laura Fenton, Tom Hulme, Sarah Crook, and many others who have read various drafts and talked through ideas with me over a drink. I have been supported by a

Acknowledgements

wide network of academics including those in the Centre for Modern British Studies at the University of Birmingham, Drinking Studies Network, Society for the History of Childhood and Youth, and Subcultures Network. Thanks also go to the anonymous readers and staff at Manchester University Press.

I owe the greatest debt to my friends and family who have ensured I made it this far. Liz, Laura, and Erin have picked me up more times than I care to count. To them, and everybody else who has made Sheffield home, I am grateful every day. Kathryn, Nat, Amy, Emma, Cat, Emily, and Liz have cheered me on for almost fifteen years. My family have always offered endless support, good humour, and much-needed distraction. My husband, David, has been a constant source of support and love. He has shared my frustrations, has celebrated my successes, and has spent many (many) hours patiently listening to me talk about this book. He has always encouraged me, never doubted me, and he has made writing this book infinitely more enjoyable. Finally, I dedicate this book to my parents, Barry and Carolyn, who have been unwavering in their love, belief, and support. This book would not exist without them.

Introduction

In 1972, a promotional film commissioned by Sheffield City Council, *Sheffield: City on the Move*, exclaimed that 'in the years when leisure and income were far less than they are now, Sheffield's nightlife was unsophisticated. Come evening, the majority of those who stopped work rested. Only a few had time and money to spend. It's different now.'[1] Indeed, the opportunities for evening leisure and culture in Sheffield had grown substantially in the years since 1945, having a remarkable effect on both the post-war redevelopment of the city and the lifestyles of young people who lived in the area. The city's first teenage beat club, Club 60, opened in 1960, while the first licensed nightclub, the Heart Beat, opened in 1965. By the time the promotional film was released in the 1970s, the city had a range of nightclubs, cabaret clubs, discotheques, and bars, and as *City on the Move* boasted, the 1,300-capacity Fiesta club – the largest in Europe. Around the same time as *City on the Move* was released, trade magazine *The Stage* pointed to the variety of Northumbria's leisure venues to argue that the region could claim the 'best nightlife outside of London', while in Birmingham there was talk of a 'revolution' in the city's nightlife.[2] This story is one that was repeated throughout Britain.

This is a book about youthful sociability and leisure; about sitting with friends round a table at the local pub, swapping stories from the last week; about walking, arm in arm, through the doors of the local discotheque, lights flashing and speakers pumping; about leaving, sometimes stumbling, and dashing into a taxi or, if lucky, the late bus home. The nightclubs and late-night bars that came to dominate the post-war urban landscape were sites of real social and cultural significance: from the first sip of coffee in a newly opened coffee bar to discos in the refurbished dance hall, youth-oriented evening leisure spaces were central to new patterns of leisure and sociability in the post-war period. The flashing lights, loud music, and dark corners of the local nightspot have held promise for generations of young people and shaped the youthful experience in post-war Britain; the exchange of glances with a crush, the prospect of meeting someone new, dancing with friends to a favourite song, or the pursuit of hedonistic escape.

2   *Growing up and going out*

Growing Up and Going Out explores how, over the course of forty short years, the urban centre after dark was reimagined and remade as a site of youthful pleasure. In the decades after the Second World War, towns and cities across the country experienced a leisure boom driven by relative post-war affluence, urban redevelopment, and unparalleled transformations to both people's lifestyle and their access to leisure time. Leisure-based consumption in the home had undoubtedly risen in the post-war period, becoming a key space for both relaxation and sociability, but a night out on the town remained an important and regular part of many people's lives. This was most true for Britain's teenagers and young adults. Public and semi-public sites of leisure became an integral part of post-war youth culture, playing an increasingly prominent role in young people's lives. Between the 1950s and the 1990s, the leisure opportunities afforded to Britain's youth changed almost beyond recognition: supervised dances were replaced by late-night coffee bars, before discos, rock bars, and nightclubs licensed until the early hours came to dominate the urban leisurescape. Despite significant economic upheaval in many areas of the country, as well as marked social and cultural shifts in young people's lives, the commercial leisure industry continued to thrive throughout the post-war period.

These spaces also transformed the post-war built environment, and the way that young people moved through it. The urban centre after dark has long been seen to hold the potential for immorality, a place associated with 'a hidden world of pleasure, transgression, and adventure'.[3] Many of these associations persisted into the latter part of the twentieth century, yet the growing popularity of late-night commerce in post-war Britain made the urban centre after dark a more accessible and desirable place for leisure. The dark corners of unlit back streets remained, but the high street, once avoided in the late hours, became filled with light spilling out from nearby pubs, the sounds of taxi drop-offs, the greeting of friends, and music escaping from briefly opened doors. Because of this, the desire to regulate the urban night continued. *Growing Up and Going Out* shows clearly how experiences of youth leisure were shaped by attempts to control and regulate these new spaces and, critically, that this was driven by longstanding associations between the urban city after dark and the dangerous lure of commercial leisure.

It is perhaps surprising, then, that the commercial spaces of evening youth leisure remain relatively overlooked in histories of post-war youth culture. More likely to be the subject of sardonic comments about cheesy pop songs and girls dancing round their handbags than the object of historical study, these spaces were in fact central to the formative leisure experiences of British youth in the second half of the twentieth century. The prevalence and importance of these spaces in the lives of young people cannot be overstated, and their relative omission in the scholarship acts as a stark reminder

Introduction

that historians of post-war Britain have far more to do in taking popular leisure cultures seriously. As Keith Gildart recently argued, 'popular music and youth culture is an area that has remained stubbornly resistant to the focus of academic historians'.[4] A sustained study of the beat clubs, pubs, bars, discos, and nightclubs that formed some of the central sites of youth leisure in the post-war period reveals much about the changing experiences of being young in post-war Britain. It also reveals how young people moved through a changing urban landscape; the emergence of the night-time economy was driven by major temporal and spatial shifts in youth leisure, and it drastically altered young people's negotiations with the urban environment. It also exposes the shifting boundaries and goalposts of adulthood; not only did young people's engagement with youth culture alter dramatically between the 1950s and the 1990s, but the traditional markers of the transition from youth into adulthood were also being challenged.

Taking its focus from the early 1950s to the late 1990s, the book charts a period of significant, sweeping, and meaningful change in the lives of young people in Britain. While discussions of wider consumption practices such as clothes shopping and record buying do feature in the following pages, the book is primarily interested in the emergence of a distinct youth-driven evening leisure economy centred around public houses, bars, nightclubs, and live music venues. The nature of these spaces shifts dramatically over the course of the post-war period and they become some of the central sites of British youth culture; *Growing Up and Going Out* demonstrates how the emergence of the night-time economy was driven by the power of youth, consumption, and commerce. With a few exceptions, underground and unlicensed spaces do not feature in this book and, for the most part, it considers spaces that were licensed and that operated within existing legal and regulatory frameworks. As will be demonstrated, though, loopholes were often found and regulations flouted.

The people and places that populate the pages of this book were engaged in a delicate interplay between international social and cultural change and local level debates about morality, regulation, and urban space. A study of youth leisure, then, offers much more than a lens through which to view wider social and cultural changes in post-war Britain; it reveals the relationship between transnational shifts in leisure and lifestyle, global commerce, and the movements of teenagers and young adults through their towns and cities. It also tells us what meanings young people attached to their leisure experiences. After all, leisure was experienced at the level of the local; the town and city was not just the backdrop to nights spent with friends, but a mutable environment that both shaped young people's access to leisure and was moulded by it.

By taking the city of Sheffield, a predominantly working-class city in the north of England, as its starting point, this book explores the many ways

4 *Growing up and going out*

in which the growth of commercial evening leisure shaped both the lives of young people and the post-war urban environment. Sheffield's experience, and the experiences of the young people who grew up and went out there, are used as a springboard through which to tell a national story of British youth culture in post-war Britain. With a population of over half a million by 1950, Sheffield is a significant urban centre that tells an important story of youth culture beyond London and the main metropoles, and beyond the well-trodden musical histories of 'Merseybeat' and 'Madchester'. Despite its size, however, the city had a modest commercial landscape in the immediate post-war period and so provides an interesting site for a study of the spatial development of youth cultures across the second half of the twentieth century.

Sheffield, popularly known as the 'Steel City', was built on an industry dominated by steel and cutlery, with a number of mining communities living on the outskirts of the city. This strong manufacturing base meant the city grew quickly during the first part of the 1800s, with the population rising from just over 31,000 inhabitants in 1799 to 111,000 in 1822, and reaching 557,050 by 1951.[5] Cutlery was one of the city's largest employers; in 1957, 650 of the 700 cutlery firms in the United Kingdom were located in Sheffield.[6] Although the industry declined significantly over the course of the post-war period, Sheffield-based tool firms were still responsible for two-thirds of the national output of cutlery in 1990.[7] As a major industrial centre, providing armaments manufacturing during both the First and Second World Wars, the city was a strategic target for bombing raids, and significant areas of the city were damaged during air-raid strikes. Faced with competition from abroad, and a lack of investment in modernisation, the city's steel industry contracted rapidly during the post-war period, causing high levels of unemployment in the city – particularly for the city's young people – from the 1970s onwards. The number of people employed in the South Yorkshire steel industry fell from 60,000 in 1971 to 43,000 in 1979 and had dropped significantly to only 16,000 by 1987.[8] As such, this period of the city's history was one of rapid change. By the 1980s, the civil service and service industries were the biggest employers in the city; by 1984, for example, 17 per cent of city residents were directly employed by Sheffield City Council, making it the city's largest employer.[9]

The physical face of the city was changing, too. Following the Second World War, the council embarked on large-scale housing projects to clear both the bomb damage and slums that had survived the first wave of housing clearance projects in the interwar period. Developments such as Park Hill, famed for its 'streets in the sky' modernist design, rehoused working-class families away from the inner city. Large swathes of the city centre were pedestrianised in the 1960s as it was reimagined as a home of retail,

Introduction 5

commerce, and leisure. The city, which had a long history of political radicalism, became known as the 'Socialist Republic of South Yorkshire' in this period, and through the 1970s and 1980s its left-wing council was committed to developing 'socially useful' goods and services in a period of economic contraction. This commitment to 'socially useful' services included a consideration of the city's leisured landscape and the effects of growing unemployment on the city's teenagers and young adults, and through the 1970s and 1980s, the council worked closely with a number of organisations to address the issue of financial marginalisation and exclusion by providing affordable spaces for young people to socialise. These included more traditional municipally funded enterprises like youth clubs and leisure centres, but financial support was also provided for more experimental spaces such as recording studios, municipal cinema and theatre, and a nightclub and arts space.[10] Through this period, the city remained a firmly working-class one, though pockets of affluence (and the majority of the city's grammar schools) could be found huddled in the south west in the leafy areas around Sheffield Hallam. Daisy Payling's recent study of the city's 'local socialism' argued that Sheffield 'remained a relatively homogeneous city into the 1960s with little migration, a continued dependence on steel and a large working class'.[11]

Using Sheffield in this way therefore enables the book to chart, with a level of detail not afforded to national studies, the transformation of the urban leisurescape and young people's movement through it. It considers how venues developed in relation to each other, how local regulatory bodies tried to control them, and how local entrepreneurs and large entertainment companies took over, converted, built, and sold venues across the city. However, this book makes no claims for the broader representativeness of Sheffield. Sheffield catered to majority cultural tastes as a predominantly white, working-class city through this period, and its broader commercial leisurescape reflected this fact. As will be seen, many of the spaces of commercial youth leisure did not appeal to all young people and, critically, could operate as spaces of marginalisation. While *Growing Up and Going Out* does not claim to speak for the experience of youth across the country, it does argue that the city of Sheffield can be used as a springboard from which to explore questions about urban development, regulation, and spatial mobility that speak to national and international transformations in the youth experience. This also shaped how these spaces were regulated and managed, and the city's leisurescape was shaped, as elsewhere, by highly racialised, classed, and gendered visions of acceptable youth leisure.

Charting the relationship between transnational changes in commercial leisure and the everyday movements of young people through their local leisure environment is not an easy task. How might we adequately represent

6 *Growing up and going out*

the changing commercial interests of national and multinational leisure corporations without losing sight of the experiences – both material and emotional – evoked by being in those spaces? *Growing Up and Going Out* is interested in doing just that. From the development of multi-city night-club chains, to debates about the appropriate amount of floor space needed for dancing, to the serving of alcohol to underage teenagers, the spaces of evening youth leisure have been the site of numerous and often competing images of the youthful experience. As spaces dedicated to hedonism and leisure, they have been positioned in equal measure as palaces of pleasure and dens of iniquity, as central to patterns of youth sociability and as causes of juvenile delinquency. As such, a thorough exploration of their role in shaping the cultures and behaviours of youth, regulatory approaches, and the urban centre as a principal space for leisure is necessary for our understanding of the changing position of youth in twentieth-century Britain.

Youth in post-war Britain

The emergence of a distinct and visible youth culture is perhaps one of the most significant socio-cultural developments of the twentieth century. While the concept of youth itself is by no means a modern one, key shifts in social reform, educational policy, and medical discourse at the turn of the twentieth century meant that adolescence was increasingly viewed as a distinct life stage.[12] As early as 1904, psychologist G. Stanley Hall identified adolescence as a period that that was characterised by 'storm and stress'.[13] Approaches to youth were shaped both by young people's supposed vulnerability to corruption and their potential as future citizens, and over the course of the late nineteenth and twentieth centuries, their actions and behaviours were put under increasing scrutiny from state and society alike. As such, young people held particular political resonance, and were often linked to the nation's success, health, and morality. In the years after the Second World War, this 'futurity' had significant implications and, as Laura King demonstrates, was a powerful rhetorical tool used as a 'driver for change'.[14]

It is undeniable that the years after the Second World War saw considerable and meaningful changes to the lives of young people in Britain. The publication of the Albemarle Report in 1960 drew attention to the changing landscape of youth in the post-war period following a decline in demand for traditional youth services. Featuring notable contemporaries such as academic Richard Hoggart and social investigator Pearl Jephcott, the report noted that 'in some periods the sense of change is particularly strong. Today is such a period.'[15] The Albemarle Report outlined several key shifts which it felt characterised youth at this particular juncture, most

Introduction 7

notably the post-war boom in births resulting in a demographic 'bulge' of young people in the early-to-mid-1960s. The shifts identified in the report included the introduction of the Butler Education Act 1944 and the 1947 extension of compulsory education to the age of 15, the ending of national service in 1960, increased economic security, and the improved health of young people, all of which were said to contribute to a cohort of young people with greater economic, social, and educational opportunities than those afforded to their parents.

Bill Osgerby has argued that the 'youth question' – the attempt to understand or make sense of changing youth behaviours – becomes more prevalent in periods of 'profound transformation', in which the metaphor of youth is extended to 'encapsulate more general hopes and fears about trends in modern life'.[16] Increasing attention was certainly being given by contemporaries to the changing position of young people in British society. Their collective visibility made for numerous debates about the 'state of youth' in post-war Britain, while researchers tried to understand the nature of these changes. The market researcher Mark Abrams published *The Teenage Consumer* in 1959, widely recognised as the first sustained study of young people's consumption and spending in Britain. Abrams's findings that these consumption patterns were driven by 'distinctive teenage spending for distinctive teenage ends in a distinctive teenage world' gave a clear indication of the newfound spending power of young people.[17] Jephcott highlighted the changing lifestyles of Scottish youth in her influential 1967 study *Time of One's Own*, while Stanley Cohen's foundational 1972 sociological study *Folk Devils and Moral Panics* considered the framing of youth following the seaside clashes of adolescent mods and rockers in 1964. These broad post-war shifts, social commentators agreed, heralded a 'revolution' in the 1950s and 1960s, culminating with the emergence of the 'modern teenager'. By the end of the 1960s, young people were at the forefront of discussions about the changing world of post-war Britain, held up in equal part as its heroes and its folk devils.

The early work on youth by social investigators and sociologists dominated scholarly approaches to youth culture for many years, yet David Fowler argues they 'seem to have been oblivious of developments in youth culture ... before the Second World War'.[18] In recent years historians have debated the making of youth culture in modern Britain, engaging critically with the emphasis placed solely on the post-war period.[19] Fowler's *Youth Culture in Modern Britain, c.1920–1970* identified an early form of youth culture in the lives of middle-class university students. Jon Savage, in his expansive 'prehistory of the Teenager', argued that 'every single theme now associated with the modern Teenager had a vivid, volatile precedent', while Melanie Tebbutt argues that while young people engaged in 'leisure-oriented

8   *Growing up and going out*

consumption' in the late nineteenth and early twentieth centuries, this was not comparable to the 'collective consumer identity' that emerged after the Second World War.[20] There were, as Tebbutt points out, striking continuities in the youthful experience over the course of the nineteenth and twentieth centuries. These continuities were highlighted in Laura Harrison's recent study of late-nineteenth- and early-twentieth-century youth, which demonstrated that young people developed distinct forms of informal street- and neighbourhood-based leisure.[21] Many of the central interests and behaviours of young people in the post-war period remained, much as they had in earlier decades, centred on friendship, courting, and forms of leisure that encouraged sociability. As this book will show, dancing in particular remained a central and important activity. Yet it was only in the post-war period, with the emergence of distinct spaces of youth leisure, that a youth culture with its own discrete customs, lifestyles, consumer products, spatial practices and temporalities was fully realised.

The historical study of youth culture remains, despite significant popular interest, a relatively young field, and until recently much historical writing on youth culture in the post-war period was to be found in broader social and cultural histories of modern Britain. As a result, youth culture was often utilised as a tool to illustrate broader shifts rather than as a topic worthy of study in its own right.[22] Much of this work relied on common tropes about the 'birth' of the teenager – the emergence of the affluent society, increased access to disposable income, the explosion of mass consumer culture, and a growing generational 'gap' – but told us very little about the lived experience of youth. However, more recently there has been a turn towards a history of youth that has sought not only to take youth cultures seriously as a topic of historical enquiry, but that also explores the lived experience of young people. While scholars have disagreed over the extent to which permissiveness and radical change shaped the 1950s and 1960s, Helena Mills has noted that there is 'a core set of assumptions and popular images about British youth culture in the period'.[23] A study of those young people who lived through the period reveals, however, that the 1960s 'were much more complex than simply either a period of revolution or stasis'.[24] Moving forwards into the 1970s and 1980s, a new generation of youth were used to explain social and political upheaval, yet Matthew Worley has demonstrated that a study of punk and youth culture reveals 'a formative and contested experience through which young people discover, comprehend, affirm and express their desires, opinions and disaffections'.[25] As this book will demonstrate, the lives of young people in post-war Britain and their interactions with youth culture were myriad and complex, dependent as much on family, friendships, and their local and regional context as on broader narratives of affluence or decline. It was recently argued that 'while the concepts of

Introduction

youth and youth culture may still be relatively new, they are no longer so novel as to deny historical investigation'.[26] For Christine Feldman-Barrett, the historical study of youth 'advocates for the longstanding and indelible importance of young people's experiences in the tapestry of cultural life'.[27] This book, therefore, can be situated within a broader movement in historical scholarship that seeks to revisit and re-evaluate the lives of young people in modern Britain as a meaningful topic of historical enquiry.

While the historical study of youth cultures remains a relatively young field, scholarship on young people in the fields of sociology, criminology, and cultural studies has a much longer past. The study of youth cultures is rooted particularly strongly in the tradition of cultural studies, and the work of theorists and researchers has done much to enrich debate on the saliency of youth, culture, and identity as categories of analysis. The Centre for Contemporary Cultural Studies (CCCS), founded by Richard Hoggart in 1964, is well-recognised as pioneering the study of contemporary British youth cultures. Established at the University of Birmingham, the centre represented a 'new generation of leftist thinkers engaged with a society increasingly dominated by affluence, new forms of mass media and the cultures of consumption'.[28] The centre was interested not only in the cultures of the young, but in what this meant for a new world in which identity could be subverted and shaped through consumption.

The legacies of the CCCS have been many and varied, but perhaps the most notable of these is the continuing focus given to visible or 'spectacular' youth cultures of the post-war period. Bill Osgerby has argued, with an ode to Churchill's famous speech, that 'never, in the field of social history, has so much been written by so many about so few. In contrast, most young people have been comparatively "normal" and "ordinary" in their cultural orientations and stylistic preferences.'[29] Despite criticisms levied at the CCCS for its emphasis on the highly visible, the centre recognised that subcultural pursuits did not account for all of young people's interactions with youth culture; John Clarke et al. noted in the centre's landmark text *Resistance Through Rituals* that 'the great majority of working-class youth never enters into a tight or coherent sub-culture at all ... their relation to the existing sub-cultures may be fleeting or permanent, marginal or central'.[30] Most importantly, they recognised that involvement in these subcultural groups 'may be less significant than what young people do most of the time'.[31] Despite this, the Birmingham school was interested in collective responses of youth, and this was found most clearly within the distinct music- and fashion-based youth movements of the post-war years.

The work of the Birmingham school was foundational for the study of British youth cultures; it offered the first sustained attempt to take the cultures of young people seriously, and has shaped the work of many scholars

10 *Growing up and going out*

of post-war youth culture. However, the approach of the CCCS has since been challenged by a range of scholars who have questioned the structural approach of the centre. Sean Albiez has argued that 'it is untenable to draw an undeviating relationship between a head of household's (usually father's) occupation or employment status, and specific musical tastes and lifestyles', while Andy Bennett and Keith Kahn-Harris have similarly argued that the CCCS's focus on class was restrictive, given 'its unqualified equation of post-war patterns of youth consumerism with notions of working-class resistance'.[32] This newer body of work, broadly united under the umbrella of post-subcultural theory, dominated scholarship on youth between the 1990s and early 2000s. Best exemplified by the work of Andy Bennett, Steve Redhead, Sarah Thornton, Keith Kahn-Harris, David Muggleton, and Rupert Weinzierl, among others, post-subcultural scholarship was defined by its focus on the individual. This school of thought reasoned that young people's lifestyles are 'more fleeting and organised around individual lifestyle and consumption choices' than the original CCCS model allowed for.[33] Sarah Thornton, for example, called the approach of the CCCS 'empirically unworkable', while Simon Frith argued that 'for every youth "stylist" committed to a cult as a full-time creative task, there are hundreds of working-class kids who grow up in a loose membership of several groups and run with a variety of gangs'.[34] Yet these revisions of CCCS theories were not without their flaws. Where post-subcultural work moved away from the class-based approach of the Birmingham school, they were perhaps too quick to overlook the material realities and structural constraints facing modern youth. Tracy Shildrick and Robert MacDonald concluded that 'the sorts of free cultural *choice* described by more postmodern, post-subcultural perspectives tend to be reserved for the more privileged sections of dominant cultural groups'.[35]

So how might we write a history of youth culture that takes into account both the fluidity of youth culture and the structural barriers that shape the youth experience? What happens when we decentre the traditional hallmarks of youth culture that have shaped the field – namely the more visible markers such as music, clothing, and style – and replace them with a study of youth in situ? This is not to suggest that these visible markers are not important; as Chapter 5 of this book demonstrates, they can play a critical and often formative role in young people's construction of self. The key purpose of *Growing Up and Going Out* is to question and re-evaluate the traditional boundaries that have dominated the history of youth culture. *Growing Up and Going Out* demonstrates clearly that youth culture in post-war Britain was a dynamic and vibrant force that had real power to shape not only the popular market but also the face of Britain's urban centres, as well as the everyday experiences of friendship, courtship, and sociability.

Youth, space, and place

The focus on spatial developments in youth leisure is one of the major methodological interventions of this book, and *Growing Up and Going Out* can be situated within a wider historiographical turn towards the local and the spatial. The coffee bar, beat club, late-night bar, and nightclub form some of the most culturally significant spaces in the lives of many teenagers and young adults in Britain. They emerged, over the course of the post-war period, as places that became increasingly distinct from and unfamiliar to the leisure spaces encountered by other sectors of society, shaped by the growing cultural and economic power of those who frequented them and by the desire of commercial leisure providers to capitalise on this. However, their arrival was mediated by interactions between governing bodies, regulators, and legislators. These urban spaces tell us not only about the shifting lifestyles of youth in post-war Britain – about their spatial mobility through the city, and about their cultures of sociability – but also reveal the myriad ways in which young people's lives have been subject to both national and local-level regulations that have shaped both their access to and use of leisure space. In short, a study of these spaces grounds post-war youth culture firmly in the lived experience of the young.

The moral panics that followed youth throughout the latter part of the twentieth century – from clashes between mods and rockers in the 1960s, to the association of violence with punks and skinheads in the 1970s, to the dangers of ecstasy and rave in the 1980s and 1990s – were rooted in much older fears concerning the 'dangers' of mass forms of leisure and a belief in the value of supervised and structured rational recreation. As Louise Jackson and Angela Bartie have demonstrated, there was 'an almost perpetual wave of public anxiety, rhetoric, and debate' relating to youth and crime in the post-war leisure that had the power to shape how young people's activities were regulated.[36] Historians have shown how leisure – particularly the leisure time of the working classes – was often subject to social and political intervention.[37] The origins of modern leisure, Peter Bailey argued, can be found in the Victorian period. It was in this period when work and leisure became separated, 'forming a separate and self-contained sector in an increasingly compartmentalised way of life'.[38] Concerns as to the 'proper' use of leisure time thus increased as higher levels of disposable income and shorter working hours made accessing leisure a reality for many more people in the years after the First World War.[39] There is a wealth of work that explores leisure in the interwar period, much of which highlights the vibrancy and importance of leisure in changing patterns of sociability, mass culture, and family life, but also considers its significance in the lives of adolescents and young adults.[40]

12   *Growing up and going out*

A significant shift in leisure provision in the 1920s and 1930s was the growing dominance of commercial leisure. Dancing, in particular, emerged as a popular pursuit among young people, providing opportunities for entertainment and sociability. The rise of commercial leisure venues such as cinemas and dance halls provided the young working classes with affordable and accessible leisure, quickly becoming sites of real social and cultural significance. These early dance halls were, in many respects, the predecessors to the post-war nightclubs that would come to dominate the late-night urban leisurescape. Indeed, many nightclubs of the 1970s and 1980s were former ballrooms and dance halls that had been renovated to appeal to the changing appetite of dancers. The work of James Nott and Allison Abra has done much to demonstrate the importance of dancing as a leisure pursuit in the twentieth century, and this book builds on their work by taking the study of commercial dancing spaces firmly into the post-war period.[41]

While historians are right to highlight continuities in youthful experience over the course of the twentieth century, as well as the *longue durée* of patterns of leisure and consumption that defined post-war youth culture, Melanie Tebbutt's argument that the consumer cultures of interwar and post-war youth are not directly comparable is an important one.[42] What marked post-war youth culture as distinct from earlier developments in commercial leisure and consumer culture were three key things: new urban spaces of youthful leisure, an unparalleled access to consumer culture, and a temporal shift that remade urban centres after dark. As this book will show, the combination of the spending power of young people alongside the development of new leisure spaces and temporalities designed solely for their entertainment sparked a seismic shift in the lives of young people, shaping not only their chosen leisure activities but their patterns of sociability, experiences of courting and sexual experimentation, spatial mobility, and their wider relationship with the urban environment. Young men and women in post-war Britain accessed, for the most part, the same types of leisure spaces as those who came earlier in the twentieth century, dominated by a focus on dancing, music, and sociability, but their leisure patterns were increasingly shaped as much by age as they were by gender, class, and race.

Despite the central place these spaces occupied in the day-to-day lives of young people in post-war Britain, they remain remarkably overlooked in histories of youth culture. Where they do appear, they are often linked to particular moments in youth cultural history, highlighted as the centre of culturally significant moments, and as places where important things happen. Soho's short-lived Ad Lib Club, for example, receives ample mention in writing about the 'swinging' 1960s. The cultural legacy of Oxford Street's 100 Club as a place of both jazz and punk is well known, while the legacy of Covent Garden's Blitz nightclub in the form of the 'Blitz Kids' is written into the cultural history of the 1980s. Overwhelmingly centred on London, and closed off to those who were not within the latest group of cultural elites, the story of these spaces is abstracted from the wider leisure landscape of post-war Britain, singled out as centres of cultural significance and artistic creativity. Yet their story, while an immensely important aspect of the cultural history of post-war Britain, can only tell us so much, and reveals little about the central role played by these new urban spaces of leisure in the lives of teenagers and young adults in towns and cities across Britain. This book argues that these spaces hold far more resonance than simply as sites of cultural significance for the world of musicians, artists, fashion designers, and socialites that moved within them. From the coffee bars of the 1950s to the sophisticated and glamorous nightclubs of the 1980s, the urban spaces of evening youth leisure played a central role in the development of a distinct youth culture. They transformed the way young people moved through the urban environment, heralding a major temporal and spatial shift that saw the city centre after dark become a place dedicated to the hedonistic pleasure of the young.

Where historians of youth culture have traditionally overlooked the spatial dynamics of youth, scholars in the fields of urban studies, cultural geography, and sociology have been far more attuned to questions of space and youth culture. Important work has been carried out by a number of scholars on the spatial dynamics of music consumption, the rise of club cultures, and the building of 'authentic' spaces.[43] The work of Robert Hollands and Paul Chatterton on late-twentieth-century urban nightscapes has shed vital light on the relationship between global cultures, local spaces, and urban regeneration, and their focus on the regulation, marketing, and consumption of modern nightlife was an important intervention in the field.[44] Indeed, they have argued that 'much youth cultural analysis has been implicitly aspatial in its orientation'.[45] This book builds on the work produced by scholars of nightlife and the night-time economy, providing a historical explanation for the post-war shifts in youth lifestyle and behaviour, and considering how these shifts interacted with leisure space and the built environment to create new ways of being for the young.

There has been, in recent years, a growing recognition of the importance of space and place to histories of youth, and *Growing Up and Going Out* is situated firmly within this body of scholarship. Julia Sneeringer's study of rock'n'roll in post-war Hamburg argued that popular music needs to be localised 'in its social and cultural contexts', and that doing so demonstrates how the cultural 'counterworld harnessed the international impulses that flowed through Hamburg'.[46] Simon Sleight's work on youth in Melbourne between 1870 and 1914 argued that 'spatial approaches to the past have been slow to embrace the lives of the young', and showed how young people

14 *Growing up and going out*

shaped Melbourne in years of significant growth 'through attempting to impress upon the city their own desires'.[47] Felix Fuhg's study of post-Victorian London utilised the 'parameters of urban studies and cultural geography [to situate] the cultural transformation Britain underwent thanks to its youth'.[48] Selina Todd, in her study of working-class life and post-war urban reconstruction, demonstrated that young people 'felt entitled to take matters into their own hands in order to convert the material landscape in which they lived into the city of their dreams'.[49] Finally, Laura Harrison's study of youth between 1870 and 1939 utilised York to demonstrate the importance of considering 'the ways young people both used and produced their own space'.[50]

The spatial approach utilised in this book is not influenced by any one key theorist, but draws on a number of approaches that recognise the fluidity of both space and place. Rather than defining space and place using geographical boundaries, many theorists have instead focused on how space and place relate to wider cultural and societal behaviours. Henri Lefebvre argued for an understanding of 'social' space and 'abstract' space, suggesting that 'the concepts of production and of the act of producing do have a certain abstract universality'.[51] Cultural and feminist geographer Doreen Massey argued that the spatial should be understood as inherently linked to social relations. The spatial, Massey argued, 'can be seen as constructed out of the multiplicity of social relations across all spatial scales, from the global reach of finance and telecommunications, through the geography of the tentacles of national political power, to the social relations within the town, the settlement, the household, and the workplace'.[52] Critically, Massey suggested that by understanding space in this way, it is possible to challenge previous conceptualisations of place. Place, Massey argued, has been subject to 'exclusivist claims ... all of them have been attempts to fix the meaning of particular spaces, to enclose them, endow them with fixed identities and claim them for one's own'.[53] Charles W. J. Withers's theoretical journey through the 'spatial turn' concluded that neither place nor space 'enjoys precise definition' and, as a result, 'we can recognize its different meanings and draw upon them in thinking about the relationships between geography and history and between place, space, and time'.[54]

Growing Up and Going Out argues that historians of youth culture have much to gain by recovering the spaces of youth leisure from debates about cultural validity, and should seek to understand how space and place shaped the youth experience, what meanings young people attached to it, and how young people themselves understood the spaces and places they moved through. Similarly, it seeks to demonstrate that the way young people experience space and place is shaped by their very position as 'young'. As Dylan Baun and Carla Pascoe Leahy have argued, 'young people across

Introduction   15

the globe have been defined by their relationship to spaces'.[55] Their movement through space, the regulation of the spaces they encounter, and their capacity to access public and semi-public space is determined by and mediated through their position as young people. As such, a study of youth that considers the spatial must also contend with the way that age functions as a category of power. Chris Jenks has argued that childhood and, by extension, youth more broadly 'is that status of personhood which is by definition often in the wrong place ... and their very gradual emergence into wider, adult space is by accident, by degrees, as an award or as part of a gradualist *rite de passage*'.[56]

While the spatial acts as a core analytical tool, this does not supersede other key categories of analysis, particularly those of class and gender. Chapters 3 and 4, in particular, consider the way in which class and gender shaped young people's access to youth leisure, how they were regulated by local authorities, by businesses, and by young people themselves, and how they intersected with wider national debates about youth, crime, sexuality, and morality. The book is particularly interested in the cultural experiences of teenage girls and young women; it considers how young men and women interacted with each other in public and semi-public spaces, examines how their experiences of – and access to – leisure space were shaped by their gender, and explores the development of gendered leisure practices through the post-war period.

Writing youth

This book is interested in charting how intersections between the international, national, and local shaped the lives of young people in post-war Britain. In doing so, it asks: how did commercial leisure respond to the emergence of a distinct youth culture? Further, what bearing did these spaces have on the lifestyles and cultural experiences of British youth? What was the significance of these spaces in young people's identity creation? Finally, how did these public and semi-public sites of youth leisure interact with the wider urban environment? To what extent were they shaped by wider legislative shifts and discourses about young people's morality? *Growing Up and Going Out* is further interested in accessing the experiences of young people that are often absent in histories of youth culture, particularly those who did not clearly identify with a subcultural grouping. The scholarship that dominates histories of post-war youth culture has tended to position subculture and popular culture as binary opposites, often preferring to focus on the spectacle of subcultural movements. Yet there were myriad ways that young people engaged with youth culture in post-war Britain that makes the binary paradigm between 'alternative' and 'mainstream' untenable. *Growing Up and Going Out* contends that there are important questions to be asked of youth culture and the experience of youth that extends far beyond subcultural identity. As Dave Russell's compelling study of the commercial 1960s cabaret club argues, 'the middle-of-the-road can be an interesting place to explore'.[57] It is for this reason that you will find limited mention of mods, punks, or skinheads in the following pages.

There are both practical and intellectual reasons for the decision to focus predominantly on licensed leisure spaces. Firstly, an exploration of these spaces challenges traditional narratives that solely privilege the experience of subcultural youth. The public houses, bars, nightclubs, and music venues that came to dominate youth leisure over the course of the post-war period reveal much about the spatial mobility, sociability, and identity creation of young people in Britain. It is also here, in the cultural and spatial 'mainstream', that we can see the disputed nature of youth in the second half of the twentieth century; youth lifestyles, their spaces of leisure, their consumption habits, and their movement through urban space exposed the contested and often contradictory attempts to control and regulate young people. As such, a historical study of youth that takes seriously the commercial sites of youth leisure is long overdue. Secondly, these spaces, while broadly overlooked in the literature, have left important traces in the archive. From planning applications and petty court sessions to the debates of licensing magistrates, we can learn much about the changing use of space and the relationship between commerce and local authority.

In focusing on the cultural mainstream, and on those spaces that flourished within it, this project also recognises the many ways in which dominant cultures act as exclusionary and marginalising forces. These spaces were culturally dominant, but they were rarely socially inclusive. While dance halls, coffee bars, and nightclubs profited from the growing popularity of Black music cultures in Britain, be that jazz, disco, soul, or reggae, they remained spaces dominated by whiteness and heteronormativity. As such, the following pages seek to address critically moments of exclusion and marginalisation. In positioning these spaces as ones dominated and, often, reinforced by whiteness and heteronormativity, the book recognises that these spaces held the potential for violence and exclusion. In a study of working-men's clubs in a similar period, Camilla Schofield demonstrated powerfully how the policing of whiteness in this traditionally masculine working-class leisure space 'reveals an extremely uneven social terrain for racialized people in post-war England – a terrain of conditional acceptance, disavowal, violence, and, sometimes, conviviality'.[58] In the new leisure arenas available to British youth, this translated clearly into the regulation of these spaces – both at the level of state governance and production of social communities – and in

Introduction

ways that prioritised and enforced 'respectability' as shorthand for whiteness and heteronormativity. As such, what follows represents a study of the social and cultural power of the youth cultural mainstream rather than a suggestion that this spoke to the experience of all youth in Britain.

The sources used in the research of this monograph shed light on local-level debates about regulation, morality, and the changing lifestyles of the young, as well as national and international shifts in the leisure industry that reshaped the post-war urban landscape. At the local level, licensing documents, police records, council minutes, and planning applications have helped construct a clear picture of the leisure landscape of the city of Sheffield, its regulatory bodies, and its shifting political and economic context over the second half of the twentieth century. The work of businesses and commercial leisure organisations have left a surprisingly scant archival trail, so their history has been traced using a combination of licensing documents, financial reports, local and national media coverage, and planning applications. The entertainment and national press, particularly publications such as *The Stage*, have been essential in establishing the changing priorities of longstanding entertainment companies such as Mecca and the Rank Organisation. Politicians, journalists, youth workers, social commentators, and researchers have created a wealth of material that speaks to the ever-changing concept of youth, and their work has been used heavily throughout this book.

While previous histories of post-war youth culture have revealed much about the consumption practices and identity creation of young people, much of this work remains abstracted from the lived experience of youth. In order to add much-needed texture and context, as well as a way in to the study of lived experience, *Growing Up and Going Out* uses oral testimony to explore the thoughts, feelings, experiences, and memories of those who grew up between the 1950s and 1990s. The pages of this book, particularly in Part II, are populated with the voices of those who grew up in Sheffield. Over twenty oral history interviews were conducted with people who grew up in Sheffield between the 1960s and 1990s during the research for this book, and their testimonies shed vital light on the spatial mobility of British youth as well as the important role the spaces of youth leisure played in shaping their consumption practices and patterns of sociability. In addition to this, testimony from men and women who have lived in Sheffield has been drawn from the University of Sheffield's Witness Oral History Project.

Oral history holds particular value for historians of youth. For those who are interested in moving beyond the 'spectacular', it holds the potential to give 'voice to the experiences of young people who are less often represented on television, in magazines, or in newspapers'.[59] As such, this book draws on David Hesmondhalgh's call to consider 'a range of experiences,

18 *Growing up and going out*

from the transgressive to the banal, without privileging the search for the rebellious'.[60] In the context of histories of youth culture, such an intervention is critical. The experiences of subcultural youth have dominated much of our knowledge and understanding about the youth experience, in part because the 'spectacular' nature of subculture 'can easily lead to the creation of myths that become deeply ingrained in popular memory'.[61]

There is a rich and extensive body of scholarship that considers the practicalities of conducting and interpreting oral history interviews, much of which considers the relationship between narrative construction, popular memory, and participant subjectivity.[62] Tess Coslett, Celia Lury, and Penny Summerfield, for example, have argued that

> Memory ... is intersubjective and dialogical, a function of personal identifications and social commitments. While it may be uniquely ours it is also objectified, a matter of public convention and shared rituals. The recovery of the past through personal testimony can have a political dimension depending on what is remembered and what is forgotten.[63]

Similarly, Maurice Halbwachs's concept of 'collective' memory – a foundational text for the study of memory – suggests that memory is constructed in accordance with the broader social and cultural context in which people move through: 'collective frameworks ... are precisely the instruments used by collective memory to reconstruct an image of the past which is in accord, in each epoch, with the predominant thoughts of the society'.[64] The construction of collective memory occurs 'because individual consciousness and its evolution are marked by the social nature of mankind'.[65] As such, working with oral history requires careful consideration of the way that memory serves not only as a function of individual recollection but as a vehicle through which people make sense of, and attach meaning to, their experiences.[66] While an analysis of oral testimony is not able to recover a true and unmediated account of youthful lives, it remains a productive and fruitful way of considering how people felt about their adolescence and young adulthood. It is, after all, the personal that makes oral testimony such a valuable resource for social and cultural historians; as Alessandro Portelli argued, 'oral sources tell us not just what people did, but what they wanted to do, what they believed they were doing, and what they now think they did'.[67]

Historians of British youth culture have, in recent years, used oral history and youth-produced sources to interrogate the everyday experience of youth. Critically, Hannah Charnock has argued that memory texts such as oral history offer insight into youthful subjectivities 'that cannot be acquired elsewhere'.[68] For Helena Mills, oral history remains one key way of

Introduction 19

addressing the 'mismatch between the popular memory and the experience of youth'.[69] Laura Harrison used a range of oral histories both to access the 'remembered experience' of youth, and as a 'critical means through which to access and explore the urban environment'.[70] Here, oral testimony is utilised to shed light on the lived experience of those people whose youthful experiences were unlikely to attract the attention of journalists, politicians, and social commentators. Moving away from London, and away from the 'celebrated' spaces of subcultural resistance and subversion, the testimonies presented here offer a way to think critically about how (and what) we value about young lives in the past.

The same call for participants was used at each stage of the recruitment process, with the recruitment of interviewees occurring over three periods between 2014 and 2015. Participants were recruited by responding to an advert calling for those who had been 'teenagers in Sheffield' to encourage anybody who was between the ages of 15 and 21 in the 1960s, 1970s, and 1980s to share their experiences and memories of being young in the city. Participants were told to expect an informal interview, with relatively open-ended questions about their memories of being a teenager in Sheffield. This technique proved particularly effective for recruiting participants who might not have come forward to discuss youth culture more explicitly as they felt that their experiences were 'middle of the road', uninteresting, or insignificant. One participant, Debbie, when discussing her involvement with ska music, caveated this by saying 'I was considered probably more middle of the road than quite a few.' Another participant, Helen, recalled growing up on the rural outskirts of Sheffield, saying: 'I mean my dad had a car but I couldn't rely on my dad to drive me everywhere so it didn't really happen, you know. It sounds really boring doesn't it!' The experiences and recollections of these individuals may not have been collected without such a broad call for participants. By asking questions about young people's broader lifestyles and habits, rather than targeted questions about specific events or movements, I was able to analyse how my participants negotiated their relationship with dominant cultural frameworks.

The definition of youth used in this book is purposefully broad. As many before me have shown, youth is an unstable category defined as much by social and cultural contexts as by age.[71] As we will see, the parameters, experiences, and expectations of youth shift significantly even between the 1950s and 1990s. The book's focus on licensed leisure spaces would, on the surface, exclude those still at school and under the age of 18. Yet we know that many young people began socialising in licensed spaces from as young as 14 and 15, and their entry into those spaces often went unchallenged. As late as 1988, politicians were questioning whether asking for proof of age from young people in bars would be an 'unjustifiable burden' on licence

20 *Growing up and going out*

holders, clearly indicating the difficulty of enforcing the age bar of 18.[72] As such, the term 'youth' is used throughout this book to denote those who fall broadly, though not exclusively, between the ages of 14 and the early 20s. This age bracket encompasses younger teenagers given a degree of freedom to socialise regularly outside of the home and away from the local neighbourhood, something not often afforded to younger children, while recognising that the patterns of consumption and sociability that define youth do not end abruptly once a person turns 20.

Summary

The book is split into five chapters over two parts, with each exploring a different facet of youth leisure, lifestyle, and nightlife in post-war Britain. Part I considers the transformation of the post-war urban environment, considering what this meant for young people growing up in post-war Britain. Chapter 1 explores the early emergence of leisure spaces in Britain in the 1950s and 1960s, and exposes important moments of transition. Community halls, coffee bars, late-night beat clubs, and converted ballrooms all offered new leisure opportunities for Britain's youth on both a temporary and permanent basis, and entrepreneurs scrambled to take advantage of this new market and appetite for late-night entertainment. Chapter 2 moves further into the post-war period, illustrating the important role played by commercial leisure organisations in developing the major spaces of post-war youth leisure. Companies such as Mecca, the Rank Organisation, and EMI played an integral role in shaping youthful experiences of leisure, and their transition into the world of nightclubs and discotheques was part of a broader reimagining of youthful leisure in this period. These swift developments in both the lifestyles of teenagers and young adults and the shaping of the urban nightscape required new approaches to regulation. Chapter 3 demonstrates the role that both national and local authorities played in influencing access to youthful leisure, showing that while many developments were national, there were also important local dimensions at play.

Part II turns towards lifestyle and lived experience, considering the influence of these new spaces of leisure on young people's behaviours, lifestyles, and patterns of sociability in the post-war period. Chapter 4's focus on alcohol consumption positions licensed leisure spaces as key sites of youthful sociability in the post-war period, both for young men and women and those under and over the age of 18. Licensed leisure spaces were the site of key behavioural shifts in the post-war period, and drinking was an important part of this. Chapter 5 turns to a bigger theme that underpins much work on youth culture in the post-war period: the link between culture

Introduction 21

and identity. Exploring young people's spatial mobility, the meanings they attached to leisure spaces, and the role these spaces played in constructing their own sense of self, Chapter 5 considers how a localised and spatial approach to histories of youth culture has the potential to challenge the way we conceptualise the major boundaries of youth culture in this period.

There is a clear need for a critical exploration of the emergence of youth-driven commercial leisure spaces in post-war Britain. Beyond the popular narratives of white stilettos and girls dancing round their handbags, these spaces have so often been written off in a sentence or two, shunned for their lack of authenticity and commitment to Top 40 pop. *Growing Up and Going Out* is the story of those young people who didn't always make the headlines, who considered their experiences too 'run of the mill' to be worthy of note, and who have been neglected in favour of more visible images of youth. Yet their experiences constituted some of the most formative moments for generations of young people in Britain; snatched moments of freedom from work and family commitments, the independence of wearing an outfit purchased with a first pay packet, the joy of dancing with friends to a favourite song. These moments carry real historical significance, and the spaces in which they occurred are sites of monumental social and cultural change.

Notes

1 *Sheffield: City on the Move* [film], directed by Jim Coulthard (Sheffield City Council, 1972).

2 'Northumbria: The Best Nightlife Outside London', *The Stage*, 23 March 1972, 11; 'The Nightlife Revolution', *Birmingham Daily Post*, 22 March 1975, 16.

3 Marion Roberts and Adam Eldridge, *Planning the Night-Time City* (Abingdon: Routledge, 2009), 15; for more on visions of the night-time city, see Henri Lefebvre, *The Production of Space* (trans. Donald Nicholson-Smith, Oxford: Blackwell, 1991); Andy Lovatt and Justin O'Connor, 'Cities and the Night-Time Economy', *Planning Practice & Research*, 10:2 (1995), 127–134, https://doi.org/10.1080/02697459550036676; Robert Williams, 'Night Spaces: Darkness, Deterritorialization, and Social Control', *Space and Culture*, 11:4 (2008), 514–532, https://doi.org/10.1177/1206331208320117.

4 Keith Gildart, *Images of England Through Popular Music: Class, Youth and Rock'n'Roll, 1955–1976* (Basingstoke: Palgrave Macmillan, 2013), 2.

5 J. Edward Vickers, *A Popular History of Sheffield* (Wakefield: EP Publishing, 1978), 41.

6 David Hey, *A History of Sheffield* (3rd edn, Lancaster: Carnegie, 2010), 280.

7 *Ibid.*, 285.

8 *Ibid.*, 288.

9 Dave Child and Mick Paddon, 'Sheffield: Steelyard Blues', *Marxism Today* (July 1984), 19.

10 Sarah Kenny, 'A "Radical Project": Youth Culture, Leisure, and Politics in 1980s Sheffield', *Twentieth Century British History*, 30:4 (2019), 557–584, https://doi.org/10.1093/tcbh/hwz006.

11 Daisy Payling, *Socialist Republic: Remaking the British Left in 1980s Sheffield* (Manchester: Manchester University Press, 2023), 9.

12 Melanie Tebbutt, *Making Youth: A History of Youth in Modern Britain* (London: Bloomsbury, 2016), 10. On the historical concept of youth and age more broadly, see Mary Jo Maynes, 'Age as a Category of Historical Analysis: History, Agency, and Narratives of Childhood', *Journal of the History of Childhood and Youth*, 1:1 (2008), 114–124, https://doi.org/10.1353/hcy .2008.0001; Laura Lovett, 'Age: A Useful Category of Analysis', *Journal of the History of Childhood and Youth*, 1:1 (2008), 114–124, https://doi.org/10 .1353/hcy.2008.0015; Laura Tisdall, 'Education, Parenting and Concepts of Childhood in England, c. 1945 to c. 1979', *Contemporary British History*, 31:1 (2017), 24–46, https://doi.org/10.1080/13619462.2016.1226808.

13 G. Stanley Hall, *Adolescence in Psychology and its Relation to Physiology, Anthropology, Sociology, Sex, Crime, Religion, and Education: Vols I & II* (Englewood Cliffs, NJ: Prentice-Hall, 1904).

14 Laura King, 'Future Citizens: Cultural and Political Conceptions of Children in Britain, 1930s–1950s', *Twentieth Century British History*, 27:3 (2016), 410, https://doi.org/10.1093/tcbh/hww025.

15 Ministry of Education, *The Youth Service in England and Wales* (London: HMSO, 1960), 13.

16 Bill Osgerby, 'Subcultures, Popular Music and Social Change: Theories, Issues and Debates' in The Subcultures Network (eds), *Subcultures, Popular Music and Social Change* (Cambridge: Cambridge Scholars Publishing, 2014), 5.

17 Mark Abrams, *The Teenage Consumer* (London: London Press Exchange), 10. There have been debates over Abrams's definition of youth, particularly given that his research defined 'teenagers' as those unmarried and between the ages of 15 and 25.

18 David Fowler, *Youth Culture in Modern Britain, c.1920–c.1970* (Basingstoke: Palgrave Macmillan, 2008), 6.

19 See for example Jon Savage, *Teenage: The Creation of Youth: 1875–1945* (London: Pimlico, 2007); Tebbutt, *Making Youth*; Bill Osgerby, *Youth in Britain Since 1945* (Oxford: Blackwell, 1998); Fowler, *Youth Culture in Modern Britain*; John Springhall, *Youth, Popular Culture and Moral Panics: Penny Gaffs to Gangsta Rap, 1830–1996* (London: Palgrave Macmillan, 1998); Selina Todd and Hilary Young, 'Baby-Boomers to "Beanstalkers": Making the Modern Teenager in Post-War Britain', *Cultural and Social History*, 9:3 (2012), 451–467, https://doi.org/10.2752/147800412X13347542916747; Gillian A. M. Mitchell, 'Reassessing "the Generation Gap": Bill Haley's 1957 Tour of Britain, Inter-Generational Relations and Attitudes to Rock 'n' Roll in the Late

1950s', *Twentieth Century British History*, 24:4 (2013), 573–605, https://doi.org/10.1093/tcbh/hwt013.

20 Savage, *Teenage: The Creation of Youth*, xiii; Tebbutt, *Making Youth*, 132.

21 Laura Harrison, *Dangerous Amusements: Leisure, the Young Working Class and Urban Space in Britain, c. 1870–1939* (Manchester: Manchester University Press, 2022), 2.

22 See for example Arthur Marwick, *British Society Since 1945* (4th edn, London: Penguin, 2003); Mark Donnelly, *Sixties Britain: Culture, Society and Politics* (Harlow: Pearson Education, 2005); Dominic Sandbrook, *Never Had It So Good: A History of Britain from Suez to the Beatles* (London: Abacus, 2006); Dominic Sandbrook, *White Heat: A History of Britain in the Swinging Sixties* (London: Abacus, 2007).

23 Helena Mills, 'Using the Personal to Critique the Popular: Women's Memories of 1960s Youth', *Contemporary British History*, 30:4 (2016), 463, https://doi.org/10.1080/13619462.2016.1206822.

24 *Ibid.*, 464.

25 Matthew Worley, *No Future: Punk, Politics, and British Youth Culture, 1976–1984* (Cambridge: Cambridge University Press, 2017), 3.

26 Jon Garland, Keith Gildart, Anna Gough-Yates, Paul Hodkinson, Bill Osgerby, Lucy Robinson, John Street, Pete Webb, and Matthew Worley, 'Youth Culture, Popular Music and the End of "Consensus" in Post-War Britain', *Contemporary British History*, 26:3 (2012), 266, https://doi.org/10.1080/13619462.2012.703002.

27 Christine Feldman-Barrett, 'Back to the Future: Mapping a Historic Turn in Youth Studies', *Journal of Youth Studies*, 21:6 (2019), 742, https://doi.org/10.1080/13676261.2017.1420150.

28 Kieran Connell and Matthew Hilton, 'The Working Practices of Birmingham's Centre for Contemporary Cultural Studies', *Social History*, 40:3 (2013), 287, https://doi.org/10.1080/03071022.2015.1043191. For more on the history of the CCCS, see Kieran Connell and Matthew Hilton (eds), *Cultural Studies 50 Years On: History, Practice and Politics* (London: Rowman and Littlefield, 2016). For discussions of the legacy of the CCCS on youth cultural studies more specifically see Shane Blackman, 'Youth Subcultural Theory: A Critical Engagement with the Concept, Its Origins and Politics, from the Chicago School to Postmodernism', *Journal of Youth Studies*, 8:1 (2005), 1–20, https://doi.org/10.1080/13676260500063629; David Hesmondhalgh, 'Subcultures, Scenes or Tribes? None of the Above', *Journal of Youth Studies*, 8:1 (2005), 21–40, https://doi.org/10.1080/13676260500063652; Tracy Shildrick and Robert MacDonald, 'In Defence of Subculture: Young People, Leisure and Social Divisions', *Journal of Youth Studies*, 9:2 (2006), 125–140, https://doi.org/10.1080/13676260600635599.

29 Osgerby, *Youth in Britain*, 74.

30 John Clarke, Stuart Hall, Tony Jefferson, and Brian Roberts, 'Subcultures, Cultures and Class: A Theoretical Overview' in Stuart Hall and Tony Jefferson (eds), *Resistance Through Rituals* (London: Routledge, 1993), 16.

24 *Growing up and going out*

31 *Ibid.*, 16.

32 Sean Albiez, 'Know History! John Lydon, Cultural Capital and the Prog/ Punk Dialectic', *Popular Music*, 22:3 (2003), 366, https://doi.org/10.1017 /S0261143003003234; Andy Bennett and Keith Kahn-Harris (eds), *After Subculture: Critical Studies in Contemporary Youth Culture* (Basingstoke: Palgrave Macmillan, 2004), 7.

33 Shildrick and MacDonald, 'In Defence of Subculture', 127.

34 Sarah Thornton, *Club Cultures: Music, Media and Subcultural Capital* (Cambridge: Polity Press, 1995), 8; Simon Frith, *Sound Effects: Youth, Leisure, and the Politics of Rock 'n' Roll* (New York: Pantheon Books, 1983), 220.

35 Shildrick and MacDonald, 'In Defence of Subculture', 133. Emphasis original.

36 Louise Jackson and Angela Bartie, *Policing Youth: Britain, 1945–70* (Manchester: Manchester University Press, 2014), 2.

37 Examples include Hugh Cunningham, *Time, Work and Leisure: Life Changes in England Since 1700* (Manchester: Manchester University Press, 2014); Peter Bailey, 'The Politics and Poetics of Modern British Leisure: A Late Twentieth-Century Review', *Rethinking History*, 3:2 (1999), 131–175, https:// doi.org/10.1080/13642529908596341; Brad Beaven, *Leisure, Citizenship and Working-Class Men in Britain, 1850–1945* (Manchester: Manchester University Press, 2005); Robert Snape and Helen Pussard, 'Theorisations of Leisure in Inter-War Britain', *Leisure Studies*, 32:1 (2013), 1–18, https://doi .org/10.1080/02614367.2011.629371.

38 Peter Bailey, *Leisure and Class in Victorian England: Rational Recreation and the Contest for Control, 1830–1885* (London: Routledge, 1978), 4.

39 For a recent study, see Sian Edwards, *Youth Movements, Citizenship and the English Countryside: Creating Good Citizens, 1930–1960* (Basingstoke: Palgrave Macmillan, 2018).

40 On interwar leisure more broadly, see Andrew Davies, *Leisure, Gender and Poverty: Working-Class Culture in Salford and Manchester, 1900–39* (Milton Keynes: Open University Press, 1992); Martin Pugh, *'We Danced All Night': A Social History of Britain Between the Wars* (London: Vintage Books, 2009); Robert Snape, 'The New Leisure, Voluntarism and Social Reconstruction in Inter-War Britain', *Contemporary British History*, 29:1 (2015), 51–83, https://doi.org/10.1080/13619462.2014.963060; on leisure and young people between the wars, see Claire Langhamer, *Women's Leisure in England 1920–60* (Manchester: Manchester University Press, 2000); Katharine Milcoy, *When the Girls Come Out to Play: Teenage Working-Class Girls' Leisure Between the Wars* (London: Bloomsbury, 2017); Melanie Tebbutt, *Being Boys: Youth, Leisure and Identity in the Inter-War Years* (Manchester: Manchester University Press, 2014).

41 See Allison Abra, *Dancing in the English Style: Consumption, Americanisation and National Identity in Britain, 1918–1950* (Manchester: Manchester University Press, 2017); Allison Abra, 'Doing The Lambeth Walk: Novelty Dances and the British Nation', *Twentieth Century British History*, 20:3 (2009), 346–369, https://doi.org/10.1093/tcbh/hwp035; James Nott, *Going to*

the Palais: A Social and Cultural History of Dancing and Dance Halls in Britain (Oxford: Oxford University Press, 2015); James Nott, *Music for the People: Popular Music and Dance in Interwar Britain* (Oxford: Oxford University Press, 2002); James Nott, 'Contesting Popular Dancing and Dance Music in Britain During the 1920s', *Cultural and Social History*, 10:3 (2013), 439–456, https://doi.org/10.2752/147800413X13661166397300.

42 Tebbutt, *Making Youth*, 132.

43 Notable examples include Ben Malbon, *Clubbing: Dancing, Ecstasy and Vitality* (London: Routledge, 1999); Thornton, *Club Cultures*; Matthew Collin, *Altered State: The Story of Ecstasy Culture and Acid House* (London: Serpent's Tail, 1997); Steve Redhead, Derek Wynne, and Justin O'Connor (eds), *The Clubcultures Reader: Readings in Popular Cultural Studies* (Oxford: Blackwell, 1997); Doreen Massey, 'The Spatial Construction of Youth Cultures' in Tracey Skelton and Gill Valentine (eds), *Cool Places: Geographies of Youth Cultures* (London: Routledge, 1998), 121–130; Jon Stratton, *Spectacle, Fashion and the Dancing Experience in Britain, 1960–1990* (London: Palgrave Macmillan, 2022).

44 The work of Chatterton and Hollands on this topic has produced a number of important publications, most notably Paul Chatterton and Robert Hollands, *Urban Nightscapes: Youth Cultures, Pleasure Spaces and Corporate Power* (London: Routledge, 2003); Paul Chatterton and Robert Hollands, 'Theorising Urban Playscapes: Producing, Regulating and Consuming Youthful Nightlife City Spaces', *Urban Studies*, 39:1 (2002), 95–116, https://doi.org/10.1080/00420980220099096; Paul Chatterton and Robert Hollands, 'Changing Times for an Old Industrial City: Hard Times, Hedonism and Corporate Power in Newcastle's Nightlife', *City*, 6:3 (2002), 291–315, https://doi.org/10.1080/1360481022000037742. Other important examples of work on nightscapes and the late-twentieth-century night-time economy include Roberts and Eldridge, *Planning the Night-Time City*; Lovatt and O'Connor, 'Cities and the Night-Time Economy'; Franco Bianchini, 'Night Cultures, Night Economies', *Planning Practice & Research*, 10:2 (1995), 121–126, https://doi.org/10.1080/02697459550036667.

45 Chatterton and Hollands, *Urban Nightscapes*, 7.

46 Julia Sneeringer, *A Social History of Early Rock'n'Roll in Germany: Hamburg from Burlesque to the Beatles, 1956–69* (London: Bloomsbury, 2018), 8.

47 Simon Sleight, *Young People and the Shaping of Public Space in Melbourne, 1870–1914* (London: Routledge, 2016), 6–7.

48 Felix Fuhg, *London's Working Class Youth and the Making of Post-Victorian Britain, 1958–1971* (London: Palgrave Macmillan, 2021), 7.

49 Selina Todd, 'Phoenix Rising: Working-Class Life and Urban Reconstruction, c.1954–1967', *Journal of British Studies*, 54:3 (2015), 696, https://doi.org/10.1017/jbr.2015.55.

50 Harrison, *Dangerous Amusements*, 5.

51 Lefebvre, *The Production of Space*, 15.

52 Doreen Massey, *Space, Place, and Gender* (Oxford: Polity Press, 1994), 4.

26   *Growing up and going out*

53 *Ibid.*, 4.

54 Charles W. J. Withers, 'Place and the "Spatial Turn" in Geography and in History', *Journal of the History of Ideas*, 40:4 (2009), 657–658, https://doi.org/10.1353/jhi.0.0054.

55 Dylan Baun and Carla Pascoe Leahy, 'Spaces and Places' in Kristine Alexander and Simon Sleight (eds), *A Cultural History of Youth in the Modern Age* (London: Bloomsbury, 2022), 41.

56 Chris Jenks, *Childhood* (2nd edn, London: Routledge, 2005), 73–74.

57 Dave Russell, 'Glimpsing "*La Dolce Vita*": Cultural Change and Modernity in the 1960s English Cabaret Club', *Journal of Social History*, 47:2 (2013), 298, https://doi.org/10.1093/jsh/sht083.

58 Camilla Schofield, 'In Defence of White Freedom: Working Men's Clubs and the Politics of Sociability in Late Industrial England', *Twentieth Century British History*, 34:3 (2023), 518, https://doi.org/10.1093/tcbh/hwad038.

59 Sarah Kenny, '"Basically You Were Either a Mainstream Sort of Person or You Went to the Leadmill and the Limit": Understanding Post-War British Youth Culture Through Oral History' in Kristine Moruzi, Nell Musgrove, and Carla Pascoe Leahy (eds), *Children's Voices from the Past: New Historical and Interdisciplinary Perspectives* (London: Palgrave Macmillan, 2019), 237.

60 Hesmondhalgh, 'Subcultures, Scenes or Tribes?', 37.

61 Bart van der Steen and Thierry Verburgh (eds), *Researching Subcultures, Myth and Memory* (London: Palgrave Macmillan, 2020), 1.

62 See in particular Robert Perks and Alistair Thomson (eds), *The Oral History Reader* (London: Routledge, 1997); Lynn Abrams, *Oral History Theory* (London: Routledge, 2010); Donald Ritchie (ed.), *The Oxford Handbook of Oral History* (Oxford: Oxford University Press, 2010).

63 Tess Coslett, Celia Lury, and Penny Summerfield (eds), *Feminism and Autobiography: Texts, Theories, Methods* (London: Routledge, 2000), 4.

64 Maurice Halbwachs, *On Collective Memory* (trans. Lewis A. Coser, Chicago, IL: University of Chicago Press, 1992), 40.

65 Sarah Gensburger, 'Halbwachs' Studies in Collective Memory: A Founding Text for Contemporary "Memory Studies"?', *Journal of Classical Sociology*, 16:4 (2016), 400, https://doi.org/10.1177/1468795X16656268.

66 For a fuller discussion of memory and critiques of oral history see Alistair Thomson, 'Memory and Remembering in Oral History' in Ritchie (ed.), *The Oxford Handbook of Oral History*, 77–91. For a consideration of gendered engagements with popular memory see Penny Summerfield and Corinna Peniston-Bird, 'Women in the Firing Line: The Home Guard and the Defence of Gender Boundaries in Britain in the Second World War', *Women's History Review*, 9:2 (2000), 231–255, https://doi.org/10.1080/09612020000200250.

67 Alessando Portelli, 'What Makes Oral History Different' in Perks and Thomson (eds), *The Oral History Reader*, 67.

68 Hannah Charnock, 'Teenage Girls, Female Friendship and the Making of the Sexual Revolution in England, 1950–1980', *Historical Journal*, 63:4 (2020), 1034, https://doi.org/10.1017/S0018246X19000396.

Introduction 27

69 Mills, 'Using the Personal to Critique the Popular', 464.

70 Harrison, *Dangerous Amusements*, 16.

71 See in particular Tisdall, 'Education, Parenting and Concepts of Childhood in England'. Other notable examples include Laura Lovett (ed.), Special Issue on 'Age as a Category of Historical Analysis', *Journal of the History of Childhood and Youth* 1:1 (2008); Jens Qvortrup, William A. Corsaro, and Michael-Sebastian Honig (eds), *The Palgrave Handbook of Childhood Studies* (London: Palgrave Macmillan, 2009).

72 HL Deb 15 March 1988, vol 494, col 1098. The government had established the Working Group on Young People and Alcohol in 1987 to assess the problem of underage drinking in Britain.

Part I

Youth and the changing urban environment

1

Out in the city

In 1963, acclaimed director Philip Donnellan and a BBC film crew visited Sheffield beat club the Esquire as part of a documentary about teenage life in 1960s Britain. Exploring young people's attitudes to sex, marriage, work, and religion, *The Long Journey* was broadcast in April 1964, and followed the life of a 16-year-old girl and her friends as they navigated their youth in the 'new' Britain of the 1960s.[1] Inspired by the BBC Radio Ballads of the late 1950s and early 1960s, *The Long Journey* positioned the voices and experiences of the 'typical' British teenager at the heart of the programme, and provided a platform for the young to describe their lives on their own terms, with their own voices.[2]

In the months running up to the broadcast of the film, the local press wrote with pride of Sheffield's place in the documentary. The *Star* noted that the Esquire had 'been chosen from hundreds of northern nightspots because of its tremendous atmosphere and originality'.[3] However, following the appearance of the club in *The Long Journey*, the initial enthusiasm shown for Sheffield's popular teenage haunt turned to outrage among many of the city's older residents, with the documentary featuring in the columns and letters of the local press in the following days and weeks. In response to criticisms labelling the venue as sordid, owner Terry Thornton explained that 'they just wouldn't understand the way the kids let off steam'.[4] While the behaviour of those young people featured in *The Long Journey* would scarcely raise even an eyebrow now, the documentary was enough to alert Sheffield's adult residents to the growing number of spaces in the city that were now beyond their knowledge and jurisdiction. The Esquire was Thornton's second venue in the city, and was one of several late-night leisure spaces for youth in Sheffield that had opened in the early 1960s.

The 1950s and 1960s are perhaps the most mythologised in Britain's recent past, and echoes of Macmillan's 'never had it so good' coupled with images of 'Swinging London' crowd the popular imagination. While historians have rightly questioned the extent to which this period can be seen as one of revolution – be that cultural, sexual, or social – it is hard to deny that

32 *Youth and the changing urban environment*

young people growing up at this time experienced significant and long-lasting changes in the realms of lifestyle and leisure.[5] Across the country a quiet revolution was taking place; in housing estates and suburbs, high streets and city centres, young people were renegotiating their place in the post-war world. Despite the many publicised and media-fuelled panics about the state of youth in the 1950s and 1960s, it was the much quieter and seemingly mundane engagements with youth leisure that truly marked the period as one of real change. Very few of Britain's teenagers were wielding flick knives in Teddy Boy gangs or fighting on the beaches of Margate on Whitsunday; they were far more likely to be found huddled round a cup of coffee in one of their town or city's newly opened coffee bars, or otherwise dancing to a juke box or live band in a local dance hall or late-night beat club. Driven by new patterns of work and leisure and growing levels of disposable income, as well as access to the products of an increasingly international youth culture, these spaces provided a place in which young people could socialise away from the home with relative freedom from the constraints and expectations of wider society.

The early post-war period saw rapid transformations in commercial youth leisure with the emergence of spaces designed to appeal solely to the cultural interests and desires of teenagers and young adults, as well as changes to the ways in which more traditional commercial leisure spaces such as the ballroom and dance hall were used. This period of transition was not necessarily a seamless one; despite the relative lack of violence and lawbreaking in the vast majority of spaces where youth socialised, they were nevertheless portrayed as having the potential to disrupt and corrupt those who entered them, helped in no small part by both the local and national press. In short, they exposed moments of real tension as older ideas about leisure and pleasure collided with the new. Responses to the increasing visibility and influence of leisure spaces held genuine power to shape young people's experiences of and access to these spaces, and this was particularly marked in provincial cities with more limited access to youth leisure. Being out in the city as a young person was by no means the preserve of the post-war period, but the emergence of coffee bars, jazz clubs, and beat nights in the 1950s and 1960s added a crucial spatial dimension that left an indelible mark on Britain's leisure landscape.[6] By the time the residents of Sheffield were writing appalled letters about the behaviour of the city's teenagers in the Esquire club, the quiet revolution was already well underway.

The response of Sheffield's residents to the behaviour of the city's teenagers was part of a wider national discourse of both concern and suspicion regarding the disruptive potential of the new spaces of youth leisure. A cursory glance at contemporary press coverage of coffee bars in the 1950s, for example, yields countless headlines about police raids, drug consumption, knife crime, and robbery. This was one of many moments over the course of nineteenth and twentieth centuries in which youth lifestyles were bought to the fore of public debate, but the particular spatial developments in youth leisure in the early post-war period gave these concerns further purchase. These responses were fuelled by a fascination with an increasingly visible form of youth culture, alongside continuing fears about the moral condition of youth. Yet these spaces hold far more significance than simply as sites of moral panic; they helped shape a generation's experience of and access to dedicated youth leisure beyond the home and youth club, and paved the way for the domination of commercial youth leisure spaces in Britain's towns and cities in the decades to come.

These new spaces of youth leisure did not emerge in a vacuum, however. This was a period of widespread urban redevelopment, and marks a very particular moment in modern British history. Major cultural and political shifts in the post-war period put leisure high on the agenda for post-war reconstruction; politicians increasingly recognised the value of quality leisure time for families, architects placed leisure and retail at the heart of the modern city, and developers recognised the potential of leisure space for profit. Towards the end of the period, upmarket cabaret clubs replaced dance halls and music halls as key sites of leisure for those who had a little extra money to spend. Of course, particular fears were articulated with regards to what might constitute appropriate youth leisure in this new cultural landscape; debates about the potential dangers of commercial leisure that had emerged in the early twentieth century continued with a vengeance, while boredom and a lack of suitable social space for young people become a common explanation for anti-social behaviour.[7] While debates about what exactly a suitable leisure space might consist of in the post-war world were abundant, this was nonetheless a moment in which the pursuit of leisure was placed high on the social and political agenda.

A fuller appreciation of the relationship between youth leisure and the urban environment in post-war Britain offers an opportunity to challenge traditional assessments of youth culture and leisure beyond the metropole. Historians have often pointed to provincial towns and cities to challenge the myth of the 'swinging sixties', demonstrating London's relative uniqueness when compared to the rest of Britain.[8] As Felix Fuhg argued, 'London differed from the rest of the country, though many people, particularly those living in the capital, were convinced of the universal appeal and relevance of the metropolitan way of life.'[9] While London can rightly be highlighted as an anomaly, many regional towns and cities were home to an increasingly diverse and vibrant set of leisure options that paint a picture of a nation undergoing far-reaching change. There were very real developments in leisure and lifestyle in this period, and these were not confined to the

34 *Youth and the changing urban environment*

metropole or isolated areas of cultural significance such as Manchester and Merseyside. By the end of the 1960s, young people could be found socialising out in the city in growing numbers and with increasing regularity, in a variety of leisure spaces that were now dedicated to their pleasure.

Leisure and the urban landscape in post-war Britain

Plans for the redevelopment of the urban environment in the years after the Second World War reveal much about hopes for the future in post-war Britain. Bomb damage, population growth, and the continuation of interwar slum clearance programmes offered the opportunity for a reimagined city, one that recognised commerce, leisure, and pleasure as key aspects of life in this period.[10] Consecutive governments took advantage of this opportunity, heralding a moment in which 'the urban fabric changed more dramatically than almost any comparable period in British history'.[11] This transformation of the urban environment – both physically and in its consideration of an imagined leisured society – is crucial to our understanding of the post-war developments in youth culture and leisure. The New Towns Act of 1946 offered real opportunity for architectural creativity, while broader programmes of redevelopment focused on pedestrianisation, upgrading road networks, and extending public transportation transformed the accessibility of the modern city. Such changes were part of a wider reimagining of the relationship between the individual and the urban, particularly in the way that the city centre was increasingly positioned as a space of retail, leisure, and pleasure.

Retail and leisure were positioned high on the agenda for post-war urban reconstruction for good reason. By the mid-1950s, Britain, alongside much of Western Europe and America, was experiencing an economic 'boom'; the end of food and clothing rationing, coupled with improved welfare services, affordable consumer products, low unemployment, and 'soaring' stock market values, fuelled 'a long-suppressed release of pent-up consumer demand'.[12] Between 1955 and 1969, Britain's workers saw significant wage rises. While retail prices rose 15 per cent between 1955 and 1960 and 63 per cent between 1960 and 1969, weekly wages rose by 25 per cent by 1960 and 88 per cent by 1969. Overall, average weekly earnings rose by 130 per cent between 1955 and 1969.[13] While it is of course possible to overstate the extent of this affluence – poverty, need, and inequality were by no means eradicated in Britain's affluent society – life did, on the whole, improve for many in this period.[14] Material shifts such as these made engaging in retail consumption and leisure a real option for a significant number of people, and planners built this into the urban fabric of the post-war city. There are

Out in the city

35

significant links to be made between the growth of retail and leisure as an accessible lifestyle choice and the growth of a distinct youth culture. Indeed, for Bill Osgerby, it is impossible to 'understand the saliency of youth as a cultural category' without contextualising it within the broader social, cultural, and political shifts of the post-war period.[15] These shifts tell us much about the potency of youth's image in this period, but also help explain the central role that youth leisure played in transforming the leisurescape of the built environment.

Sheffield in the 1960s, like many regional urban centres, was a city in transition. The 1972 film *Sheffield: City on the Move* showcased the city's new leisurescape and was indicative of the language of modernism and aspiration that surrounded the post-war city. Promising clean air, green open spaces, and 'world-class' shopping and leisure facilities, the modern city was held up as a symbol of the affluent society. Civic pride was alive and well in the early post-war period, 'no longer mirrored in the choice of Gothic or classical styles of design, but through the dirtfree and the modern, promised by concrete and glass'.[16] As elsewhere, post-war redevelopment sought to reimagine Sheffield as a site of leisure. A great deal of the city's redevelopment was focused on creating a modern and accessible shopping precinct, with much of the city centre being pedestrianised in the 1950s and 1960s. Following the removal of central slums in the interwar years, it was hoped that large-scale pedestrianisation of the city would create a more homogenous shopping district. Construction of one of Sheffield's most iconic city-centre schemes, the 'Hole in the Road', began in 1967 and created a large pedestrianised area running beneath the city centre, acting as a thoroughfare to department stores such as C&A Modes but also housing independent retailers. The building of the Hole in the Road demonstrated the council's commitment to a more homogeneous and shopper-friendly retail centre, and it is indicative of the wider feeling of optimism and prosperity in the city in the early post-war years.

Similar developments were seen in Leeds with the building of the Merrion Shopping Centre, which was seen by a local developer 'as an extension of the city's status as a leading centre in the country', while architect Donald Gibson created an entirely pedestrianised shopping district called the Precinct in his vision for the bomb-ravaged Coventry.[17] In a study of 1960s Blackburn, Otto Saumarez Smith has shown how the city's Victorian legacy was swept away and replaced with Blackburn Shopping Centre: 'a megastructural melange, a consumerist paradise, a beacon for an affluent and modern age'.[18] Shopping centres such as these, containing cinemas, hotels, and restaurants alongside shops and services, appeared across the country yet now represent 'a banal, everyday modernism that is invisible and unloved'.[19] These centres, while overlooked in the legacies of post-war

Figure 1.1 Cover image for 'Sheffield: City on the Move' campaign, 1970. © Sheffield City Council and Picture Sheffield.

urban planning, shed light on the cultural potency of post-war affluence; access to quality leisure and retail opportunities was no longer designed to appeal solely to middle-class tendencies and instead was held up in and of itself as a sign of the successful modern city. This was a moment, argues Selina Todd, in which working-class lives 'were central, rather than marginal, to Britain's civic centers'.[20]

The language of civic pride was amalgamated into a broader narrative of the period; at the start of 1967, the *Daily Mirror* launched its 'Boom Cities' campaign, designed to 'salute the thrusting, thriving cities whose enterprise is key to Britain's future'.[21] 'The whole world knows about swinging London', declared the front page, 'but these cities are swinging too'. Further cementing this post-war image of prosperity and modernity, the campaign asked readers to nominate their favourite cities; Sheffield was highlighted as one of Britain's 'boom cities', alongside Manchester, Liverpool, Birmingham, and others. By 1967 Sheffield was, according to the *Daily Mirror*, 'a Boom City in step with all the young ideas of today'.[22] The redevelopment of the city centre was said to be done 'with the shopper in mind'; 'just pause along any of the main shopping centres', the article explained, 'and you will hear Sheffield booming'. Significantly, the campaign highlighted the importance of growing opportunities for urban leisure as central to the successful modern city. While one 15-year-old youth from Gloucester wrote in to nominate the city as 'the biggest raspberry of the lot' – 'by all means keep the Cathedral, but let's also have a bowling alley, sports arena, and a decent dance hall which would cater more for people of my age' – Bristol was celebrated for its range of coffee bars, youth clubs, and 'the liveliest ice rink in the West country'.

The consumer products of post-war youth culture 'opened up a new kind of active engagement with consumption as an aim in itself', and this was reflected in the urban environment.[23] Boutiques, department stores, and record stores, as well as cinemas and dancing, became central facets of the youthful experience, making the city centre an important site of youth leisure. Marnie Fogg, for example, has outlined the particular cultural importance of the boutique as a place for young people to congregate.[24] For those with limited access to disposable income, window shopping provided a viable alternative, and the displays of modern stores provided ample inspiration for those who sought to replicate the latest fashions at home. Unlike their parents who were increasingly – though not exclusively – moving towards home-based consumption, young people's consumption of consumer goods and entertainments 'primarily took place in public realms'.[25] The emergence of these public and semi-public sites of youth leisure were driven by the same economic 'boom' that saw sales of washing machines and television sets soar; rising levels of disposable income were as important for Britain's teenagers and young adults as they were to their parents. Between 1945 and 1950, the wages of young people rose at twice the rate of adults, and by the late 1950s, the incomes of young people in Britain had risen by at least 50 per cent when compared with pre-war levels.[26] Young people had more money to spend, and far more opportunity to spend it on themselves. The spending power of youth in the early post-war period had a marked impact on the towns and cities where they lived, and unlike their parents, they were far more likely to spend and consume in the public realm.

The urban centre therefore emerged as an important leisure space in the post-war period, and these broader transformations in the urban environment played a crucial role in reshaping the way young people spent their time in the city. Town and city centres were well-served by public transport, providing a central and mutually accessible space for young people to meet and congregate. The redevelopment of the central parts of many of Britain's towns and cities represented a physical manifestation of the importance of commerce, retail, and leisure in this period, and as such should be understood as part of a wider reimagining of the relationship between public space and leisure time. These shifts did not exclude young people, and the emergence of a distinct youth culture at this particular juncture in the urban history of modern Britain left its mark on the built environment. Tracing

38 *Youth and the changing urban environment*

the emergence and development of spaces of youth leisure can therefore tell us much about the changing lifestyles of young people in this early post-war period, but also reveals their spatial mobility and use of the changing cityscape.

Coffee bars and youth clubs

Within this transforming urban environment, the coffee bar emerged as a socially and culturally significant space for Britain's youth. Found both in town and city centres, offering an opportunity to rest and socialise after a day's shopping or browsing, as well as in residential areas and housing estates, the coffee bar provided a cheap and accessible leisure space for Britain's young people. Coffee bars grew in popularity at an astonishing rate during the 1950s and, by 1957, there were estimated to be over a thousand of them across Britain.[27] By the end of the 1950s, there was perhaps no space that was so closely associated with the image of the British teenager. Their emergence and immediate popularity marked an important cultural shift; before the wholesale growth of commercial leisure venues from the mid-1960s onwards, coffee bars were one of the earliest commercial spaces where young people could socialise away from the adult gaze. While youth clubs had long provided dedicated space for young people, their formal programming and activities were fast losing appeal to British youth. The coffee bar not only offered the opportunity for cheap and accessible amusement, but it was also a space where young people could gather simply to socialise. Their growth had a marked impact on youth leisure in the early post-war period; the accessibility of coffee bars forced the hand of church groups and youth clubs who were increasingly struggling to attract and retain members, and heralded a real shift in approaches to youth work.

The milk bar had become an increasingly common sight in Britain from the 1930s, but it was from the 1950s that the espresso or coffee bar soared in popularity.[28] What marked the coffee bar apart from other similar establishments in this period were two key things: the introduction of juke boxes, and opening hours that often extended past the closing hours of public houses. The fast rise of coffee and milk bars in London's Soho district in the mid-1950s earned it the title 'Little Europe', and the city's 'coffee bar capers' featured regularly in the press.[29] They became a cultural symbol of the time, seen to represent Americanisation, affluence, and modernity. Richard Hoggart's now infamous passage on the 'juke box boys' in his landmark 1957 text *Uses of Literacy* cemented their status as icons of 1950s youth culture. Hoggart's observations of the boys and their cafe, the type of which he estimated there to be 'one in almost every northern town with more than say, 'fifteen-thousand inhabitants', were less than complimentary.[30] Hoggart described the 'nastiness of their modern knick-knacks, their glaring showiness', with the main visitors being 'boys aged between fifteen and twenty, with drape-suits, picture ties, and an American slouch'.[31] In what could be perceived as a rather cynical attack on their interests, Hoggart described how the youths put 'copper after copper into the mechanical record player … living to a large extent in a myth-world compounded of a few simple elements which they take to be those of American life'.[32] For many, coffee bars came to represent the immediacy and crassness of modern youth culture.

The coffee bar was singled out in part because of its sheer popularity. Much like the cinema and dance hall of the 1920s and 1930s, the coffee bar was seen as distracting young people from better, more wholesome pursuits. In his assessment of teenage spending in 1959, Mark Abrams found that soft drinks, snacks, and meals out accounted for 15 per cent of all teenage expenditure.[33] Abrams's popular 1959 marketing study reveals much about teenage spending habits, but far less about exactly *where* young people were spending. By contrast, pioneering social investigator Pearl Jephcott focused far more on the behaviours and lifestyles of young people, and her 1967 study of Scottish youth, *Time of One's Own*, outlines the leisure pursuits of young people in the 1960s.[34] Jephcott's study confirmed Abrams's findings on youth spending on soft drinks and snacks, finding that while the cinema and dancing remained highly popular leisure activities, 51 per cent of those interviewed went into cafes on a regular basis.[35] Geographical location was highlighted as particularly important with regards to the coffee bar; young people growing up Glasgow had access to a range of late-night leisure spaces, but in Armadale, West Lothian, which in 1961 was a town of only 6,195, the coffee bar emerged as a central space. In Armadale, 44 per cent of boys and 33 per cent of girls between the ages of 15 and 19 had been in a cafe in the previous seven days.[36] Jephcott noted that alongside cheapness and accessibility, the young people involved in *Time of One's Own* highlighted the 'social assets' of the youth cafe; this was a space where 'ideas could be exchanged more readily … than at the street corner or when just walking round'.[37] Peter Willmott's five-year study of adolescent boys in east London in the early 1960s similarly found that coffee bars acted as 'social centres'.[38] For John Barron Mays, the coffee bar was not the 'nadir of moral depravity', but simply filled with 'ordinary young people having an evening out'.[39]

The social and cultural significance of the coffee bar has not gone unnoticed by historians, either. In revisiting Hoggart's extract in *The Uses of Literacy*, Joe Moran considers how Hoggart's response to the coffee bar 'had less to do with fears about Americanization … than with concerns about the relationship between the public and private sphere, and the losses and

40 *Youth and the changing urban environment*

gains of rising affluence'.[40] Kate Bradley has explored the role the coffee bar played in social reformers' ideas of 'rational recreation' in the period, while Louise Jackson has demonstrated the central place that Manchester's coffee bars played in the moral regulation of the young in the mid-1960s.[41] Adrian Horn argued that the introduction of juke boxes into coffee bars in Britain meant that 'the social needs that had been catered for by amusement arcades were transferred to the youth café'.[42] While making a clear argument for the significance of the coffee bar in the 1950s, Moran argued that outside of London, 'the espresso bar was a more mundane but still popular venue for young people largely deprived of other forms of evening entertainment'.[43] The coffee bars of London were known for their unconventionality, often adopting eye-catching or risqué concepts to separate them from their many competitors, but such a comparison risks undermining the significance of such venues to youth outside of London. As this chapter will show, these spaces were central to the leisure experiences of many young people across the country. Indeed, Katie Milestone has argued that in this period the north 'was frequently imagined as a parochial, friendly but dull place, with little to offer culturally'.[44] Yet, as Keith Gildart has powerfully shown in his study of popular music and working-class youth, 'the industrial communities of northern England were positively buzzing with new soundscapes, fashions, and forms of expression'.[45] In order to reach a fuller understanding of the way youth culture developed across Britain, historians must explore these spaces on their own terms, and in their own local contexts.

The coffee bar has been highlighted by historians and social commentators because it became a particular site of moral panic for both the establishment and wider society, but what can the popularity of the coffee bar reveal about the growing prominence of youth leisure in the urban environment? In 1958, in response to a column in the *Peterborough Advertiser* decrying the lack of suitable spaces for young people, a local businessman wrote to announce the opening of the city's first coffee bar, the Moderno. The coffee bar was to be designed 'so that the business man and lady shoppers in the morning will feel equally as ease there as the "young man about town" will in the evenings'.[46] While not advertising itself solely as a destination for the city's youth, the owner's decision to open until ten o'clock in the evening was a clear indication of his desire to capitalise on the youth market. In an article tackling youth boredom in New Towns, the *Daily Herald* highlighted the importance of coffee bars in towns that had other limited leisure facilities. Welwyn Garden City's first coffee bar, for example, was 'sprinkled with housewives sipping coffee in the daytime and jammed with youngsters listening to the juke box each night'.[47]

The rise of coffee and milk bars was prominent in Sheffield as elsewhere in Britain. By the 1960s, there were a number of coffee bars in Sheffield city centre and the suburbs, including the Side Walk, La Favourita, the Leprechaun, El Mambo, La Strada, Paramount, the Zodiac, Disc Jockey Café, Flamingo, the Mustard Seed, the Octopus, Chez Brion, and the Teenager Tavern, located in the downstairs area of Marsdens' Milk Bar.[48] Despite not selling alcohol, coffee bars often gained a negative reputation for the people they attracted. One Sheffield resident recalled her memories of the El Mambo coffee bar in Sheffield's city centre, saying: 'if my mum ever caught a sniff of me going near that place she'd have killed me. She told me it was frequented by the dodgiest people'.[49] My own interviewee, Trish, a teenager in Sheffield in the mid-1960s, echoed this sentiment. She explained that:

> Sometimes at the end of the evening there was a coffee bar somewhere, I think it was Carver Street, called La Favourita, because the pubs kicked out at eleven, half ten, eleven, and that was open until midnight which was very daring and very late and after the last bus and you were in big trouble.

Trish's interview highlighted a key concern surrounding coffee bars by the 1960s: their late opening hours immediately made them, in the eyes of many parents, a space of transgression. This transgression was heightened by the way these spaces were racialised. Sheffield's El Mambo coffee bar, for example, was known to be frequented by young men of Yemeni heritage, many of whom worked in the city's steelworks.[50] The cafe culture of coffee bars, for many a more welcoming alternative to the city's traditional public houses, were therefore viewed with suspicion by many of the city's older white residents, and the temporal shift to late-night socialising in the city centre was framed clearly as cause for concern. Coupled with racialised media portrayals of coffee bars and links to 'Teddy Boy violence' in both the local and national press, many young people faced opposition when socialising in these spaces late into the evening. This image was also something young people themselves were aware of. Jephcott's teenagers proved themselves to be very knowledge about the range of coffee bars in their vicinity, being able to 'pin its social character onto any one of them'.[51]

The later opening hours of coffee bars were central to their popularity in the years after the Second World War. The minutes of licensing magistrates give an indication as to how these spaces were being used in this period. The meeting of Sheffield's licensing magistrates in May 1966 shows three Sheffield coffee bars being granted Music and Singing licences until 10 p.m., enabling them to install juke boxes on the premises, a key factor in attracting a younger clientele.[52] The meeting of July 1966 similarly shows another three coffee bars being granted extensions to their hours, allowing them to open until 10 p.m.[53] Many of these spaces were open all day, and coffee bars

42   *Youth and the changing urban environment*

such as Sheffield's La Favourita or Peterborough's the Moderno were ideally placed in the centre of town, appealing to young people socialising in the city centre in the day and at night, and thus offering an important level of accessibility. However, not all of these spaces were situated in the town or city centre; throughout this period, the suburbs and residential areas, particularly in larger cities, were an important site of youth leisure. All three Sheffield cafes granted extensions to their opening hours in the July 1966 meeting were in large residential areas where there were high populations of young people: Maisie's Cafe on Duke Street was located near the Park Hill housing development; Hilo Cafe on Cuthbert Bank Road was located in the well-connected suburb of Hillsborough; and Harlequins Cafe was located on the high street of Crookes, a western suburb of Sheffield near the University. The applications to authorities to extend opening hours and install juke boxes are demonstrative of the ways in which businesses were becoming more aware of the growing desire for, and commercial benefits of, spaces more attractive to young people.

For young people who were unable to – or did not want to – socialise in public houses, the later opening hours of coffee bars provided a much-needed space for sociability. While dance halls and cinemas remained a popular leisure space for many young people, the new coffee bars provided an important alternative. Crucially, young people were able to socialise over a relatively cheap cup of coffee, making this an important space for working-class youth who were excluded from regularly participating in other forms of commercial leisure. As Kate Bradley has argued, coffee and milk bars were not simply a place where adolescents went to 'dress up and show off; they were also spaces where many had the opportunity to "do nothing" while casually building social skills and confidence outside of the parental home or school'.[54] The significance of the coffee bar in the 1950s and early 1960s also signalled a broader temporal and spatial shift in youth leisure; young people no longer had to huddle on street corners or walk the streets in the dark if they wanted to socialise in the evenings, but were now able to gather in the bright and warm environment of the coffee bar. This had a marked effect on the relationship between young people and the urban environment; they were at once more removed from the public gaze and offered the opportunity to socialise in comfort in the evenings.

The coffee bar's influence

Nowhere was the influence of new commercial spaces of youth leisure more apparent than in the work of youth clubs and church groups in the years after the Second World War. The work of youth clubs in the 1950s and

1960s was shaped by this particular moment in the history of youth leisure; debates about rational recreation and worthwhile leisure pursuits came into clear conflict with young people's desire for unstructured and adult-free leisure time. Designated space for young people had existed in the form of youth clubs for a number of years, but these were often tied to churches, schools, and other official institutions. Groups existed for younger children, including Boy Scouts, Brownies, and the Boys Brigade, and were similarly organised through more formal structures.[55] These spaces were controlled and shaped by the presence of supervising adults, and the often formal structure of these clubs was highlighted as one of several potential issues with the recruitment and retainment of older club members from the late 1950s onwards. Fears about 'competition' from commercial leisure were by no means unique to the post-war period, but took on a new urgency in the 1950s given the increasing leisure options for young people and access to rising levels of disposable income. The rise of coffee bars in particular, often designed with the young person in mind, created a greater availability of space for young people to socialise in and created a threat to the long-established popularity of the youth club.

In November 1950, the National Association of Mixed Clubs and Girls' Clubs (NAMGC) drew particular attention to three categories of youth they felt to be particularly vulnerable to misbehaviour: the older club member, the adolescent working girl, and the 'unattached'.[56] The older club member, they argued, needed help to 'find their place in adult society', while the adolescent working girl required 'careful planning' of club programmes to alleviate problems caused by work which was 'so often dull and monotonous'.[57] Indeed, Penny Tinkler and Emma Latham have considered the continuing importance of gender to youth work in the immediate post-war period, with Latham arguing that in Liverpool the Liverpool Union of Youth Clubs increasingly 'advanced a version of femininity alien to that of female club members'.[58] The 'problem' of attracting unattached youth became a particular focus throughout the 1950s and 1960s, and experimental programming was encouraged to try and attract these young people. The publication of Mary Morse's *The Unattached* in 1965 outlined the national association's approach, categorised by informality, a lack of structure, and youth-driven activities.[59] This approach, the NAMGC felt, would provide a real alternative to commercial leisure provision that was attracting so many young people but that lacked the moral guidance of the association youth clubs.

As part of this new approach, many youth clubs began to embrace and incorporate particular aspects of commercial leisure into their clubs. In 1958 H. J. Frank, the deputy general secretary of the NAMGC, promoted the idea of running coffee bars to attract the 'sixty per cent of young people who did not belong to an organisation', an idea based on a 'flourishing' club in Sheffield.[60] Frank explained that 'no group had changed its tastes and habits so much in the past twenty years as the adolescent'.[61] In a commentary of the 'modern youth club' the *Liverpool Echo* noted in 1959 that 'today youth has money and many organisations, not all of them reputable, are competing for it ... members of the dirty, dingy, ill-lit clubs will compare them with the colour and comfort of new homes, new schools, cinemas, coffee bars and dance halls'.[62] Youth clubs and organisations across Britain – both affiliated and unaffiliated – were taking inspiration from commercial leisure provision to attract potential club members. The Y.M.C.A. in Eastbourne, for example, began the 'Coffee Pot Club' in 1957 following the redecoration of the club's premises, while in 1958 the secretary of the Aberdeen Youth Council spoke of the importance of the coffee club for attracting older youth.[63] In Harrow, the Education Committee financed a teenage coffee bar in 1960, 'designed to take off the street young people who were not likely to join a more conventional youth club'.[64] In Sheffield, the Sheffield Association of Mixed Clubs and Girls' Clubs sponsored the opening of a jazz club.[65] The '552' Jazz Club's premises opened on 1 November 1960, and John Clement, assistant organiser for the association, explained at the time that 'it's got the ideal coffee bar type atmosphere ... and will be the only jazz club in this area of the city'.[66] The decision to open the club came, explained Mr Clement, after a series of articles in local newspaper the *Star* which 'dealt with the lack of clubs for teenagers too young to hear most of the local bands, which play in pubs'.[67] A similar article in the *Guardian* from 1960 reported on a Salford youth club being given initial approval for 'all the things they [teenagers] appear to be interested in, including [a] coffee bar, music, dancing, and possibly boxing'.[68] The club hoped that 'youngsters could realise the advantages of getting together and eventually could be attracted to more worthwhile activities'.[69]

Alongside youth clubs, the role of churches in running activities for young people remained a significant feature of youth provision in this period. Indeed, Charlotte Clements has argued that despite a wider narrative of secularisation, the role of the church in youth work was an important continuity in the post-war period.[70] In October 1960, Wesley Hall Methodist Church in Crookes, a western suburb of Sheffield, proposed the building of a coffee bar. The coffee bar, explained Reverend R. G. Jones, would be for young people, 'without ramming religion down their throats'.[71] He went on to explain that 'there will be opportunities for these youngsters to enter into youth club activities, but they will be able to sit in the coffee bar and do nothing if they so wish'.[72] In Eastbourne, the Central Methodist Youth Club unveiled their redecorated premises in 1959, featuring a soft drinks and coffee bar, which would 'provide more attractive and comfortable surroundings for informal conversation, discussions, and small social gatherings.'[73]

Out in the city

In Birkenhead, members of Oxton Road Congregational Church established the 'Drawbridge Club' in the Church's basement. Featuring a coffee bar and stage for live gospel and rhythm music, the club was designed to 'draw young people in and bridge the gap between them and the church'.[74] The desires of the Church to attract young people 'to more worthwhile activities' through these ventures was indicative of the continuing importance of rational recreation in the approaches of youth workers and organisations in this period. However, the incorporation of aspects of commercial leisure such as coffee bars, juke boxes, and live music to achieve this marked a significant development from the youth work of the pre-war era.

These shifts were in line with national trends; as live music became increasingly more common in public houses, and juke boxes provided music in commercial coffee bars, youth clubs and church clubs needed to provide viable and attractive alternatives. Bradley demonstrates the fear that the young would 'ape' behaviours seen in supposedly less reputable spaces such as public houses and bars, and the work of youth clubs in this early post-war period demonstrates the continuing desire to 'guide' young people towards adulthood.[75] However, the need to adapt to the changing lifestyles of the young reflected the growing significance of commercial leisure in the lives of Britain's teenagers and young adults. Young people were increasingly able to dictate and influence how and where they wished to spend their time, and as the period progressed, older teenagers were more likely to be drawn to these alternative commercial spaces. As a 'respectable' space under the supervision of adults, the youth club remained an important stepping-stone for younger adolescents to begin to socialise and build social networks outside of the traditional spaces of home and school. The growth of commercial leisure provision fuelled major shifts in approaches to youth work, as organisations recognised the growing importance of staying relevant in the ever-shifting landscape of modern youth. The new coffee bars, then, represented not only the emergence of a distinct youth culture but a distinct youth lifestyle, increasingly characterised by separate spaces of commercial youth leisure.

However, the growth of the coffee bar and other commercial entertainments did not necessitate the total decline of the youth club as an influential space for young people. While many youth clubs struggled to compete with the attractions of commercial youth leisure, others provided a much-needed space for young people to have greater control over their cultural activities. The drive for youth clubs and organisations to reflect the interests of their young members therefore provided young people with a degree of agency over their interests and activities. This was driven by youth workers – often unpaid and volunteers – who sought to provide a space for young people in their community. In Sheffield, as in other areas like Birmingham, Bradford,

46 *Youth and the changing urban environment*

and Manchester, young people of Asian heritage found community and opportunities for activism in local youth clubs and organisations. As one young student at Sheffield Polytechnic recalled upon entering a youth club associated with the Asian Youth Movement in the late 1970s:

> I realised that what I'd experienced in terms of the racist abuse and racism, the insecurities I experienced, a sense of not belonging – that was shared by a whole group of individuals and it was not unique to me and I found a collective support and strength in that.[76]

Daisy Payling has outlined the importance of safe spaces for Black and Asian youth in the city in this period, noting that a number of important organisations including Sheffield and District African Caribbean Community Association (SADACCA), formed in 1955 and heavily involved in youth work in the city, were located in the 'so-called "Black area" of the city', in areas surrounding the Wicker near the city centre.

As well as opportunities for community building and activism, youth clubs and organisations also offered spaces for young people to produce and consume music that wasn't being played in the mainstream dance halls. As William 'Lez' Henry and Les Back have demonstrated, reggae's development in London and elsewhere emerged from 'the network of youth clubs, house parties, and churches that offered alternative public spheres' for young people of colour.[77] Juan, a Black teenager growing up in Sheffield in the 1970s, recalled the important influence that his local youth club held for him as a young teenager:

> we had a state of the art youth club that had its own disco room and all sorts of stuff like that ... absolutely amazing in the sense that every so often she brought up DJs from London, so we were hearing, so I was into jazz funk, so they would come up with funky jazz ... then they had a local DJ who again, was playing a lot of important jazz funk sort of stuff and he became quite big in the northern ... jazz funk scene.

The popularity of these events brought together young people across the city, who would often travel for this music. As Juan remembered, 'you were all into that sort of stuff so you started to build up ... a wider range of friends'. The youth club, in Sheffield and elsewhere, not only responded to the growing threat of commercial entertainment by incorporating coffee bars, music, and activities that prioritised sociability into their offerings, but also provided important opportunities for teenagers to encounter a wider range of cultural activities, in a safe space, than the growing commercial leisure landscape could offer. For many young people who were racialised in

Out in the city   47

post-war Britain, events such as these held additional significance as places that offered 'physical and psychological refuge in an otherwise hostile city'.[78]

Ballrooms, church halls, and beat clubs

The growth in demand for spaces dedicated to youth leisure, and in particular for dancing, through the 1950s and 1960s ushered in an important moment of transition in youth leisure across Britain. Established spaces of leisure such as the cinema, youth club, and dance hall were adapting their leisure provision, while new spaces were emerging to cater for the growing demand for cheap leisure from Britain's teenagers and young adults. In a period of urban redevelopment and decline of traditional inner-city industry, abandoned storage buildings, workshops, factories, and cellars were repurposed in this new era of youth leisure. The late 1950s and early 1960s also emerge as a historically distinct moment in the spatial development of youth leisure, during which the entrepreneur is established as a central actor in the urban youth leisure scene. So far this chapter has outlined national shifts in leisure, lifestyle, and consumption, positioning them within the changing urban environment of post-war Britain. This next section considers two major spatial transitions in youth leisure: the role of hired venues and the rise of unlicensed beat clubs, tracing them through the development of leisure space in the city of Sheffield.

Before the widespread opening of dedicated late-night clubs for young people, the hired or occasional venue played an important role in providing teenagers with leisure opportunities in the early post-war period. The continued popularity of dancing, and of dance halls as sites of sociability and leisure, is one of the key continuities in youthful leisure between the inter-war and post-war period. The traditional dance hall maintained its popularity in the immediate post-war period, with the number of people estimated to be dancing regularly ranging from three to five million.[79] However, by the 1960s, significant social and cultural changes, including the liberalisation of licensing laws, the growth of solo dancing, and the increasing variety of leisure opportunities, all served to undermine the popularity of the traditional dance hall.[80] As such, the ballrooms and dance halls that had dominated the leisurescape of the 1920s–1950s were finding new ways to remain profitable in the post-war period as tastes in music and dancing changed, and many began hiring out their halls to local promoters and adding jive and twist sessions to their programming.[81] While the period from the mid-1950s to the early 1960s saw a relative collapse in the popularity of dance halls and ballrooms with traditional audiences, these spaces emerged as significant sites

48 *Youth and the changing urban environment*

of youth leisure in the years before nightclubs and late-night bars dominated the urban leisure scene.

In Worthing, local businessmen renovated parts of the Dome Ballroom, formerly a cinema and ballroom, into a 'super coffee-dance bar', while in Kenilworth, just outside of Coventry, the Chesford Grange Hotel opened a 'twist den', where dancers could twist until midnight.[82] The Rialto Ballroom in Liverpool similarly introduced a 'beat policy' at weekends in the early 1960s to ensure it remained competitive amongst the city's growing club scene.[83] In Sheffield, as elsewhere, traditional ballroom venues such as City Hall, Cutlers Hall, and the Empress Ballroom could be found advertising 'beat' nights in the early 1960s.[84] These venues recognised the attraction of these nights to teenagers and as such began to advertise regularly in both the local newspaper the *Star* and its teenage supplement the *Top Star Special* throughout the early 1960s. After its reopening in July 1962, the *Top Star Special* wrote that the Central Ballroom in Attercliffe was 'already attracting teenagers from miles around with twist and bop sessions on four evenings every week'.[85] 'All the customers at the Central Ballroom', the article explained, 'are teenagers who can twist the night away for as little as two shillings.' Nether Edge Hall, in the south west of the city, similarly held 'teenage' nights throughout the 1960s. As a venue, it had a capacity of 460 for dancing, and these events were popular enough to attract the special attention of the licensing magistrates, who ensured that 'the service of alcohol shall cease one hour before the dancing' on teenage nights.[86]

However, the introduction of youth-driven leisure activities to these more traditional venues was not always met with enthusiasm. These spaces represented important sites of social and cultural transition, and while not representative of insurmountable generational conflict, they were certainly the site of tension. Sheffield musician Terry Thornton was denied use of the City Hall's ballroom for rock'n'roll nights in the late 1950s, while in Ealing, the town council only reluctantly lifted a ban on twist and jive in the Town Hall in 1963.[87] Twist and jive dancing caused particular concern, and in 1956 Blackpool Tower Company, owner of the three largest ballrooms in Blackpool, cancelled all jive nights due to their association with Teddy Boys.[88] Indeed, James Nott has demonstrated that while dance hall owners resented restrictions placed on them in the years before the Second World War, the threat of violence – or at least the perception of it – at dance halls by Teddy Boy gangs in the 1950s meant they turned towards authorities to help maintain respectability.[89]

'Getting up with the beat': entrepreneurs and provincial leisure provision

Hired venues provided important opportunities for youth leisure through the 1960s and beyond, particularly in provincial towns and cities with smaller youth populations, but they came with a number of restrictions not least regarding decor and access being limited to individual nights. However, where there was demand for evening leisure, there were scores of businesses and individuals that were keen to cater for it. Such demand fuelled a new phenomenon: the late-night coffee club. These clubs, usually serving tea, coffee, and soft drinks, were often members only and as such bypassed licensing restrictions placed on other public spaces of leisure. These clubs, Louise Jackson has argued, were 'spaces removed from the normative gaze of adults'.[90] Their use of membership acted as an important technique to limit entry to those within a specific age range, thus ensuring adults weren't able to enter. Age ranges varied from club to club, but generally encompassed the ages between 16 and the early 20s. Indeed, the late-night coffee club or beat club formed some of the first spaces of late-night youth leisure in many major cities. These clubs were open well after the last call of pubs, often beyond midnight, and many ran frequent 'all-nighters' that ended the following morning. As such, the introduction of beat clubs into the urban leisure scene marked a major spatial and temporal transformation to the post-war leisurescape.

While historians can look to the cosmopolitanism of London in the early twentieth century to view a leisurescape of dance halls, jazz clubs, and bohemian clubs, the development of areas like Soho and Bloomsbury as leisure destinations were in many ways a national anomaly. It was only in the 1950s with the rise of late-night jazz and beat clubs that the wheels were put fully in motion for the growth of a more distinct and nationwide youth lifestyle. Jackson's study of Manchester coffee bars in the 1960s shows a significant number of late-night venues in the city, many of which 'attracted coach parties of youngsters from Cheshire, Yorkshire and Humberside'.[91] As the birthplace of Merseybeat, the popularity of Liverpool's beat club scene has also been well documented, but similar scenes could be found in major cities up and down the country.[92] The beat clubs of the late 1950s and 1960s, while by no means accessible or desirable for all young people, nonetheless emerge as a significant space for youth leisure.

The formal structures of licensing played an important part in the development of youthful leisure, and the emergence of late-night beat clubs and coffee bars is no exception to this. In 1967, the government introduced the Private Places of Entertainment Act, designed explicitly to tackle the rise of unlicensed beat clubs that had emerged over the course of the late 1950s and 1960s.[93] This Act gave local licensing committees powers to shut down 'undesirable' clubs, but the years before the introduction of this Act mark an important moment in the history of youth culture during which local entrepreneurs had real power to shape young people's access to leisure. As such, this moment of legislative uncertainty led to an often tense relationship between club owners and authorities, with proprietors playing 'a game of cat and mouse with the police and licensing authorities'.[94]

50   *Youth and the changing urban environment*

Leisure entrepreneurs materialised during this particular juncture in the history of post-war youth culture as the success of coffee clubs, juke boxes, and the explosion of rock'n'roll and beat music amongst young people provided a ready supply of consumers for the leisure industry. However, while the larger commercial ballrooms were increasingly holding beat nights alongside their traditional programming, there was, in many towns and cities, a distinct lack of dedicated youth spaces for evening leisure. The early beat clubs in Britain were opened not by large commercial organisations, but by local business owners and young entrepreneurs who recognised the desire for spaces of this type. The influence of individual figures such as Alan Sytner and the Abadi brothers, respectively the founders of Liverpool's Cavern Club and Manchester's Twisted Wheel, are well known, but the influence of entrepreneurs stretched beyond cities with a booming music scene. Birmingham's Eddie Fewtrell became a major player in the city's nightlife scene following success in the 1960s, while the Levy brothers made a name for themselves in Newcastle following the opening of the La Dolce Vita club. By focusing on several key figures in Sheffield's early leisure industry, Terry Thornton and the Stringfellow brothers, this next part of the chapter will demonstrate the importance of leisure entrepreneurs in transforming the leisure opportunities for youth in provincial towns and cities.

Local musician Terry Thornton opened Sheffield's first club for teenagers, Club 60, on 5 October 1960. Situated in Shalesmoor, about a fifteen-minute walk from the city centre, Thornton wanted to create a space for young music lovers after being refused use of the City Hall for rock'n'roll by the council.[95] Club 60 was housed in an old pub cellar and was originally billed as a jazz club; however, after introducing 'pop' nights on a Saturday, Thornton discovered that these were much more popular than the jazz that he had originally planned for the club, and so the venue proceeded to host a mixture of jazz, twist, and beat.[96] Entrance to the club was by membership only, and within eighteen months of opening, the venue had 1,800 members.[97] Campbell Page, writer for the local teenage newspaper *Top Star Special*, visited the club's Saturday beat night in May 1962, detailing 'the members, mostly late teens and early twenties... sitting round the barrel-end tables waiting to be rocked'.[98] The venue had a capacity of 250, but its popularity and large membership made clear that a much larger venue would flourish. Within two years of opening Club 60, Thornton opened his second venue, the Esquire.

Upon its opening in 1962, the Esquire was the city's first major beat club, with a much larger capacity than other coffee bars and jazz bars in the city. The Esquire was housed in an abandoned industrial building on Leadmill Road, only a short walk from the city's train station. The central location of the club made it accessible by public transport, while its lack of alcohol licence ensured it was accessible to those under the age of 18. Thornton spoke to the *Top Star Special* about the conversion and opening of the venue in September 1962.[99] The Esquire was to open until 11 p.m. four nights a week, from Thursday to Sunday, with two evenings each dedicated to twist and jazz. The club was set over three floors, with a balcony created on the top floor to view the dance floor below. Thornton told the *Top Star Special* that a rehearsal room had been provided to allow groups to practise during the three days when the club wasn't open. Given that the bills for both Club 60 and the Esquire were dominated by live acts, often featuring local artists such as Joe Cocker, Dave Berry, Frank White, and others, this addition provided further support for Sheffield's growing music scene. Annual membership for the Esquire was only 2s and 6d., making the space an affordable leisure venue for many of the city's working-class teenagers.[100] In an interview with the *Top Star Special* in February 1963, four months after opening, Thornton noted that rock had been added to the club's roster, alongside beat and jazz, while the venue was also planning to run a number of 'all-nighters' until dawn.[101]

The success of Thornton's late-night beat and twist venues in the city encouraged others who were similarly business-minded. Peter and Geoff Stringfellow opened a number of venues in the city, with Peter Stringfellow later making an international name for himself in the club industry. The brothers' first venue, the Black Cat Club, opened on Friday nights in St Aidan's church hall, City Road, in 1962, with the Blue Moon Club opening in September 1963. Peter Stringfellow gained a reputation in the city for booking acts on the brink of success, and this was cemented by his booking of the Beatles in 1963. The gig coincided with the rise of 'Beatlemania' and had to be moved from St Aidan's church hall to the much larger Azena Ballroom in Gleadless, in the south east of the city, as a result of high ticket demand. In an interview with the *Top Star Special* in 1962, Peter Stringfellow, then 21, explained that 'there is not enough room in some pubs for a really swinging session, and a lot of young people do not like going in to pubs anyway'.[102] The Stringfellow brothers recognised the importance of creating spaces in the city that were solely dedicated to the leisure needs of teenagers and young adults. Less than a year later, in May 1963, *Top Star Special* reporter Carole Newton wrote about the Black Cat Club:

> Peter began by hiring St Aidan's Church Hall, City Road, for a couple of nights a week and has done so well that he opens four nights a week and the church authorities have allowed him to hold his own club there and decorate the premises as he wishes. He does in fact help the hall to support itself.[103]

However, the brothers had larger ambitions, and when speaking to the *Top Star Special* about plans for their clubs in the future, Peter Stringfellow said in 1962: 'if we make money, my idea is to get a hall of our own which we can decorate as we like and have rock and twist sessions every day of the week'.[104]

It wasn't long before the Stringfellow brothers moved on from the Black Cat and Blue Moon clubs, and in 1964 they opened the much larger King Mojo Club; on being handed to a new manager, the Black Cat Club had over 1,800 members.[105] While not confined solely to the early part of the 1960s, hired venues such as church halls and community centres played an important role in the formation of the cultural landscape of Sheffield in the early 1960s. They provided a space for entrepreneurs such as Thornton and the Stringfellow brothers to test what was commercially viable, yet their lack of permanent status and licensing mean their central role in the early development of youth leisure in provincial cities has often gone overlooked in broader histories of post-war youth culture.

The Stringfellow brothers' move to the King Mojo Club in 1964 marked the opening of the city's second beat club, both of which were owned by local entrepreneurs. The King Mojo's location was somewhat unusual; rather than

Figure 1.2 Exterior of The King Mojo Club, Pitsmoor, Sheffield, 1966. © Sheffield Newspapers Ltd and Picture Sheffield.

Out in the city

being situated in the city centre, the club was housed in a converted house in Pitsmoor, about two miles from the centre. The venue had been used as a dance studio and ballroom earlier in the century, but its location in a residential area of Sheffield's working-class neighbourhood of Pitsmoor was somewhat incongruous with its ambitions as a late-night leisure venue. The King Mojo Club quickly gained fame due to Peter Stringfellow's approach to publicity; unlike Thornton, Stringfellow frequently advertised in the *Star*, and was interviewed on a regular basis in the *Top Star Special*. Despite its location, the club was a resounding success, and within two months of opening it had eight hundred members. The King Mojo Club became particularly well-known for its all-nighters, advertising these in the local press, and between 1965 and 1966 the club hosted a total of thirteen all-night and late-night sessions.[106] The Whitsun weekend of 1965, for example, was host to an all-nighter on Whit Monday which ran from 7.30 p.m. to 7.30 a.m.[107] Similarly, an advert in December 1966 promoted the Mojo's Christmas opening hours: the Mojo was to be open until 2 a.m. on 23 December, Christmas Eve, and Boxing Day with the celebrations culminating on New Year's Eve with an all-night session.[108]

Given the reputation of late-night coffee clubs by the mid-1960s, Stringfellow was keen to maintain a respectable image for his venue. Press headlines such as 'Coffee Bar Cowboys', alongside high-profile police raids and debates around regulation, meant that the late-night coffee clubs of the early 1960s, much like the coffee bars of the 1950s, were increasingly being singled out as spaces of transgression.[109] An advert placed in the *Star* in July 1965 specified that 'only the city's smart teens and twenties [are] allowed in'.[110] The club's membership was only open, in theory, to those over the age of 16, and following the response of the public to Terry Thornton's Esquire in the weeks after the broadcast of *The Long Journey*, Stringfellow was quick to issue an open invitation to parents in the *Top Star Special* to visit his clubs to see that everything was 'above board'.[111] Stringfellow added 'the club shown in the film was not one of mine, and I happen to know it is a perfectly respectable club. Every teenage club in Sheffield is attended, in the most part, by decent, fun loving youngsters who love dancing and rhythm and blues'. Aside from the clear opportunity for publicity, Stringfellow's invitation to parents is an example of the importance of the appearance of respectability in the early club scene, particularly to appease local authorities and local residents.

The *Top Star Special* noted in May 1963, a year before the venue had opened, that 'there's nothing sinful or vice-ridden about these places ... yet for some strange reason Sheffielders, especially the powers-that-be, are suspicious of these clubs'.[112] Indeed, from its opening in February 1964, the venue was subject to ongoing issues with police, local residents, and licensing magistrates. The case of the King Mojo highlights the value of situating histories of youth culture within its local context; whilst there was a national narrative of suspicion around beat clubs, in Sheffield the King Mojo Club came under far more pressure from Sheffield's citizens and local authorities than the Esquire due to its physical location in the city. Its suburban location meant local residents were far more attuned to the behaviour of the club's patrons, while late-night noise and disturbance from scooters and motorcycles became a much bigger problem than its city-centre counterpart. While people were shocked by the televised interviews with Esquire club members, it was the King Mojo Club that faced regular attempts to intervene in the club's activities and shut the venue down.

The venue was faced with numerous complaints from local residents about noise and the behaviour of those who attended the King Mojo Club, and in 1965 an eighty-six-name petition complaining of noise and disruption was submitted to the council. Local residents presented the petition 'in the form of complaints of various undesirable nature taking place in the vicinity of this club'.[113] The complaint continued, explaining that 'the behaviour is causing alarm and unrest in adjacent dwellings and the surrounding district'. Despite much sympathy from local authorities, the subsequent investigation by the Town Planning, Watch, and Health committees concluded that they were unable to take firm action against the club. The venue had formerly been used as a dance studio and community dance hall, and the final report noted that 'no planning permissions have ever been required for its continued use as a dancing establishment ... provided the main function of the building remains dancing then no material change of use has taken place requiring planning permission'.[114] However, following this report, the Town Clerk explored the option of invoking the Noise Abatement Act 1960 and the Public Health Act 1936 to gain 'effective control' over the club.[115] In March 1966, the Stringfellow brothers found themselves in court, having been served with a notice relating to noise under the Public Health Act.

Following the initial investigation into the club, a member of the council stepped forward in partial defence of the Mojo. Alderman Sidney Dyson told the *Top Star Special*: 'I take the view that in the main clubs help to dissipate the energies of youth by letting them get up with the beat. This is in a sense filling up a kind of vacuum. It allows them to let steam off'.[116] However, Dyson continued by saying of the all-nighters: 'I think they want limiting. I do not think it is quite reasonable to expect that young people should stop all night.' Despite continued assurances by the management that the Mojo club was not the source of excessive noise or disruption, or the centre of immoral behaviour, the club continued to face problems.

Although the council showed clear concern when faced with the complaints of residents, the biggest issues facing the Mojo came from the licensing magistrates. In 1966, the Mojo applied for an alcohol licence. In an article covering the application of the licence, Peter Stringfellow told the *Star*:

> It is still going to be very exclusive. We shall be very careful about the types we shall allow into the bar. We don't want any roughs. And we are not going to allow anyone in above the age of 30. At the moment we are going to settle for the 18s and late 20s.[117]

Despite assurances, the club was denied its alcohol licence. The management swiftly appealed against this decision, and in the hearing Geoff Stringfellow argued that club members were not able to go into local pubs before they went to the Mojo because of their 'mod gear'. Stringfellow's statement highlighted the problems faced by many young people in Sheffield during the early 1960s: the city's drinking establishments were the mainstay of traditional drinkers, particularly outside of the city centre, and flamboyant groups of youths were not welcome, and were actively excluded from these places. Because of their 'mod gear', members were not welcome in Pitsmoor's pubs. To demonstrate to the Justices what was meant by 'mod gear' (and likely in search of a little extra publicity), Peter Stringfellow sported 'a grey and white pinstriped jacket with an orange tie'.[118] However, the Stringfellow brothers were told that their club attracted 'the undesirable element', and the licence was refused.

Problems with the licensing magistrates continued in 1967, when the Mojo applied for a Private Places of Entertainment licence and was again refused. The appeal documents demonstrate the continuing concerns of local residents about the behaviour of young people attending the club. One licensing magistrate commented that:

> So far as catering for customers aged sixteen to twenty-five is concerned, I am not sure it is right for people to speak of those ages as if they were a strange and different race. It seems to me they are perfectly entitled to dress as they like and should have whatever amusements they like, but at the same time they have exactly the same rights and obligations as any other section of the population.[119]

Addressing the arguments presented by residents who lived near the club, the magistrate argued that:

> All of them speak of frequent occasions of people urinating in their gardens, on their gates, in their drives. All of them have found a variety of different kinds of objects left in their gardens, contraceptives, panties, brassieres, sanitary

56   *Youth and the changing urban environment*

> towels and objects of that kind. They have, in addition, been subjected to a considerable measure of rudeness.[120]

Concerns of drug taking were raised in the appeal, and police had raised particular anxieties about all-night events attracting dealers and users of amphetamines.[121] A number of drug raids had taken place at the club, and the appeal noted 'the number of arrests and number of convictions ... [and] a considerable volume of evidence about the finding of packets which are used for passing pep pills'.[122] Fifteen people had been arrested and charged on drug offences between the King Mojo's opening in 1964 until its closure in October 1967. This was enough to secure the fate of the King Mojo Club, and the appeal was rejected with the statement that investigators were 'not satisfied that this particular club is in the interests of all sections of the population'.[123] The complaints against the Mojo were fuelled in part by its disturbance of a residential area, but the argument presented both by those who lived nearby and the authorities focused as much on the supposedly immoral behaviour of the young people who attended the club as on the disturbance and noise.

The emergence of beat clubs in Sheffield in the mid-1960s raises important questions about the history of youth leisure in this period. While Jackson's work on Manchester beat clubs demonstrates clearly the particular forms of moral regulation carried out by local authorities, something also happening in Sheffield, the debates taking place around the King Mojo Club and the Esquire expose these clubs as sites of spatial tension. The Esquire Club, while subject to low-level concern about the attitudes and behaviour of those who attended, was subject to far less regulation than the King Mojo. Its city centre location meant that it was somewhat removed from the gaze of Sheffield's citizens, while the King Mojo's residential location put on full display the activities of those in attendance. In refusing the King Mojo's appeal for a Private Places of Entertainment licence, counsel for the licensing magistrates was quick to explain that 'it is very nice for either the young or people of any other age to have any amusements they wish and it is very proper to have dance halls and dance clubs ... as one of the ordinary amusements of life'.[124] Alderman Sidney Dyson's claims that clubs 'in the main help to dissipate the energies of youth' and were a place 'parents can send their teenage daughters with confidence', while arguments from the licensing magistrates that the young 'are entitled to dress as they like and should have whatever amusements they like' do not suggest wholescale rejection of the beat-club scene by authorities.[125] Indeed, Callum Brown has argued that Sheffield's licensing magistrates could be viewed in this period as being 'significantly more liberal than some other licensing jurisdictions' in their approach, though they remained concerned with temperance and Sabbatarianism.[126]

Out in the city 57

While reactions to the jazz bars, beat clubs, and late-night coffee clubs of the 1950s and 1960s can rightly be read as a moment of moral panic regarding the state of British youth, their emergence also signals an important moment of transition. In a period in which access to leisure and retail was increasingly seen as essential in the modern urban environment, these early spaces of youth leisure enabled teenagers and young adults to form cultures and patterns of sociability of their own. The role of entrepreneurs to shape the leisurescape of individual towns and cities was significant in this period, and the development of these spaces within the urban landscape reveals much about the vibrancy of youth leisure beyond the metropole. By the time the Stringfellow brothers closed the King Mojo in 1967, Sheffield 'had fostered a structure for youth culture free from effective civil control'.[127] However, local authorities were quick to respond to the changing leisurescape, and made numerous attempts to wrest back their control. It marks a historically distinct moment in the years between a domination of the national and international commercial youth leisure market and the development of regulatory powers aimed more directly at spaces of youth leisure.

Conclusions

The period between the early 1950s and mid-1960s was one of meaningful transition and significant change in the development of post-war youth cultures. Far from being barren wastelands of leisure, provincial towns and cities were home to a growing number of leisure spaces dedicated solely to the hedonistic pursuits of youth. Free from the formality and structure of youth organisations and youth clubs, the steamed-up windows of late-night coffee bars and overheated basements of jazz clubs where young people talked and danced until the early hours were culturally and socially significant spaces for British youth. They provided a space beyond the street corner to meet people with no other goal than sociability and dancing, and they laid the groundwork for major transformations to youth leisure and lifestyle in the following decades.

These spaces emerged in a period of broader urban change; the relationship between the city, the individual, and leisure was shifting as urban centres became increasingly dedicated to commerce and leisure. In this new environment, the coffee bar took its place alongside the department store and the boutique, with the juke box, modern surroundings, and prospect of cheap coffee and soda attracting local youths when the storefront shutters went down and shoppers returned home. Entrepreneurs took advantage of derelict and abandoned buildings in the developing city to provide more frequent spaces to dance and meet beyond the local ballroom's Saturday-night twist sessions. Yet these changes to more traditional spaces of leisure were equally as significant, and signal the extent to which young people were able to shape their local environment. Faced with competition from the success of the coffee bar, youth organisations increasingly recognised the importance of youth-led leisure and incorporated coffee bars into their premises. Dance halls and ballrooms, once the site of more formal and structured dances, began hosting jive, twist, and beat as tastes in both music and dancing changed, despite fears about trouble from gangs of youths.

The success of beat nights early in the late 1950s and early 1960s, often held in church halls and hired venues, provided a platform for a small number of entrepreneurs to capitalise on the growing demand for youth-oriented space. In turn, the emergence of these evening leisure spaces provided many young people with the opportunity to socialise until the early hours of the morning for the first time, creating a temporal shift in young people's cultural experiences. These shifts were by no means seamless, however, and a study of spaces such as Sheffield's King Mojo shows how both residents of the city and local authorities could shape young people's access to leisure. Respectability began to emerge as a key concern for late-night venues; this was true of ballrooms and dance halls that were adapting to the post-war leisurescape as well as new venues keen to gain the support of authorities.

Exploring the way these spaces were used exposes both intergenerational tension and intergenerational support for youth leisure in the early post-war period. At the same time that jive was banned in some ballrooms for fear of violence, and drug raids were taking place in late-night coffee bars, others were recognising the value of these spaces in keeping young people off the streets and entertained. The rise of city-centre youth-oriented pubs, bars, and nightclubs would come to dominate the lifestyles of many young people in Britain over the following two decades. While a Friday or Saturday night out with friends did not necessarily present a new or novel way to spend one's time, the wider variety of venues and spaces available to young people by the end of the 1960s created an environment in which young people were able to construct lifestyles and patterns of behaviour that were increasingly distinct and separate from those of their parents and wider adult society.

By the end of the 1960s, the making of a distinct youth culture was woven into the fabric of the urban environment; from the ballrooms that hosted live music and dances, to the repurposing of abandoned industrial buildings and basements for late-night coffee clubs, decorated with the murals of local art-college students, the power of youth to transform the urban environment was clear. The young people who came of age at the end of this period traversed the streets of their towns and cities in new ways, moving through spaces of leisure and engaging in patterns of sociability that could increasingly be defined as their own.

Notes

1 *The Long Journey* [film], directed by Phillip Donnellan (BBC, 1964).
2 The BBC Home Service broadcast six Radio Ballads between 1958 and 1964. A 1963 Ballad, *On The Edge*, featured the experiences of teenage youth and provided the inspiration for the television documentary. For more on the cultural significance of the BBC Radio Ballads see Paul Long, 'British Radio and the Politics of Culture in Post-War Britain: The Work of Charles Parker', *The Radio Journal*, 2:3 (2004), 131–152, https://doi.org/10.1386/rajo.2.3.131/1.
3 'TV Film Planned on City Club', *Star*, 8 November 1963, 3.
4 *Top Star Special*, April 1964, 21.
5 See Arthur Marwick, *The Sixties: Cultural Revolution in Britain, France, Italy, and the United States, c.1958–c.1974* (Oxford: Oxford University Press, 1998); Trevor Fisher, 'Permissiveness and the Politics of Morality', *Contemporary Record*, 7:1 (1993), 149–195, https://doi.org/10.1080/13619469308581241; Sandbrook, *Never Had It So Good*; Sandbrook, *White Heat*; Jonathon Green, *All Dressed Up: The Sixties and the Counterculture* (London: Random House, 1998); Donnelly, *Sixties Britain*; Mills, 'Using the Personal to Critique the Popular'; Charnock, 'Teenage Girls'.
6 For more on youth and public space in the nineteenth and early twentieth centuries, see Laura Harrison, '"The Streets Have Been Watched Regularly": The York Penitentiary Society, Young Working-Class Women, and the Regulation of Behaviour in the Public Spaces of York, c. 1845–1919', *Women's History Review*, 28:3 (2019), 457–478, https://doi.org/10.1080/09612025.2018.1477105; Pamela Cox, *Gender, Justice and Welfare in Britain, 1900–1950: Bad Girls in Britain, 1900–1950* (London: Palgrave Macmillan, 2003); Samantha Caslin, *Save the Womanhood! Vice, Urban Immorality and Social Control in Liverpool, c.1900–1976* (Liverpool: Liverpool University Press, 2018); Sleight, *Young People and the Shaping of Public Space in Melbourne*; Simon Sleight, 'Rites of Passage: Youthful Walking and the Rhythms of the City, c.1850–1914' in Chad Bryant, Arthur Burns, and Paul Readman (eds), *Walking Histories, 1800–1914* (London: Palgrave Macmillan, 2016), 87–112.
7 See Kate Bradley, 'Rational Recreation in the Age of Affluence: The Café and Working-Class Youth in London, c.1939–1965' in Erika Rappaport, Sandra Trudgen Dawson, and Mark J. Crowley (eds), *Consuming Behaviours: Identity, Politics and Pleasure in Twentieth-Century Britain* (London: Bloomsbury, 2015), 71–86; Springhall, *Youth, Popular Culture and Moral Panics*; Charlotte Clements, 'Lady Albemarle's Youth Workers: Contested Professional Identities in English Youth Work 1958–1985', *History of Education*, 48:6 (2019), 819–836, https://doi.org/10.1080/0046760X.2019.1588395.
8 For a more thorough exploration of this, see John Griffiths, '"Rivalling the Metropolis": Cultural Conflict between London and the Regions c.1967–1973', *Contemporary British History*, 33:4 (2019), 524–547, https://doi.org/10.1080/13619462.2018.1519434.
9 Fuhg, *London's Working Class Youth*, 4–5.

60   *Youth and the changing urban environment*

10 For more on post-war urban planning, see Guy Ortolano, 'Planning the Urban Future', *The Historical Journal*, 54:2 (2011), 477–507, https://doi.org/10.1017/S0018246X11000100; Otto Saumarez Smith, 'Central Government and Town-Centre Redevelopment in Britain, 1959–1966', *The Historical Journal*, 58:1 (2015), 217–244, https://doi.org/10.1017/S0018246X14000077; Otto Saumarez Smith, *Boom Cities: Architect Planners and the Politics of Radical Urban Renewal in 1960s Britain* (Oxford: Oxford University Press, 2019); James Greenhalgh, *Reconstructing Modernity: Space, Power and Governance in Mid-Twentieth Century British Cities* (Manchester: Manchester University Press, 2017); Peter Mandler, 'New Towns for Old: The Fate of the Town Centre' in Becky Conekin, Frank Mort, and Chris Waters (eds), *Moments of Modernity: Reconstructing Britain, 1945–1964* (London: Rivers Oram Press, 1999), 208–227; Simon Gunn, 'The Rise and Fall of British Urban Modernism: Planning Bradford 1945–1970', *Journal of British Studies*, 48:1 (2010), 849–869, https://doi.org/10.1086/654912; Catherine Flinn, '"The City of Our Dreams?" The Political and Economic Realities of Rebuilding Britain's Blitzed Cities, 1945–54', *Twentieth Century British History*, 23:3 (2012), 221–245.

11 John R. Gold, *The Practice of Modernism: Modern Architects and Urban Transformation, 1954–1972* (Abingdon: Routledge, 2007), 108.

12 Donnelly, *Sixties Britain*, 23.

13 Marwick, *British Society Since 1945*, 88.

14 A good example of this is the broadcast of Ken Loach's television play *Cathy Come Home* on the BBC in 1966, which shed light on the continued problem of poverty and poor housing in post-war Britain. For more on this, see Tanya Evans, 'Stopping the Poor Getting Poorer: The Establishment and Professionalisation of Poverty NGOs, 1945–95' in Nick Crowson, Matthew Hilton, and James McKay (eds), *NGOs in Contemporary Britain* (Basingstoke: Palgrave Macmillan, 2009), 147–163.

15 Osgerby, *Youth in Britain*, 30.

16 Peter Shapely, 'Civic Pride and Redevelopment in the Post-War British City', *Urban History*, 39:2 (2012), 314, https://doi.org/10.1017/S0963926812000077. For more on civic pride in the nineteenth and twentieth centuries, see Simon Gunn, *The Public Culture of the Victorian Middle Class* (Manchester: Manchester University Press, 2007); Charlotte Wildman, *Urban Redevelopment and Modernity in Liverpool and Manchester, 1918–1939* (London: Bloomsbury, 2016), Tom Hulme, *After the Shock City: Urban Culture and the Making of Modern Citizenship* (London: Royal Historical Society, The Boydell Press, 2019).

17 Shapely, 'Civic Pride', 320; Louise Campbell, 'Paper Dream City/Modern Monument: Donald Gibson and Coventry' in Iain Boyd Whyte (ed.), *Man-Made Future: Planning, Education and Design in Mid-Twentieth-Century Britain* (London: Routledge, 2007), 121–144.

18 Saumarez Smith, *Boom Cities*, 65.

19 *Ibid.*, 67.

20 Todd, 'Phoenix Rising', 680.

Out in the city 61

21 'The Boom Cities!', *Daily Mirror*, 2 January 1967, 1.

22 'The Boom Cities!', *Daily Mirror*, 12 January 1967, 7.

23 Tebbutt, *Making Youth*, 143.

24 Marnie Fogg, *Boutique: A '60s Cultural Icon* (London: Mitchell Beazley, 2003).

25 Osgerby, *Youth in Britain*, 38.

26 Tebbutt, *Making Youth*, 147.

27 Harry Hopkins, *The New Look: A Social History of the Forties and Fifties in Britain* (London: Secker & Warburg, 1963), 460.

28 For an overview of the rise of the milk and coffee bar, see Joe Moran, 'Milk Bars, Starbucks and the Uses of History', *Cultural History*, 20:6 (2006), 552–573, https://doi.org/10.1080/09502380600973911.

29 'It's War to the Last Cup of Coffee', *Daily Mirror*, 13 November 1954, 3; 'Coffee Bar Capers', *Daily Mirror*, 18 November 1959, 25.

30 Richard Hoggart, *The Uses of Literacy: Aspects of Working-Class Life* (6th edn, London: Penguin, 2009), 221.

31 *Ibid.*, 220–221.

32 *Ibid.*, 221.

33 Abrams, *The Teenage Consumer*, 11.

34 Pearl Jephcott published widely on British youth, including studies on high-rise housing and the lives of working-class girls. For more on Jephcott's legacy, see the special issue John Goodwin and Henrietta O'Connor (eds), 'Pearl Jephcott: Reflections, Resurgence and Replications', *Women's History Review*, 28:5 (2019), 711–813.

35 Pearl Jephcott, *Time of One's Own* (London: Oliver and Boyd, 1967), 68.

36 *Ibid.*, 70.

37 *Ibid.*, 71.

38 Peter Willmott, *Adolescent Boys of East London* (2nd edn, London: Pelican, 1975), 37.

39 John Barron Mays, *The Young Pretenders: A Study of Teenage Culture in Contemporary Society* (London: Michael Joseph, 1965), 24.

40 Moran, 'Milk Bars', 570.

41 Bradley, 'Rational Recreation', 71–86; Louise Jackson, 'The Coffee Club Menace', *Cultural and Social History*, 5:3 (2015), 289–308, https://doi.org/10.2752/147800408X331407.

42 Adrian Horn, *Juke Box Britain* (Manchester: Manchester University Press, 2009), 177.

43 Moran, 'Milk Bars', 556.

44 Katie Milestone, 'Swinging Regions: Young Women and Club Culture in 1960s Manchester', *Film, Fashion, and Consumption*, 7:2 (2018), 181, https://doi.org/10.1386/ffc.7.2.179_1.

45 Gildart, *Images of England*, 6.

46 'Letters: Plans for City's First Coffee Bar', *Peterborough Advertiser*, 21 February 1958, 8.

47 'New Towns? They're Ghost Towns Say the Teenagers Who Live in Them', *Daily Herald*, 21 October 1959, 6.

48 Neil Anderson, *Dirty Stop Out's Guide to 1960s Sheffield* (Sheffield: ACM Retro, 2011), 15–16.

49 *Ibid.*, 15.

50 On the growth of Black- and Arab-owned shops and cafes in Sheffield in 1950s and 1960s, see Kevin Searle, *From Farms to Foundries: An Arab Community in Industrial Britain* (Oxford: Peter Lang, 2010), 113–138.

51 Jephcott, *Time of One's Own*, 70–71.

52 Sheffield City Archives, Sheffield (hereafter SCA), MC 2008/146, Sheffield Corporation, Licensing Justices, Minutes, Box 85, 10/11/1965–06/01/1970, 47.

53 *Ibid.*, 56.

54 Bradley, 'Rational Recreation', 82.

55 For more on twentieth-century youth workers and youth movements, see Edwards, *Youth Movements, Citizenship and the English Countryside*; Bernard Davies, *From Voluntaryism to Welfare State: A History of the Youth Service in England, Volume 1 1939–1979* (Leicester: Youth Work Press, 1999); Rhys Jones, Peter Merriman, and Sarah Mills, 'Youth Organizations and the Reproduction of Nationalism in Britain: The Role of Urdd Gobaith Cymru', *Social and Cultural Geography*, 175 (2016), 714–734, https://doi.org/10.1080/14649365.2016.1139166; Simon Bradford, 'Managing the Spaces of Freedom: Mid-Twentieth-Century Youth Work' in Sarah Mills and Peter Kraftl (eds), *Informal Education, Childhood and Youth* (Basingstoke: Palgrave Macmillan, 2014), 184–196; Clements, 'Lady Albemarle's Youth Workers', 819–836.

56 Cadbury Research Library, Birmingham (hereafter CRL), MS 227/1/1/1/3, National Council and AGM Minutes, 14/11/50. Note: the unattached was a label given to young people who were not part of affiliated youth clubs.

57 CRL, MS 227/1/1/1/3, National Council and AGM Minutes, 14/11/50.

58 Emma Latham, 'The Liverpool Boys' Association and the Liverpool Union of Youth Clubs: Youth Organisations and Gender, 1940–1970', *Journal of Contemporary History*, 35:3 (2000), 429, https://doi.org/10.1177/002200940003500306. On a similar theme, also see Penny Tinkler, 'An All-Round Education: The Board of Education's Policy for the Leisure Time Training of Girls', *History of Education*, 23:4 (1994), 384–403, https://doi.org/10.1080/0046760940230404.

59 Clements, 'Lady Albemarle's Youth Workers', 9.

60 'Getting Near to Young People: Coffee Bars Experiment', *Manchester Guardian*, 12 May 1958, 4.

61 *Ibid.*, 4.

62 'Modern Youth Clubs', *Liverpool Echo*, 8 January 1959, 6.

63 'Losing Faith with Youth?' *Eastbourne Herald*, 14 September 1957, 16; 'Coffee Bars Would Attract Youth', *Aberdeen Evening Express*, 12 June 1958, 15.

64 'Teenage Bar Success: Another Planned', *Harrow Observer*, 25 February 1960, 1.

65 'City Group Lays on "Young" Jazz', *Star*, 29 October 1960, 6.

66 *Ibid.*, 6.

67 *Ibid.*, 6.

Out in the city
63

68 'Coffee Bar Bait: Enticing Youth to Better Things', *Guardian*, 24 June 1960, 20.

69 *Ibid.*, 20.

70 Clements, 'Lady Albemarle's Youth Workers', 6.

71 'Coffee Bar at Church', *Star*, 21 October 1960, 6.

72 *Ibid.*, 6.

73 'Coffee Bar for Church Youth Club', *Eastbourne Gazette*, 29 April 1959, 4.

74 'Gospel Rhythm Groups Play at Church Beat Club', *Liverpool Echo*, 12 September 1966, 16.

75 Bradley, 'Rational Recreation', 78.

76 Anandi Ramamurthy, *Black Star: Britain's Asian Youth Movements* (London: Pluto Press, 2013), 154.

77 William 'Lez' Henry and Les Back, 'Reggae Culture as Local Knowledge: Mapping the Beats on South East London Streets' in William 'Lez' Henry and Matthew Worley (eds), *Narratives from Beyond the UK Reggae Bassline: The System Is Sound* (London: Palgrave Macmillan, 2020), 31.

78 Henry and Back, 'Reggae Culture', 51.

79 Nott, *Going to the Palais*, 87.

80 *Ibid.*, 96. See also Jon Stratton, 'Disco Before Disco: Dancing and Popular Music in the 1960s and 1970s in England', *Journal of Popular Music Studies*, 33:1 (2021), 50–69, https://doi.org/10.1525/jpms.2021.33.1.50.

81 For more on the popularity of dance halls in the earlier twentieth century, see Nott, 'Contesting Popular Dancing'; Abra, *Dancing in the English Style*; Abra, 'Doing the Lambeth Walk'.

82 'Entertainments', *Worthing Gazette*, 23 December 1959, 6; 'Entertainments', *Coventry Evening Telegraph*, 17 January 1964, 2.

83 'Dancing Time', *Liverpool Echo*, 6 June 1964, 12.

84 'Entertainments', *Star*, 14 August 1964, 2.

85 *Top Star Special*, September 1962, 10.

86 SCA, MC 2008/146, Sheffield Corporation, Licensing Justices, Minutes, Box 83, 19/11/1965–06/01/1970, 198.

87 Dave Haslam, *Life After Dark: A History of British Nightclubs and Music Venues* (London: Simon and Schuster, 2016), 95; 'Twist and Jive in Town Hall on Saturday Nights!', *Middlesex County Times*, 26 January 1963, 13.

88 'Ballroom Ban on Teddy Boys', *Manchester Guardian*, 24 July 1956, 12.

89 Nott, *Going to the Palais*, 291.

90 Jackson, 'Coffee Club Menace', 290.

91 *Ibid.*, 290.

92 For example, see Spencer Leigh, *Twist and Shout: Merseybeat, The Cavern, The Star Club and The Beatles* (Liverpool: Nirvana Books, 2004); Eric Woolley, *The Golden Years of Merseybeat* (Liverpool: Bluecoat Press, 2008); Manfred Kuhlman, *The Sound with the Pound: An Anthology of the 60s Merseybeat Sound* (London: Best Books Online, 2009).

93 The Private Places of Entertainment Act was introduced in 1967 to regulate the activities of 'members' clubs – predominantly coffee bars and beat clubs – that

provided entertainment in the form of music and dancing, but did not serve alcohol. The broader significance of the Private Places of Entertainment Act as a regulatory act is explored in more detail in Chapter 3.

94 Gildart, *Images of England*, 102.
95 Haslam, *Life After Dark*, 95.
96 Anderson, *Dirty Stop Out's Guide to 1960s Sheffield*, 21.
97 *Top Star Special*, May 1962, 10.
98 *Ibid.*, 10.
99 *Top Star Special*, September 1962, 10.
100 As a point of comparison, the cost of membership to one of Sheffield's recently opened cabaret clubs, the Cavendish, was £1 1s. This was around ten times the cost of membership to the Esquire.
101 *Top Star Special*, February 1963, 6.
102 *Top Star Special*, September 1962, 10.
103 *Top Star Special*, May 1963, 3.
104 *Top Star Special*, September 1962, 10.
105 *Top Star Special*, June 1964, 22.
106 SCA, CA 674/49, Correspondence relating to the Mojo Club, press cutting dated 10 March 1966.
107 *Star*, 28 May 1965, 2.
108 *Star*, 16 December 1966, 2.
109 'The Big Menace from the Coffee-Bar', *Daily Mirror*, 8 June 1961, 7.
110 'Entertainments', *Star*, 9 July 1965, p. 2.
111 *Top Star Special*, April 1964, 21.
112 *Top Star Special*, May 1963, 3.
113 SCA, CA 674/49, Correspondence relating to the Mojo Club, petition dated May 1965.
114 SCA, CA 674/49, Correspondence relating to the Mojo Club, Watch Report dated 17 June 1965.
115 SCA, CA 674/49, Correspondence relating to the Mojo Club, letter from Town Clerk dated 26 November 1965.
116 *Top Star Special*, September 1965, 21.
117 'Mojo Club to Apply for Drinks Licence', *Star*, 11 June 1966, 5.
118 '"No" to Drinks Please for Mojo Club Mods', *Star*, 6 July 1966, 5.
119 SCA, MC 2008/146, Sheffield Corporation, Licensing Justices, Minutes, Box 83, 19/11/1965–06/01/1970, 188.
120 *Ibid.*, 188.
121 *Ibid.*, 192.
122 *Ibid.*, 190.
123 *Ibid.*, 192.
124 *Ibid.*, 188.
125 *Top Star Special*, September 1965, 21.
126 Callum Brown, *The Battle for Christian Britain: Sex, Humanists and Secularisation, 1945–1980* (Cambridge: Cambridge University Press, 2019), 199.
127 *Ibid.*, 197.

2

The business of leisure

Sheffield's first licensed nightclub, the Heart Beat Club, opened in 1965. It marked a new stage in the city's nightlife, and for many of the city's young people, it represented a shift away from the dance halls of their parents' youth towards something that felt more distinctly their own. Large, spacious, and well-lit dance floors were gradually replaced with tight crowds and flashing lights, while the disc jockey replaced the live band. The Heart Beat Club, which successfully applied for a provisional publican's licence in January 1965, was granted its full licence in November the same year.[1] Sheffield's teen newspaper supplement the *Top Star Special* visited the club a year after its opening, reporting that the Heart Beat had a healthy membership of over ten thousand and three resident disc jockeys.[2] Located on Queens Road, a few miles south east of the city centre, the Heart Beat Club was part of the Silver Blades ice-skating complex, an entertainment centre owned and operated by Mecca Leisure Ltd. It was one of several leisure venues owned by Mecca in Sheffield in the mid-1960s, and its opening heralded a new era in the availability of late-night entertainment in the city. It was a sign of changing mores amongst Britain's youth, a signal that they valued the diversity of leisure space that was increasingly being made available to them. The commercial success of the club was also a clear indication of the staying power of the leisure industry's old guard, whose capacity to adapt to these changes ensured their survival.

Writing the commercial history of youth culture in Britain is no easy task. Individual venues are bought, sold, renamed, and redesigned on a regular basis. Entertainment companies, often the power and finance behind the sale and resale of individual venues, are themselves the subject of various takeovers, mergers, and liquidations. Both venues and companies change hands with astonishing regularity. As such, the archive trail is often disjointed and offers only a partial view of the individuals and companies involved in reshaping the post-war leisure landscape. Yet, despite its difficulties, this remains an essential task. As this chapter will demonstrate, the years between the 1950s and 1990s were characterised by the growing presence of leisure chains on the British high street. Their presence transformed the way that young people engaged with the urban environment and, by the end of the twentieth century, the very purpose of the urban centre. Many of these chains were already established as household names by the post-war period. Others were newly established, seemingly regional ventures, but increasingly financed by national and international conglomerates that profited from the growing demand for leisure. As Chapter 1 demonstrated, leisure providers were only too happy to adapt to new trends and increasingly recognised the potential profitability of those venues that catered solely or primarily to young people's desire for distinct spaces of their own.

Despite their familiarity to those who grew up in Britain over the course of the second half of the twentieth century, the story of these venues remains under-explored in academic literature on youth. Often detached from the alternative underground network of clubs and venues that have captured the imagination of generations of journalists and researchers, commercial chain venues nevertheless provide a central way of understanding the experience of youth leisure across the twentieth century. For urban historians, their presence is more commonly linked to the later twentieth century, telling a story of regeneration and the triumph of public–private renewal. As Alistair Kefford argues, private commerce played a remarkable role in recasting post-war cities as 'centres for the new business of shopping, leisure, and pleasure'.[3] The roots of this, however, run much deeper. The emergence of popular leisure is one of the defining features of everyday life in Britain in the last two hundred years. Yet, more often than not, its history is told via the activities and spaces through which it was practised. What is considered less often is how those spaces came to be, who financed them, and, critically, what that meant for people's access to and experience of leisure. This chapter tells the story of those venues, from their establishment to their growth and, ultimately, to their domination of the high street. Focusing on three major entertainment corporations – Mecca, the Rank Organisation, and EMI Dancing – it demonstrates how major commercial leisure organisations played a driving role in transforming late-night leisure in Britain and, critically, that the emergence of a series of seemingly separate venues and franchises was connected to an increasingly global leisure industry. While such a story might tempt us to reach a rather critical conclusion about the homogenising power of corporate leisure – indeed, such a conclusion is not entirely unwarranted given the enormous power these corporations come to wield by the end of the century – it is nonetheless the case that they were a driving force in transforming the late-night leisurescape and held, for generations of post-war youth, a central and formative place in their leisure experience.

The business of leisure in twentieth-century Britain

The cultural power of commercial leisure was not, of course, confined to the post-war period. Its presence is a defining feature of the changing landscape of working-class life from the end of the nineteenth century and is central to how historians have explored the emergence of an increasingly defined youth culture in the interwar period.[4] Indeed, the establishment of large-scale entertainment corporations in the first half of the twentieth century laid the very groundwork for the post-war transformation of the urban centre into a hub for recreation and pleasure. This section outlines how, by the 1950s, commercial leisure organisations were a firmly established feature of the British town and city centre and why, by the end of the twentieth century, they had taken the lead in transforming how young people experienced the late-night urban environment. In many cases, it was the same leisure and entertainment organisations that established dominance in the early twentieth century that then diversified into youth leisure in the post-war period. Where there were opportunities for leisure, there were opportunities to make money and, more than ever, post-war leisure provision was an industry.

From nineteenth-century gin palaces to pubcos, music halls to nightclubs, picture houses to multiplexes, popular leisure and commerce have long been intricately connected. It was, as Lee Jackson argued, the Victorians who first 'created' the leisure industry in Britain. The now long-recognised societal and economic changes heralded by the industrial revolution – urban growth, changing patterns of work, a growing and more accessible consumer market – meant that pleasure, and its provision, formed part of a growing commercial marketplace. The new institutions of leisure and entertainment that emerged to cater to the growing urban working class were 'substantial businesses, requiring considerable investments of capital, and collectively patronised by millions of customers'.[5] If the Victorians heralded the start of the leisure industry in Britain, then the developments of the twentieth century only further entrenched its cultural, social, political, and economic significance.

Technological advancements in myriad areas including audio, film, and manufacturing meant that across large swathes of the globe, the expansion of leisure time went hand-in-hand with the expansion of accessible and affordable amusements. Cinema, perhaps the most dominant commercial leisure form of the early twentieth century, offers us a clear indication of how quickly the growing appetite for leisure and industry collided. Following the introduction of film into Britain at the end of the nineteenth century, it rose 'from little more than a scientific toy in a sideshow at fairs to one of the most important social institutions of the country'.[6] Between 1926 and 1938, the number of cinemas in Britain had grown from an estimated 3,000 to 4,967.[7] Indeed, so important was the expansion of commercial cinema in the first half of the twentieth century that, during the Second World War, cinema attendance was recognised as a clear 'barometer for the mood of ordinary Londoners'.[8] Not only had a trip to the cinema become a central part of everyday life for millions of Britons, it had become a multi-million-pound industry with companies competing against each other to attract patrons. They battled to provide the best value, most glamorous surroundings, and latest releases, which were 'suggestive of luxurious fantasy'.[9] In Rotherham, for example, the reopening of the Cinema House in 1931 detailed the 'elaborate scale' of the venue's refurbishment, including velvet runner curtains, Wedgewood-blue ceilings, and a proscenium designed to look like 'old castle walls'.[10] Meanwhile, in Stockport, the approach to the newly opened Empress Cinema was 'across a forecourt, attractively laid out in flower beds and borders'.[11]

Dance, another area where commercial leisure made significant inroads, benefitted from the rising popularity of American music and dance styles in the years after the First World War and, thanks to the growing accessibility and affordability of radio and gramophones, a public that was well-versed in these new musical forms. Following the introduction of the country's first purpose-built commercial dance hall in 1919, London's Hammersmith Palais, it is estimated that up to eleven thousand new dance halls opened in the six years that followed.[12] These spaces were affordable and, argues Allison Abra, increasingly followed a 'basic dance hall model' in their design and construction, featuring sprung dance floors surrounded by tables and chairs and, in larger venues, viewing balconies.[13] The years between 1919 and 1945 thus heralded the entrenchment of public commercial leisure in a meaningful way in Britain. Designed to be affordable and accessible to the masses, and responding to profound transformations in working conditions, access to leisure time, urban infrastructure, and relative wage increases, leisure was big business. Among the most profitable sections of the customer base? The young.

Historians of youth leisure have considered at length the many ways in which youth lifestyles have intersected with the consumer market. Young people were at the forefront of post-war developments in consumer culture, increasingly able to exercise choice over their financial decisions and, critically, recognised as a distinct type of consumer. From the explosion of Carnaby Street to the growth of Biba clothing boutiques, the importing of Italian Gaggia coffee machines and the influence of American design on juke boxes, being able to orient a product towards the youth market had become, by the 1950s and 1960s, an indication, if not always a guarantee, of commercial success.[14] Nowhere is the intersection of youthful leisure and

The business of leisure   69

commerce more clear than in the post-war development of teenage magazines. The pages of teenage magazines are where ideas about youth, girlhood, and boyhood were constructed and played out.[15] However, nestled in amongst pinup posters of musicians and interviews with the stars of film and television were adverts for clothing, cosmetics, and records. These decisions were deliberate, themselves a product of the publishing industry's desire to profit from growing youthful affluence. Put another way, they demonstrate clearly the interconnectedness of youthful consumption and the powerful role that corporations came to play in 'commercially mediated' constructions of youth.[16] This interconnection is what came to define the growth and eventual domination of leisure-based multinationals.

However, this is not simply a story of growing youth affluence or the emergence of a distinct teenage market. The transformation of youth spending took place in the context of the growing globalisation of business and industry and, in particular, in an era in which multinational corporations were becoming increasingly powerful forces, both economically and politically. Changes in 'finance, production, technology, and policies' have, since the nineteenth century and into the twenty-first, 'pushed multinationals to centre stage of the international economic system'.[17] As this chapter demonstrates, the leisure industry developed in significant ways over the second half of the twentieth century. The 'leisured masses', driven by post-war affluence and peacetime stability, demanded access to an ever-growing landscape of leisure in the domestic, public, and commercial spheres. While the dominance of cinemas and traditional dance halls declined, there was growing demand for camping and holiday parks, swimming pools and leisure centres, bingo, cabaret, variety shows, bowling, and squash.[18] New entertainment 'centres', driven by suburbanisation and rising levels of car ownership, increasingly sought to provide these amenities under one roof. By the end of the twentieth century, the leisure industry was global and, according to Chatterton and Hollands, 'distinguishable by a concentration of corporate ownership, increased use of branding and theming, and conscious attempts to segment its markets'.[19]

While the following pages are less interested in questions surrounding the mechanics of globalisation than a chapter on national and multinational businesses might suggest, they do chart how and why an ever-smaller number of businesses come to have a claim in the leisured experiences of mid-to-late twentieth-century British youth. In doing so, this chapter seeks to untangle the messy and often intricate relationship between private commerce and urban development, between youth consumption and commercial leisure, at both a national and a local level. It will demonstrate that considering the history of youth leisure without asking how it intersects at a local and national level with global commerce can only provide the

70 *Youth and the changing urban environment*

historian with a partial account of youthful lives. Leisure provision was big business, and young people remained one of the largest consumer groups in the industry. As such, a consideration of how, why, and when large corporations transformed their provision of youth-oriented leisure offers us a critical way of exploring young people's access to leisure at the most intricate level. It explains how, via a touring circuit of Rank-owned cinemas and ballrooms, the Beatles were bought to Crewe, Birkenhead, and Hull, and why Europe's largest bowling alley found its home in Leicester in 1963. In short, doing this work reveals, as Leif Jerram says, 'the rendezvous between big and small' in modern Britain.[20]

'We are the leaders in our field and the future is ours': Mecca Leisure

Of all the commercial leisure institutions that came to dominate the British leisure landscape in the twentieth century, none held the national reputation of Mecca. A household name, the company became synonymous with dancing and entertainment by the mid-twentieth century. After all, it was Mecca that had been able to capitalise on the interwar dancing boom and bring dance to the masses. Mecca's journey through the British leisure landscape tells the story of British commercial leisure in microcosm, and offers a clear indication of the changing leisure patterns of the British public across the twentieth century. From relatively humble beginnings in the catering industry, it recognised the importance (and commercial value) of working-class entertainment, establishing an empire of ballrooms and dance halls, before diversifying into gambling, late-night entertainment, and large-scale recreation centres. Throughout this period, Mecca adapted its existing venues to better suit the national appetite, and these changes to the built environment of leisure offer us perhaps the most revealing way to understand changing youth behaviours.

Mecca Dancing, which became the largest dance-hall chain in Britain, was established by Carl Heimann in 1934. Mecca Dancing was an offshoot of a catering company running 'Ye Mecca Cafes' that Heimann had worked for since 1924, but it was Heimann's decision to take advantage of the fashion for dancing in the late 1920s that transformed the company's fortunes.[21] Persuading the company to purchase a number of dance halls, the first in Brighton in 1928, Heimann started the company's transition into popular entertainment. By 1934, Heimann was general manager of Mecca Dancing and, following his partnership with Scottish entertainment operator Alan Fairley the following year, the two went on to become board members of the now fast-growing Mecca company.[22] Such was the corporate power of Mecca by the end of the 1930s that social research organisation Mass

The business of leisure   71

Observation called Heimann 'one of the "cultural directors" of the nation' in 1939.[23] In 1946, Heimann and Fairley became leading shareholders and joint chairs of the new Mecca Ltd, a company that would become 'synonymous with popular entertainment'.[24] Between them, Heimann and Fairley revolutionised Britain's dancing landscape.

Mecca's success through this period was testament to the popularity of dancing as a pastime in Britain, and to their commitment to providing a recognisably 'Mecca' experience. The company had been particularly effective in creating a brand identity, ensuring that the Mecca name became associated with reliability and quality entertainment. This public image was one the company relied on heavily, and was central to their strategy in the changing leisure landscape of the post-war period. As both Allison Abra and James Nott have demonstrated, the desire to dance in Britain was significant and, by the 1950s, the numbers of people dancing was 'higher than ever before', with estimates putting weekly dancing figures at around five million by 1959.[25] However, through the early to mid 1960s, numbers began to decline as an increasingly affluent working class demanded more from their leisure pursuits. Dancing itself, as we will see, remained a popular activity, but the traditional dance hall went into swift decline. By the mid-1960s, Mecca had begun the process of diversification to ensure not only its survival, but that it retained a central place in the leisure experiences of the British public.

The decline of popular ballroom dancing did not spell the end for Mecca. As James Nott notes, the company was 'always abreast of changes in customer preferences' and it shifted its operations accordingly.[26] Mecca's repertoire expanded significantly and diversification in the post-war period moved the company's portfolio of interests into a 'new scale', encompassing gambling, motorway service stations, ice skating, and roller skating, alongside its continuing dance operations.[27] In 1964, the company assured shareholders that 'there is no slackening in the expansion of your Company'.[28] Perhaps the most significant development in Mecca's diversification was the company's investment in 'entertainment centres'. These centres spoke clearly to Mecca's desire to be a 'one stop shop' for leisure and recreation, catering to all sections of society regardless of age or income. They also capitalised on the growth of car ownership and suburban living, providing customers with a range of entertainment options accessible by car. In doing so, Mecca hoped it could satisfy the leisure and entertainment needs of the whole family, from children and teenagers through to grandparents, in one purpose-built space.

The first of these centres was in Bristol, and comprised a 'Mecca Dance Hall, a Mecca Banqueting Suite, a Silver Blades Ice Rink, a Top Rank Bowl, a Cinerama Theatre and Car Parks'.[29] The development, it was reported in

Figure 2.1 Advert placed in the local press for Mecca's 'New Bristol Centre', 20 May 1966. © Reach PLC and Mirrorpix.

1962, was to cost upwards of £1 million and 'regarded as possibly the most advanced in Britain as, in the car era, it combines so many amenities under one roof'.[30] Upon opening in 1966, Mecca's advertising touted it as 'the world's newest and greatest entertainment centre'.[31] The development opened in stages over the course of the year, and was a prime example of the company's policy of diversification. In collaborating with industry rivals Top Rank, alongside others, Mecca was able to keep overhead costs down while ensuring the Mecca name remained associated with quality and accessible leisure.

The company was buoyant in the mid-1960s despite a difficult trading period in the summer of 1964. Diversification meant that dancing in its traditional sense made up an increasingly small part of Mecca's business operation, something they were keen to emphasise rather than shy away from. Reflecting on the company's future in 1965, the board highlighted a 'total membership of two-and-a-half million people'. These millions, they exclaimed:

> Support us in our Shops, visit our Gaming Rooms for a little flutter, park their cars and use our garages. They can join Mecca Postal Bingo with all the

The business of leisure

security that our name imparts, read Dance News, and give parties for almost any number in our Banqueting Suites. Just imagine that all age groups and all income groups can enjoy the range and variety of these things that we sell. Our responsibility is indeed immense for we are the leaders in our field, and the future is ours.[32]

While the 'golden age' of dancing had come to an end, Mecca's role in Britain's leisure landscape continued unabated. The diversification away from traditional dancing meant that dancing and late-night leisure spaces formed only one portion of their profits into the later twentieth century, but their continued interest in this sphere meant that the company retained a strong presence in the vast majority of Britain's towns and cities. A £33 million merger with industry giant Grand Metropolitan in 1970 also marked a new moment in the company's history, though they maintained a significant degree of independence in their operations. In Swindon, the organisation's refurbishment of the historic Locarno ballroom demonstrated its capacity to absorb 'its historic past and adapts [sic] to the future'.[33] The Locarno was snuggled 'inside Swindon's old Corn Exchange like a cuckoo inside another bird's nest', updating its decor and entertainment provision to cater to the young crowd.[34] By 1970, Mecca had turned away from traditional ballrooms and towards 'smaller, more intimate establishments'.[35] It is to these intimate establishments that this chapter now turns.

In an interview with industry publication *The Stage* in 1974, Ivor Rabin and Phil Tate, the deputy managing directors of Mecca Agency International – a subsidiary of the company responsible primarily for live entertainments – reflected on Mecca's recent business investments. The company, Rabin and Tate insisted, 'still regard[ed] dancing as the foundation of its business'.[36] While Mecca had made important moves to diversify the use of their more traditional ballrooms, they insisted that dancing remained the primary function. Mecca ballrooms and dance halls were not, it was made clear, cabaret clubs. 'There are many big clubs in the provinces, not owned by Mecca, which can be called theatre restaurants, in that the show is the focal point of the evening and the dancing fills the gaps. Our halls for the most part fulfil the function of the ballrooms – the "boy meets girl" thing, you know.'[37] That sociability remained at the heart of Mecca's post-war business model is undoubtedly a significant factor in the company's continued success through this period. While formal partnered dancing fell out of fashion, the importance of the dance hall and, increasingly, the nightclub and discotheque, as a place for romantic or sexual encounter remained.

In the sphere of youth leisure, it was Mecca's decision to renovate and re-brand their late-night entertainment spaces that marked the most significant change to young people's engagement with these spaces. Alongside

74 *Youth and the changing urban environment*

many other companies, including industry rival the Rank Organisation, Mecca recognised the growing demand for licensed nightspots that catered to young adults. Unlike the growing cabaret scene that prioritised glamour and live entertainment, these nightspots were to focus on disc jockeys and static dancing, and would provide alcoholic refreshment. 'Dancehalls are a thing of the past', argued the head of operations in Mecca's leisure division in 1984.[38] 'Yet in a sense they are still there, but in a different guise. What we are selling now is an environment, primarily, but not exclusively, for young people.'[39] Following the demise of many of the country's membership-only beat clubs in the aftermath of the Private Places of Entertainment Act in 1967, the new – or, in many cases, revamped – discotheques stepped in to fill the gap. These new clubs shed the more formal social requirements often found in older dance halls, and instead moved to provide multi-functional leisure spaces where young people could dance, socialise, and drink into the early hours.

For Mecca, the desire to licence their premises had been an ongoing battle, and it was one that required careful navigation of the country's disparate licensing committees. Licences 'had to be fought for, with great risks taken', recalled Alan Fairley's wife Roma Fairley in her 1966 memoir.[40] In 1958 Alan Fairley took one such risk, challenging Birmingham's reluctance to allow a licensed club in the same premises as a ballroom, arguing that Mecca's approach favoured responsible consumption of intoxicants. 'Give people facilities for social drinking, in a dignified way, over the period of an evening in order to put them off stoking up too quickly in pubs and trying to gain entrance when drunk', Fairley argued in a court hearing.[41] The Chief Constable's case, which sought to argue such an approach would encourage instances of drunk and disorderly behaviour, fell down when counsel for Mecca reminded justices that they had not yet granted a licence within a dance hall, and as such the police had 'no evidence' to prove the link.[42] As Mecca's interests turned towards late-night entertainments from the early 1960s onwards, the precedent for combining an alcohol licence with music and dancing was put in place.

Mecca's move into licensed late-night entertainment was firmly established by the end of the 1970s, with the company owning a total of 104 venues across England, Scotland, and Wales. The dominance of Mecca leisure spaces in the post-war period is perhaps one of the most significant facets of the post-war youth experience – particularly for young people in smaller provincial towns – yet the company's post-war transition remains woefully under-explored. Mecca's nightclubs provided a place for young people to socialise until the early hours, away from the traditional public houses and social clubs that still dominated the leisurescape of many areas of Britain. Critically, they provided access to live music and industry stars, with Mecca

The business of leisure 75

venues retaining a central place on many national and international touring circuits. For example, the opening of a Mecca nightclub and music venue in Merthyr Tydfil, an industrial town in the south of Wales, formed an essential facet of youth leisure for the town in the 1970s. Incorporated into the newly opened shopping precinct early in the decade, the club comprised one of only two major venues for music and dancing in the town, and featured well-known bands including Elvis Costello and the Attractions and Dexy's Midnight Runners.[43]

It is in this context that Mecca's diversification into late-night leisure was most transformative for provincial towns in Britain. As well as access to licensed late-night dancing, Mecca also bought with it significant economic and cultural resource. Carolyn Downs has demonstrated how, in the fast-growing bingo division of the company, no expense was spared in bringing 'the glitz of Hollywood to small towns', with celebrities such as Lulu, Cilla Black, and Tommy Steele brought in to call bingo.[44] The company sought, in many ways, to be self sufficient. For every major element of the supply chain needed to run its operations, another part of the Mecca family could offer the relevant services.[45] Mecca Agency, which was established in 1973, enabled the company to deploy its significant power and contacts in the entertainment market by booking artists to perform across the Mecca circuit. Their establishment of a concert division in 1974 meant Mecca could attract big-name bands, often from America, to perform 'at suitable locations' within the organisation.[46]

The 'new' discotheques of the 1960s and 1970s were, more often than not, renovations of old premises, though Mecca was expanding its property portfolio significantly both through the purchase and construction of new buildings throughout this period. The transformation of ballrooms and dance halls into nightclubs and discotheques was a gradual process, but it was one that ensured Mecca retained a considerable presence across Britain. Of these transformations, it was the establishment of the Tiffany's brand of discotheque that most closely tied Mecca to the late-night entertainment industry. This shift marked the company's initial move away from dance halls in the 1960s towards the more static discotheque that had the disc jockey at its centre. It was a real moment of transformation for the company, which attached the Tiffany's name to seventy of its newly renovated dance halls in the 1960s in an attempt to capture the demand for more informal dancing 'as quickly as possible'.[47]

By 1977, Mecca owned a total of fifty-one venues with the Tiffany's branding, making the company the owners of one of the largest nightclub chains in the country. Tiffany's clubs could be found in large cities – Birmingham, Edinburgh, Sheffield, and Newcastle, for example – and much smaller towns – Darwen and Coalville, for instance. Tiffany's clubs were initially aimed at a slightly older demographic, though they inevitably attracted younger people in their teenage years and upwards (providing they could convince the door staff to let them enter). Tiffany's in Bristol, for example, advertised 'soft lights' and 'intimate music', while Newcastle's branch was branded as a 'luxury nightspot'.[48] Of course, such language spoke to the desire to shed Mecca's old dance-hall image as well as to the company's key selling point of 'affordable glamour'. However, it also hinted at the significant financial investments Mecca was making in redeveloping these spaces.[49] The more iconic venues retained the historic names attached to them, such as Locarno and Palais, which drew on the company's rich and established history.

Mecca's continued commercial success in the realm of late-night entertainment came primarily from two key factors: the company's structure and the autonomy given to individual venues. Tiffany's was not the only name given to Mecca's newly opened bars and discotheques. Despite the partial franchising of portions of its business under names such as Locarno, Tiffany's, and Samantha's, Mecca resisted the homogenisation of these spaces. While each venue retained a relative flexibility, allowing it to host live music and entertainment, disc jockeys, and private functions, it was the company's policy to be driven by the needs of each venue in its local setting. Tiffany's in Ilford reverted to its original name of the Palais following its renovation in 1983, as 'all the locals still referred to it as the Palais so we decided to change it back'.[50] Indeed, by the 1980s, the company was actively moving away from the standardisation of its late-night spaces. Instead each venue was 'individually designed ... in keeping with the clientele it hope[d] to attract'.[51] The result? Step into a Mecca venue and it 'is difficult for a casual customer to detect that he is in a Mecca establishment'.[52] The company maintained a clear management structure that provided individual venue managers with a surprising degree of autonomy regarding the decor and entertainment. This meant that, increasingly, Mecca's portfolio of nightclubs did not look or feel as though they were united under one company. From Norwood Rooms and Samson and Hercules in Norwich to Dolly Gray's and Raquel's in Wakefield, Mecca's operations were responsible for a significant portion of the country's late-night leisure between the 1960s and early 1980s.

Across the 1980s, Mecca's growth in this area slowed and their share of the market challenged, and by 1990 the company was in debt to the tune of £450 million.[53] The company was taken over by long-time rivals the Rank Organisation in the same year as part of a £537 million deal, making them one of the largest entertainment groups in the country. In the sixty years since its establishment, Mecca had transformed the provision of late-night leisure in Britain and demonstrated the importance of listening to young

The business of leisure 77

consumers. In transforming dance halls into nightclubs, maintaining a distinctly local presence, and upholding a strong reputation for reliable leisure provision, Mecca played a crucial role in transforming Britain's late-night leisurescape. While it eventually fell foul of the growing 'cartelisation' of the British leisure industry, Mecca's survival in a period of dramatic transformation to leisure provision was testament to its commitment to adapt to young consumers.[54]

'Industry has seized the initiative and charts the way': the Rank Organisation

Originally specialising in film distribution and cinema, the Rank Organisation made similar attempts to diversify their trading in the post-war period, making significant inroads into the leisure and entertainment industry through the 1960s. While their growth in this area was somewhat more limited than Mecca's, the much larger scale of Rank's wider operations provided the organisation with the capital to invest significant sums of money into their new ventures and, by the 1990s, the company was one of the largest providers of leisure in Britain.

The Rank Organisation was, in some ways, an unexpected entrant into the arena of late-night entertainment. While the company had its roots firmly in the leisure industry, its interests were historically concentrated in the film industry. J. Arthur Rank, the company's founder and a lifelong Methodist, made his entrance into the world of film by distributing projectors to Sunday Schools in the early 1930s. This 'curious collision between business and missionary enthusiasm' was not one that suggested the meteoric ascent that was to come and yet, by the early 1940s, the Rank Organisation was a central player in the country's film industry.[55] J. Arthur Rank and his business partners focused their interests in two key areas: the production and distribution of British films. The organisation gained full control of its first studio, Pinewood, in 1937, and soon turned to the missing link in its chain: cinema. It was through cinema that the Rank Organisation and its subsidiaries became a household name, in particular by taking ownership of well-known cinema companies Odeon and Gaumont-British. These two acquisitions combined to give Rank a total of 724 cinemas by the end of the 1940s, a significant number of which were large capacity 'flagship' venues.[56] J. Arthur Rank was, according to Jeffrey Richards, 'the colossus of the British film industry' by the end of the Second World War.[57]

Despite this success, the early 1950s marked a difficult period in Rank's history. As cinema attendances fell across the country, so too did the company's profits. The company had embarked on a period of significant cost-cutting at the end of the 1940s and, while the company's overdraft was reduced by the mid-1950s, they were certainly not out of the woods.[58] The answer to these financial challenges? Diversification. In the early 1950s, the company's trading base was expanding and, as a 1955 article on the growing threat posed to cinema by television claimed, it was 'probably as widely based as any could be while remaining broadly within the cinema business'.[59] As such, the company's end-of-year report for 1957 explained that while profits had been 'maintained in a difficult trading year', their policy of diversification would continue.[60] The challenge, they claimed, was the various burdens placed on the industry by taxes and levies. In particular, the Sunday Entertainments Act (1932) was highlighted as being an outdated and 'iniquitous burden' that did not reflect the changing entertainment landscape of 1950s Britain.[61] The reasons behind the industry's contraction were varied, with historians pointing to causes including the growth of television and more varied opportunities for leisure.[62] However, as Sam Manning argues, the changing behaviours of young people were also a significant factor. Young people 'remained the cinema's core audience', but also took advantage of the opportunities to spend their money in the growing number of dance halls, coffee bars, and youth clubs that increasingly vied with the cinema for their income.[63]

It was in this context that the Rank Organisation looked to move beyond the film industry to shore up the organisation's finances and ensure its survival. Geoffrey Macnab termed this period in the company's history the 'Xerox years', denoting Rank's investment in, and subsequent commercial success of, the Rank Xerox photocopying machines.[64] Such was the scale of Xerox's success that Rank became known by the late 1960s for only one product, 'and that product wasn't anything to do with movies'.[65] However, alongside Xerox, the company recognised, much like Mecca in this period, that the national appetite for leisure was increasing and 'their job was to identify profitable new ventures, whether they be ten-pin bowling alleys, dance halls, or motorway service stations'.[66] Leisure space emerged as a significant remit for the organisation, with Rank focusing on two core areas through the 1960s: ten-pin bowling and dancing. 1962 was announced as 'one of the most significant in the group's history', with significant financial diversification and growth.[67] The 'greatest potential' in this area, the organisation argued, was in ten-pin bowling. Following a pilot installation of a venue in London's Golders Green in 1960, Rank was confident of its financial viability and, of the twenty-four ten-pin bowling sites in Britain in 1962, Rank owned eight. It was also in this period that the organisation turned towards the 'highly competitive' field of ballrooms and dance halls, operating a total of twenty-five by the same year.[68] However, its experience in this field suggested the need for 'careful forward planning', particularly

The business of leisure 79

in relation to location, decor, furnishing, and equipment, in order to mark them apart from their competitors – namely Mecca. In 1963, the organisation spoke of a quiet revolution in which 'industry has seized the initiative and charts the way'.[69] This 'new world' of the Rank Organisation was dictated by three revolutions: technological, societal, and entertainment. By the time of J. Arthur Rank's death in 1972, the company had deviated significantly from its origins in British cinema, and was increasingly turning towards the broader remit of leisure.

Rank focused, in the late 1950s and early 1960s, on the acquisition and, later, the conversion of cinemas and ballrooms. In doing so, the organisation was able to quickly expand the number of dancing and entertainment venues under the Rank name. The Majestic chain of ballrooms, which included venues in Glasgow, Chester, and Portsmouth, formed a significant part of the organisation's early dance hall offering which, by 1962, stood at twenty-five strong. The conversion of these venues meant Rank was able to adjust their business interests without significant financial outlay; converting the Majestic cinema to a ballroom in Luton, for example, cost £125,000.[70] Indeed, all four ballrooms added to Rank's collection in 1962 – Luton, Oldham, Plymouth, and Preston – were conversions of existing leisure venues including cinemas and ten-pin bowling.[71] Rank's full expansion into the world of dancing and late-night entertainment came comparatively late when considered alongside rivals Mecca, and its ownership of large numbers of cinemas in a period of declining attendance meant that conversion was the most sensible route. One implication of this was that the scale of Rank's early dancing venues tended to be much smaller than Mecca's, and its share of the consumer market more limited.[72]

At the heart of Rank's foray into dancing was the Top Rank chain of 'entertainment suites' and ballrooms. Much like Mecca, Top Rank's leisure division sought to capitalise on the post-war redevelopment of Britain's towns and cities and built relationships with local authorities and planners. The opening of new large-scale entertainment facilities catering for upwards of two thousand people, in comparison to the conversion of existing spaces such as ballrooms and cinemas, marked a new stage in the organisation's expansion and capital expenditure. Such ventures were expensive and often required upwards of £1 million, in comparison to the relatively cheaper route offered by the conversion of existing venues. Rank's milestone move into the world of the entertainment centre came with the opening of the Brighton Top Rank Entertainment Centre, phase one of Brighton's major post-war redevelopment scheme, which opened in 1965. Promising to be one of Britain's 'most lavish-ever entertainment centres', it was a clear sign of Rank's commercial commitment to what it considered to be the quiet revolution in leisure.[73] The venue was a significant one, designed by the

Figure 2.2 Couple dancing the twist, Majestic Ballroom, Newcastle, 1962. © NCJ Archive and Mirrorpix.

Brutalist architect Russell Diplock and located in a prominent sea-front location. Original plans for the entertainment centre promised a multi-site complex encompassing dance halls, banqueting suites, cinema, bowling, and ice skating.[74] By the early 1970s, both the bowling lane and ice rink had closed, but the Top Rank Suite – the venue's 2,500-capacity dance hall and primary attraction – retained a strong audience. Similar ventures were opened across the country, ensuring Rank was able to continue its expansion into the youth market.

The business of leisure

81

This expansion was volatile, however, and demonstrates the instability of the leisure market in a moment of momentous change. Growing competition between venues meant businesses had to work hard to maintain their share of the market and to keep their venues up to date. Through the 1970s and 1980s, a number of Rank-owned late-night venues opened and closed, many of which changed hands between a handful of corporations with marked regularity. In 1972, Rank sold their prominent city-centre location in Leicester to the Bailey Organisation, while in 1979 leisure group Leisure 2000 took ownership of a flagship Liverpool venue that had been owned by Top Rank, Baileys, and EMI.[75] In 1984, Rank sold twenty-one of their smaller discos and public houses in the midlands to brewing group Whitbread in a £4.5 million deal, reflecting both Rank's decision to focus on larger leisure ventures and the entrance of pub corporations, more commonly known as pubcos, onto the late-night leisure market in the later twentieth century.[76]

The dominance of Top Rank in the leisure sphere was further compounded in 1990 by their takeover of industry rivals Mecca. Rivalry between the two firms' leisure offering was longstanding, with the 'battle of the ballrooms' stretching back to the 1960s.[77] The Rank Organisation first attempted a takeover of Mecca in 1964 with an offer of £30 million. Combined, the two organisations ran a total of seventy-two ballrooms and dance halls in Britain and they battled continuously in this period for their share of the market. Through the 1960s, Mecca retained a larger share of the dancing market but was unable to keep pace with Rank's later expansion, despite its move into the profitable arenas of gambling and holiday resorts. Between 1985 and 1990, Rank spent £1 billion on acquisitions, with more than half of that in the leisure industry, and rivalry between the two ended following Rank's £512 million takeover.[78] By 1992, following its takeover of Mecca, Rank was operating over three hundred leisure venues including discos, social and bingo clubs, holiday camps, and conference suites.

Rank was initially an unlikely contender in the business of dancing and late-night entertainment, but it was its commitment to laying 'heavy emphasis on more modern trends' that ensured its success amongst young consumers.[79] By converting cinemas to dance halls and bowling alleys, collaborating with commercial developers and redevelopment programmes, and establishing its venues on the live music circuit, the Rank Organisation became a prominent part of the reimagined post-war city, and demonstrated the commercial potential of staying abreast of the changing leisure demands of youth.

Lavish and luxurious: the Bailey Organisation and EMI Dancing

While Mecca and Rank were undoubtedly the two largest players in Britain's dancing and entertainment industry, they were by no means the only organisations operating in this sphere. Rank and Mecca dominated the large capacity and historic venues, setting up dance halls in prominent locations and converting existing leisure venues already in their ownership. The pace of change in this industry was quick, however, and a much smaller company entered the fray in the 1960s with a singular focus on late-night dancing and entertainment. Its story offers a clear indication of the changing behaviour of young people – some of the primary consumers of late-night leisure – and the relationship between the local, national, and international consumer market. The Bailey Organisation had humble roots in South Shields in the early 1960s, and in less than twenty years had become Europe's largest nightclub chain before being incorporated into one of Britain's biggest multinationals, EMI.

Established in 1960 by Stanley Henry and John Smith, former draughtsmen at Reyrolle's engineering firm on Tyneside, the Bailey Organisation quickly built a standing for providing reputable and quality nightlife. After running a dance academy with Henry's mother, the pair took over the defunct Cavendish Club in Newcastle city centre, swiftly followed by the already established nightclub La Dolce Vita.[80] By 1973 the organisation had venues in twelve towns and cities, including seven with the company's namesake: Baileys. With a focus on glamorous interiors, quality sound, lighting, and fixtures, Baileys venues sought to 'bring to countless people standards of nightlife and entertainment most of them had only dreamed about'.[81] Much like Mecca's drive to bring 'affordable glamour' to the masses, the Bailey Organisation responded to the growing appetite for late-night leisure by seeking to diversify, and profit from, the venues available in England's provinces. The adverts for the opening of the Cavendish in Sheffield, for example, touted it as a 'new King-Spot of nightclubs' that was 'luxurious ... lavish ... inexpensive'.[82]

An interview with the firm's public relations consultant in 1969 suggested that 'it is no accident that the name of the Bailey Organisation is synonymous with all that is good in the night club scene, that the company is constantly one step ahead of its competitors, or that a unique and profitable relationship of family togetherness exists between the organisation and its patrons'.[83] What the Bailey Organisation demonstrated was the value of good business acumen in the fast-growing and ever-changing sphere of late-night leisure. Much like other leisure entrepreneurs of the late 1950s and early 1960s, the duo took advantage of the growing desire for late-night entertainment in the provinces, but they coupled this with a recognition

The business of leisure 83

of the power of branding to establish a regional chain. Indeed, Smith and Henry were keen to distance their outfit from 'the man who wants to play at running a night club'.[84] It was a job, Smith argued, 'for experts, a job for businessmen using modern business methods'. The Bailey Organisation's success came from its well-timed entry into the cabaret market which, Dave Russell argues, 'helped reshape the pleasure economy of provincial England'.[85]

The organisation's rise in the 1960s and 1970s was testament to its desire to do good business. It was established on the national 'clubland' circuit; had launched a booking agency, SAS Ltd; and was able to attract popular entertainers and cabaret artists by ensuring them performance slots across numerous Baileys locations.[86] Indeed, the sheer speed and scale of their growth caused a number of independent entertainment club owners to express concern at the competition posed by the Bailey Organisation's consolidation in the north of England as early as 1967.[87] Its growth was only compounded by the attention it paid to young consumers. While the cabaret for which it had made its name tended to attract a more mature audience, the Bailey Organisation recognised that late-night entertainment was an industry increasingly driven by the shifting consumption habits of teenagers and young adults. In 1968 it announced the opening of 'Sloopy's Club' in Newcastle, a club designed 'for the single set'. While younger teenagers were relatively well catered to by the growing number of jazz bars and existing dance halls, there was not, Henry argued, 'a great deal of opportunity for the young single person to meet unattached members of the opposite sex and strike up new friendships'.[88] With a more relaxed dress code, and a focus on music and dancing, Sloopy's indicated the growing need for smaller, more intimate late-night discotheques alongside the existing larger entertainment centres and dance halls.

By the mid-1970s, the Bailey Organisation was a well-known name in late-night entertainment, with a reputation for providing quality entertainment, cabaret, and dancing. The organisation captured the attention of the leisure division of Electric and Music Industries (EMI), one of Britain's largest multinational corporations, which had been expanding its interests into the leisure industry from the 1960s. In 1977, EMI Leisure purchased all twelve of the Bailey Organisation's nightspots for £1.87 million, stating that the purchase of a 'national chain of night spots for dancing and cabaret ... will provide the Group with an important expansion of its present leisure businesses'.[89] This purchase gave EMI a stake in nightspots across England, from Bristol to Hull, with the largest concentration in the midlands and north west. The new acquisitions would trade under the new name of EMI Dancing, the aim of which was to create 'highly stylised discotheques and clubs'.[90]

EMI's move into the leisure industry was driven, much like Rank and Mecca before it, by a desire to diversify, thus 'ensuring continued growth'.[91] The organisation's most high-profile leisure acquisition had been the renowned Blackpool Tower Company in 1968, and in 1974 it established EMI Leisure Enterprises Ltd and the subsidiary EMI Dancing to better reflect the 'growing programme of new leisure enterprises'.[92] This included sporting activities such as squash and bowling, entertainment complexes, and licensed premises. The latter was part of EMI's expansion project and included twenty-three licensed venues including the western-themed Painted Wagon pubs and, by 1977, the Empire Ballroom in London.[93] Their take-over of Baileys was simply the latest stage in the organisation's diversification, but it provided EMI with a clear opportunity to capitalise on the growing popularity of disco. Utilising existing Baileys venues, EMI launched a new twin-nightclub concept, Romeo's and Juliet's, hosting live music and entertainment alongside disc jockeys and disco. Large-scale refurbishments were undertaken, including a £300,000 relaunch in Liverpool. EMI were keen to establish a clear link between its venues and disco, organising the World Disco Dancing Championships in conjunction with the *Daily Mirror* and staging the semi-finals and finals at various venues operated by EMI Dancing.[94]

EMI Dancing's success was short lived, however, and by 1979 the organisation had sold its Leicester venue Baileys and was monitoring the remaining eleven. Demonstrating the precariousness of the night-time economy, the managing director of EMI Dancing told *The Stage* that a 'large organisation like EMI cannot be interested in units which return low profits'.[95] By the end of 1980 EMI had sold the majority of its leisure interests, including its London dance hall and national disco chain, to the global restaurateur and hotelier Trusthouse Forte for £16 million.[96]

Towards a commercial history of youth culture

Between them, Mecca, Rank, and for a while the Bailey Organisation followed by EMI Dancing and Trusthouse Forte, became powerful players in the British leisure industry. Their commitment both to expansion and diversification ensured their survival in an ever-changing marketplace. Critically, their interventions in the commercial leisure industry contributed to a meaningful transformation in the experience of youthful leisure. As town and city centres were remade in the post-war decades, these organisations ensured their leisure provision was at its heart. As cinemas and ballrooms turned to dancing, discos, ice skating, or ten-pin bowling, the vast majority of towns and cities across Britain were, by the 1990s, home to a venue (or, in many

The business of leisure 85

cases, multiple venues) owned or leased by a subsidiary of Mecca, Rank, EMI, or Trusthouse Forte. The sheer speed at which these organisations expanded and consolidated their share of the leisure industry in Britain was remarkable, and meant that almost all young people growing up in the years between the 1960s and 1990s would, at some stage, have socialised in their spaces.

The growing consolidation of the entertainment industry in the hands of an increasingly small number of companies had myriad impacts at the local level, and did not go without notice from young patrons. One Plymouth-based letter writer to the *Sunday Mirror* argued that the rebranding of well-known local venues demonstrated a distance from the cities in which they were based. 'London decisions, presumably. Why?' asked the frustrated writer.[97] This consolidation also had the potential to leave young people in provincial towns and cities at the mercy of corporate reorganisation. In Crewe, a group of forty-five teenagers submitted a petition to the Rank Organisation following their decision in 1965 to close the town's Majestic Ballroom. Rank's 'scandalous' plans to convert the large ballroom into a site for bingo left the town's young people with a far more limited leisure landscape, with many noting the already crowded nature of the town's leisure facilities and the need to travel to neighbouring towns and cities for late-night dancing. One disgruntled teenager explained that 'Top Rank must have made an enormous amount of money from the young people of Crewe and now they are just forsaking us all in favour of middle-aged bingo fans'.[98] Organisations were quick to expand, but equally quick to identify venues that weren't running a profit. As such, venues changed hands and were renamed and rebranded with remarkable regularity. EMI's launch of Romeo's and Juliet's in late-1970s Liverpool followed ownership of the same venue by both Rank and Baileys, who had left the building on Lime Street 'empty, like a giant concrete and glass white elephant'.[99]

The implications of this were felt harshly by those young people growing up in smaller towns and cities. The turn towards large-scale entertainment centres and purpose-built leisure facilities, favoured by Mecca and Top Rank in particular, meant the majority of new ventures required a population of at least one hundred thousand in the venue's 'catchment area', while tight profit margins ensured that financial viability came before social need.[100] In Cambridge, the closure of the city's only public ballroom in the early 1970s led to calls for the city council to 'tempt the big dance and entertainment organisations, such as Mecca and Top Rank'.[101] The city's young people were travelling as far as Stevenage, to the Mecca-owned Locarno, to dance in the absence of any dedicated late-night spots in the city. The calls being made to the city council demonstrate, in stark terms, the important role that commercial leisure organisations came to play in the provision of

86 *Youth and the changing urban environment*

youthful leisure. Their absence, and in the case of Cambridge City Council, the perceived inability to attract their investment, was touted as a failure of the city's young people who, it was felt, were not catered to adequately.

The growth of these commercial leisure companies, and the cultural power this afforded them, was central in determining the type of leisure that was available to young people. This relationship was, at times, fraught and complicated. As licensed venues, many of these new nightclubs were limited to those young people who were over the age of 18, though, as Chapter 4 demonstrates, this exclusion was not always enforced. More important to these venues was public image and profitability. In particular, the desire to avoid attracting 'troublemakers' was often couched in a classed and racialised vision of respectability. For young men and women of colour, the implications of this were keenly felt. As James Nott demonstrates, Mecca in particular had attracted controversy for decades due to its imposition of an informal 'colour bar' in a number of its ballrooms.[102] Companies like Mecca and the Rank Organisation rarely had coordinated or formal door policies, yet the desire to maintain their established and historic public image was, in their eyes, of paramount importance. Mecca justified their approach to door management as aiding the 'prevention of trouble', an approach which drew widespread criticism and saw the company investigated by the Race Relations Board on a number of occasions.[103] In a study of Leicester, Sue Zeleny Bishop demonstrated that 'people of colour were not always guaranteed admission' to the city's public houses and nightclubs and, as a result, 'members of Leicester's new black, Asian and ethnically minoritised communities established their own "in" places'.[104] These door policies therefore both placed young people of colour at risk of harassment and violence by security and bouncers seeking to 'reinforce' the company's door policy and encouraged their marginalisation from the dominant spaces of youthful leisure.

The question of respectability was further extended to speak to the connotations between particular youth movements and societal violence. The Rank Organisation, for example, became deeply embroiled in the public panic around punk violence in 1976. Following the Sex Pistols' appearance on the *Today Show* with Bill Grundy, during which the band was infamously goaded into on-air profanity, the Rank Organisation, whose venues had been scheduled to host a number of dates on the group's 'Anarchy in the UK' tour, pulled out. Rank's public statement on the matter said that the group did not 'appear to be the kind of entertainment we want to be associated with'.[105] In the same week, Rank announced a 'ban' on young people under the age of 25 in a number of its dance halls, following a supposed rise of hooliganism. 'It has cost us a fortune', argued one Rank official, who

The business of leisure

suggested that growing violence at dance halls meant 'innocent kids have stopped coming because they are worried about being involved in fights'.[106]

However, these spaces also held an important yet complicated place in the development of local and national subcultural scenes. Despite their reputation, they were not solely places for dancing to Top 40 pop though, admittedly, this is where the bulk of their dancing income lay. Mecca, for example, played an important role in the Northern Soul scene of the early-to-mid 1970s, hosting a number of soul sessions in its venues across England. Many nightclubs also sought to capitalise on the popularity of jazz, soul, disco, and funk by hosting Black bands and disc jockeys, often from America and the Caribbean, offering an 'authentic' experience for customers.[107] In this way, the role that commercial leisure organisations played in the leisure landscape of Britain could be fraught. While racist door policies and the risk of harassment or violence were felt keenly by many young people who were racialised in Britain, these were also venues that often sought to capitalise on Black and alternative music cultures. The space given to less 'mainstream' music cultures was, of course, contingent on its success and commercial viability. Samantha's, housed above Sheffield's Mecca ice rink on Queens Road, was host to regular soul nights on Wednesdays, reportedly attracting up to six hundred dancers within a few years of opening.[108] With a total capacity of seven hundred, the venue's mid-week soul nights seemed a successful endeavour.[109] However, the venue made clear to their disc jockeys not to play soul outside of these nights as 'the soul crowd tended to drink nothing but cokes which was not very profitable'.[110] As Felix Fuhg has argued, while commercial venues offered opportunities for interaction between young people of different races, 'the market for music and style was designed primarily to serve white teenagers'.[111] While the relationship between large entertainment leisure corporations and alternative music scenes was complex, it does serve as an important reminder that the history of youth leisure and consumption cannot be separated from the commercial context of the wider British leisure industry.

Taken together, what did these commercial transformations mean? At the macro level, it is clear to see how these developments demonstrate a marked change in young people's appetite for leisure that was driven by rising levels of affluence and post-war urban reconstruction. However, it is at the micro level, at the level of individual venue and street, where it is possible to chart the intersection of global, national, and local. In doing so, it becomes clear to see both the extent of commercial investment in urban leisure and the implications of this for young people's access to leisure space. By returning to the streets of Sheffield, this final part of the chapter explores how the introduction and eventual expansion of commercial late-night leisure into

88   *Youth and the changing urban environment*

the city transformed young people's relationship to the city in two key ways: spatially and temporally.

When Mecca opened their Heart Beat Club above the Silver Blades ice rink in 1965, it was the first licensed nightclub in the city that was explicitly geared towards younger patrons. While small – initially licensed for a maximum of 250 people in an entertainment complex holding thousands – the club was open until 2 a.m. and offered youth-oriented entertainment that stood in stark contrast to the cabaret clubs or occasional youth dances offered elsewhere in the city.[112] The venue was immediately popular, with the membership list of the club stretching to ten thousand within a year of opening. Its focus on disc jockeys and pop records was clearly a welcome addition for the city's young people. This venue was one of several that Mecca opened or renovated in the city over the following years, and their provision of entertainment for Sheffield's young people demonstrates the tangible impact that the organisation's policy of diversification had for the city. Alongside the Silver Blades complex, Mecca also owned the Locarno Ballroom, which opened in the city in 1954. The Locarno was situated in a former cinema that had closed due to bomb damage during air raids on the city in 1940, and alongside the City Hall, it was one of Sheffield's most popular spots for dancing. By the mid-1960s the Locarno Ballroom was incorporating jive, twist, and beat sessions into its schedule and, in 1968, Mecca took the decision to transform the venue into a licensed nightclub under the Tiffany's branding. Mecca took ownership of other venues in the city in the following years, including the 450-capacity Crazy Daizy in the city centre. Perhaps more well known as the venue where the second line-up of Sheffield band the Human League formed, the Daizy was licensed between 8 p.m. and 12 a.m. Monday to Thursday, and until 1 a.m. on a Friday and Saturday.[113] Mecca's expansion in Sheffield was, as this chapter has shown, part of a wider process of expansion and diversification of their leisure provision that encompassed dance, bingo, skating, and bowling. However, it is also demonstrative of the tangible way in which leisure conglomerates transformed access to late-night leisure in the city.

The arrival of the Rank Organisation on Sheffield's late-night leisure scene came with the opening of the city's Top Rank Suite on Arundel Gate, in the heart of the city centre, in 1967. Its opening marked the first purpose-built late-night and licensed entertainment centre in the city, and the scale of the new Top Rank Suite was significant: with a capacity of 2,500 people and opening until 2 a.m. (or 11.30 p.m. on Sundays), it rivalled the City Hall and converted dance halls, and marked the start of a new era of late-night entertainment in Sheffield.[114] The venue was multi-use, hosting conferences, functions, and live events alongside club nights. It was most well known, however, for its dancing, and alongside its regular club nights the venue

The business of leisure 89

hosted under-18 nights on Tuesdays and under-16 discos on Saturday mornings, providing an introduction to commercial dancing culture to countless of the city's teenagers. It wouldn't be matched in scale until the 1970 opening of the Fiesta Club, also on Arundel Gate, though with its focus primarily on cabaret and live performance, the two venues offered something very different. Baileys and, later, EMI, were also early entrants into the city's latenight leisure circuit, opening the Cavendish Club (later renamed Baileys and then Romeo's and Juliet's) in 1967. The venue promised patrons luxurious and lavish surroundings, and it represented a £70,000 investment from the Bailey Organisation.[115]

The period between 1966 and 1970 saw a rapid expansion in the number of licensed late-night clubs dedicated to evening entertainment and music in Sheffield. Of the four largest – Top Rank Suite, Tiffany's, the Cavendish Club, and the Fiesta Club – three were owned by major entertainment corporations. All four clubs were licensed until 2 a.m. on most nights of the week, and the rapid extension of opening hours alongside the growing number of venues catering to young people until the early hours (combined, the four venues catered for just shy of six thousand people) constituted a significant and material shift in the way that young people experienced the city. Critically, it extended the temporal transformation of young people's relationship to the urban centre, first introduced in the city's beat clubs and coffee bars, and made this available en masse. Late-night dancing was now another stop on the city's growing entertainment circuit, meaning that young people increasingly moved across the city from venue to venue as part of a night out. A day that started at one of the city's new boutiques, or on the recently opened Mecca ice rink, may well have ended with a disc jockey and dancing until the early hours of the morning.

Conclusions

The transformation of Britain's late-night leisurescape in the decades after the Second World War was nothing short of meteoric. In thirty short years, the face of Britain's urban landscape had transformed and, with it, the lives of the young people who moved through it. In towns and provincial cities, where once the final call of the publican's bell signalled the end of the night, young men and women could continue dancing into the early hours. In larger cities, the ballroom, dance hall, and theatre were no longer the sole preserve of late-night leisure. Huddles of late-night revellers had been replaced with crowds, with young people able to choose between any number of bars, clubs, and discos depending on their mood.

The entrance and eventual domination of commercial leisure providers in the youth market had myriad effects on youthful leisure in post-war Britain. It demonstrates the extent to which the post-war urban environment was reimagined as a centre for leisure and recreation and, in particular, that young consumers wielded sufficient economic power to contribute in significant ways to the spatial and temporal remaking of the urban centre. In many respects, the expansion of leisure provision for the young was part of a wider leisure boom in Britain, represented in the growing number of cabaret clubs, ice rinks, bowling alleys, restaurants, and holiday parks found dotted across the country. Similarly, it demonstrates in tangible ways how the youth consumer was increasingly connected to global business interests. This connection – between an increasingly affluent young consumer and corporate expansion in the leisure industry – also heralded a growing commonality of the youth experience in Britain. That commonality does not, it must be made clear, necessitate homogeneity. While these venues were becoming more standardised in their layout and offering, providing bars, dance floors, seating, and music in the form of a disc jockey or live band, they remained rooted in the local environment. Older venues in particular, despite being purchased, sold, and remodelled at regular intervals, often retained their historic links in the public imagination. These changes were not inevitable, nor were they predictable developments in response to changing lifestyles in post-war Britain. The expansion and consolidation of the leisure industry was a reflection both of the desire to reimagine the urban centre as a site of leisure and the particular recognition of the popularity of late-night leisure spaces amongst Britain's youth.

However, the consolidation also had myriad effects for Britain's youth. In smaller towns, it is clear that the capital and connections brought by large companies such as Mecca and the Rank Organisation provided access to live music and entertainments that local leisure entrepreneurs were unlikely to be able to afford. Young people living outside of Britain's large cities were provided with access to late-night commercial leisure venues, many of which enabled them to share in the cultural experiences once reserved for youth in large urban areas. However, this investment could be quickly removed and young people remained at the behest of company-wide financial strategies. In bigger cities, heightened investment in a new post-war leisurescape meant the construction of large entertainment centres that left a significant mark on the landscape. This investment also meant that the number of venues owned by an ever-smaller number of companies was a firmly established facet of the post-war leisure industry, with distinct ramifications for those who moved through them. Further, the use of racist door policies and privileging of white consumers contributed to the marginalisation of many young people of colour from their local leisurescape. The drive for

The business of leisure 91

'respectability' and profitability ruled, and it acted as an important reminder that while these organisations were happy to provide leisure outlets for and profit from the new youth market, this provision remained on their terms.

Notes

1 SCA, MC 2008/146, Sheffield Corporation, Licensing Justices, Minutes, Box 83, 19/11/1965–06/01/1970, 173.
2 *Top Star Special*, December 1966, 4.
3 Alistair Kefford, 'The Arndale Property Company and the Transformation of Urban Britain, 1950–2000', *Journal of British Studies*, 61:3 (2022), 563, https://doi.org/10.1017/jbr.2022.54.
4 See for example Tebbutt, *Making Youth*; David Fowler, *The First Teenagers: The Lifestyle of Young Wage-Earners in Interwar Britain* (London: Routledge, 1996); Savage, *Teenage: The Creation of Youth*; Fowler, *Youth Culture in Modern Britain*; Harrison, *Dangerous Amusements*; Langhamer, *Women's Leisure*.
5 Lee Jackson, *Palaces of Pleasure: From Music Halls to the Seaside to Football, How the Victorians Invented Mass Entertainment* (New Haven, CT: Yale University Press, 2019), 257.
6 Quoted in Jeffrey Richards, *The Age of the Dream Palace: Cinema and Society in 1930s Britain* (3rd edn, London: I.B. Tauris, 2010), 11.
7 *Ibid.*, 12.
8 Richard Farmer, *Cinemas and Cinemagoing in Wartime Britain, 1939–1945: The Utility Dream Palace* (Manchester: Manchester University Press, 2016), 4.
9 Bruce Peter, 'The Impact of the Talkies on Scottish Cinema Architecture', *Visual Culture in Britain*, 20:3 (2019), 209, https://doi.org/10.1080/14714787.2019 .1686415. Into the 1930s, there was a move away from 'ornate picture palaces' towards a more modernist design, spearheaded by the founder of Odeon Cinemas, Oscar Deutsch. For more, see Allen Eyles, *Odeon Cinemas: Oscar Deutsch Entertains Our Nation* (London: BFI Publishing, 2002); Richards, *The Dream Palace*, 37–38.
10 'Rotherham Reconstruction: Cinema House Attractive Decorations', *Kinematograph Weekly*, 10 September 1931, 72.
11 'Stockport Empress Opened', *Kinematograph Weekly*, 11 May 1939, 17.
12 Abra, *Dancing in the English Style*, 81.
13 *Ibid.*, 81. On the space of the dance hall, see also James Nott, 'Dance Halls: Towards an Architectural and Spatial History, c. 1918–65', *Architectural History*, 61 (2018), 205–233, https://doi.org/10.1017/arh.2018.8.
14 See for example Horn, *Juke Box Britain*, 90–114; Moran, 'Milk Bars'; Osgerby, *Youth in Britain*, 30–50.
15 The scholarship in this area is extensive, but for examples see Angela McRobbie, *Feminism and Youth Culture: From Jackie to Just Seventeen* (Basingstoke: Palgrave Macmillan, 1991); Penny Tinkler, *Constructing Girlhood: Popular*

Magazines for Girls Growing Up in England, 1920–1950 (London: Routledge, 1995); Penny Tinkler, '"Are You Really Living?" If Not, "Get With It!"', *Cultural and Social History*, 11:4 (2014), 597–619, https://doi.org/10.2752/147800414X14056862572186.; Alexander Clarkson, 'Virtual Heroes: Boys, Masculinity and Historical Memory in War Comics 1945–1995', *Boyhood Studies*, 2:2 (2008), 175–185, https://doi.org/10.3149/thy.0202.175.

16 Fan Carter, 'A Taste of *Honey*: Get-Ahead Femininity in 1960s Britain' in Rachel Ritchie, Sue Hawkins, Nicola Phillips, and S. Jay Kleinberg (eds), *Women in Magazines: Research, Representation, Production and Consumption* (London: Routledge, 2016, ebook edn), 184.

17 Robert Fitzgerald, *The Rise of the Global Company: Multinationals and the Making of the Modern World* (Cambridge: Cambridge University Press, 2016), 15.

18 On the growing demand for leisure in post-war Britain, and in particular the role played by municipal government, see Otto Saumarez Smith, 'The Lost World of the British Leisure Centre', *History Workshop Journal*, 88:1 (2019), 180–203, https://doi.org/10.1093/hwj/dbz007.

19 Chatterton and Hollands, *Urban Nightscapes*, 19.

20 Leif Jerram, *Streetlife: The Untold History of Europe's Twentieth Century* (Oxford: Oxford University Press, 2011), 1.

21 Ye Mecca Cafes were established in the 1880s in Coventry. See Roma Fairley, *Come Dancing Miss World* (London: Neamme, 1966), 18.

22 Nott, *Music for the People*, 157.

23 Quoted in Abra, *Dancing in the English Style*, 13.

24 Nott, *Music for the People*, 157; Fairley, *Come Dancing Miss World*, ix.

25 Nott, *Going to the Palais*, 87. Allison Abra also explores Mecca's meteoric rise as a commercial force in *Dancing in the English Style*, 86–88.

26 Nott, *Going to the Palais*, 95.

27 Carolyn Downs, 'Mecca and the Birth of Commercial Bingo 1958–70: A Case Study', *Business History*, 52:7 (2010), 1092, https://doi.org/10.1080/00076791.2010.523460.

28 'Mecca Ltd', *The Economist*, 20 June 1964, 1418.

29 *Ibid.*, 1418.

30 '£1,000,000 Entertainment Centre for Bristol', *The Stage*, 23 August 1962, 3.

31 'Mecca Advertisement', *Wells Journal*, 22 April 1966, 7.

32 'Company Meeting Reports: Mecca', *The Economist*, 19 June 1965, 1452.

33 'Night Life – The Changing Scene', *Petticoat*, June 1970, 15.

34 *Ibid.*, 15

35 'Company Statements: Mecca', *The Economist*, 27 June 1970, 92.

36 'Facing Mecca', *The Stage*, 24 January 1974, 8.

37 *Ibid.*, 8.

38 'A "Ballrooms and Bingo Halls" Image; But a Most Consistently Successful Company', *The Stage*, 14 June 1984, 4.

39 *Ibid.*, 4.

40 Fairley, *Come Dancing Miss World*, 124.

The business of leisure 93

41 *Ibid.*, 125.

42 *Ibid.*, 126.

43 Paul Carr, 'The Lost Musical Histories of Merthyr Tydfil', *Popular Music History*, 12:1 (2019), 112–140, https://doi.org/10.1558/pomh.v12i1.2775.

44 Downs, 'Mecca', 1093.

45 *Ibid.*, 1089.

46 'Facing Mecca', *The Stage*, 24 January 1974, 8.

47 'Entertainment: A Business of Making Pleasure for You', *The Times*, 18 May 1971, 21; 'Mecca: Annual General Meeting', *The Economist*, 27 June 1970, 92.

48 'What's On In and Around Bristol', *Bristol Evening Post*, 28 June 1969, 6; 'Nightspots', *Newcastle Evening Chronicle*, 19 June 1974, 6.

49 Downs, 'Mecca', 1092.

50 'A "Ballrooms and Bingo Halls" Image; But a Most Consistently Successful Company', *The Stage*, 14 June 1984, 4.

51 *Ibid.*, 4.

52 *Ibid.*, 4.

53 'Shock as Mecca Director Walks Out', *Daily Mail*, 22 June 1990, 39.

54 Nott, *Going to the Palais*, 92.

55 Geoffrey Macnab, *J. Arthur Rank and the British Film Industry* (London: Routledge, 1994), 17.

56 'Future for Films', *The Economist*, 10 December 1949, 1309.

57 Richards, *The Dream Palace*, 43.

58 Macnab, *J. Arthur Rank*, 214–219.

59 'When Screens Overlap', *The Economist*, 17 September 1955, 963.

60 'The Rank Organisation Ltd', *The Economist*, 19 October 1957, 116.

61 *Ibid.*, 116.

62 See Sam Manning, *Cinemas and Cinema-Going in the United Kingdom: Decades of Decline, 1945–65* (London: Royal Historical Society, The Boydell Press, 2020).

63 *Ibid.*, 69.

64 Macnab, *J. Arthur Rank*, 214.

65 *Ibid.*, 227.

66 *Ibid.*, 228.

67 'Rank Advertisement', *The Times*, 12 October 1962, 19.

68 *Ibid.*, 19.

69 'The Quiet Revolution', *Financial Times*, 11 February 1963, 25.

70 'Soft Lights, Sweet Profits', *Financial Times*, 7 November 1962, 8.

71 'Four New Rank Ballrooms', *The Times*, 12 October 1962, 19.

72 'Soft Lights, Sweet Profits', *Financial Times*, 7 November 1962, 8.

73 'It's Top Rank', *Newcastle Journal*, 20 December 1962, 2.

74 Timothy Carder, *The Encyclopaedia of Brighton* (Brighton: Brighton and Hove Libraries, 1990), 121.

75 'Bailey's in Leicester', *The Stage*, 24 August 1972, 3; 'Leisure 2000 Group Buy City Nightspot', *The Stage*, 11 October 1979, 4.

76 'Whitbread Pays £4.5m for 21 Pubs', *The Times*, 25 January 1984, 16.

77 'Mecca v Rank Dance Battle', *Daily Mirror*, 11 June 1964, 32.

78 'Rank Launches Hostile £512m Bid for Mecca', *The Times*, 2 June 1990, 17.

79 'No Partners on the Dancefloor', *Financial Times*, 17 June 1964, 15.

80 'Final Extinction', *The Stage*, 12 June 1969, 11.

81 *Ibid.*, 11.

82 'Now Sheffield Gets Britain's Finest Night Club', *Star*, 20 April 1967, 2.

83 'Teeside Clubland's Top P.R.C.', *The Stage*, 16 October 1969, 17.

84 'Cautious Optimism', *The Stage*, 19 March 1970, 13.

85 Russell, 'Glimpsing "*La Dolce Vita*"', 303.

86 'Bailey's Go Marching On!', *The Stage*, 19 October 1972, 15.

87 'Club Owners Hit Back', *The Stage*, 21 September 1967, 3; 'Bailey's Build Bridges', *The Stage*, 12 October 1967, 19.

88 'Niterie For In-Betweens', *The Stage*, 21 March 1968, 3.

89 'Bailey's Shed 12 Dance Halls', *The Stage*, 29 September 1977, 3.

90 'EMI Report: Report and Accounts, Chairman's Review' (1978), 40, via https://web.archive.org/web/20170624051043/http://www.kronemyer.com/EMI/EMI%20Music%20AR%201978.pdf [last accessed 19 May 2023].

91 'Electric & Musical Industries Ltd', *The Economist*, 19 November 1968, 90.

92 'EMI Report: Report and Accounts, Chairman's Review' (1974), 32, via https://web.archive.org/web/20170624071641/ttp://www.kronemyer.com/EMI/EMI%20Music%20AR%201974.pdf [last accessed 19 May 2023].

93 'EMI Report: Report and Accounts, Chairman's Review' (1978), 39.

94 'See the Top Disco Dancers', *Daily Mirror*, 7 August 1978, 19.

95 'Wheatley Moves in for EMI Bailey's Venue in Leicester', *The Stage*, 20 December 1979, 3.

96 'THF Buys £16m Thorn EMI Leisure Interests', *The Times*, 1 November 1980, 17.

97 'Letters', *Sunday Mirror*, 14 February 1965, 26.

98 'Ballroom Closes, and Teenagers Are "Disgusted"', *Crewe Chronicle*, 12 August 1965, 11.

99 'Romeo and Juliets', *The Stage*, 5 January 1978, 7.

100 'No Partners on the Dancefloor', *Financial Times*, 17 June 1964, 15.

101 'All Set To Take Your Partners?', *Cambridge Daily News*, 15 December 1972, 19.

102 Nott, *Going to the Palais*, 271.

103 The National Archives, London (hereafter TNA), CK 2/358, Commission for Racial Equality and Predecessors, Letter from E. Morley to T. Connelly, 22 July 1975.

104 Sue Zeleny Bishop, 'Inner-City Possibilities: Using Place and Space to Facilitate Inter-Ethnic Dating and Romance in 1960s–1980s Leicester', *Urban History*, 50:2 (2023), 233, 242, https://doi.org/10.1017/S0963926821000742.

105 Quoted in Keith Gildart, '"The Antithesis of Humankind": Exploring Responses to the Sex Pistols' Anarchy UK Tour 1976', *Cultural and Social History*, 10:1 (2013), 139, https://doi.org/10.2752/147800413X13515292098313.

The business of leisure 95

106 'Crackdown on Dance Vandals', *Daily Mirror*, 6 December 1976, 9.
107 See Felix Fuhg, 'Ambivalent Relationships: London's Youth Culture and the Making of the Multi-Racial Society in the 1960s', *Britain and the World*, 11:1 (2018), 22, https://doi.org/10.3366/brw.2018.0285; Stephen Catterall and Keith Gildart, *Keeping the Faith: A History of Northern Soul* (Manchester: Manchester University Press, 2020), 215. On the importance of Caribbean music cultures in post-war Britain, see in particular Eddie Chambers, 'The Jamaican 1970s and Its Influence on the Making of Black Britain', *Small Axe*, 23:1 (2019), 134–149, https://doi.org/10.1215/07990537-7374502; William 'Lez' Henry, 'Reggae, Rasta and the Role of the Deejay in the Black British Experience', *Contemporary British History*, 23:3 (2012), 355–373, https://doi.org/0.1080/13619462.2012.703024.
108 Catterall and Gildart, *Keeping the Faith*, 112.
109 SCA, MC 2008/146, Sheffield Corporation, Licensing Justices, Minutes, Box 83, 19/11/1965–06/01/1970, 225.
110 TNA, CK 2/358, Yorkshire and North-East Conciliation Committee, 27 August 1975.
111 Fuhg, 'Ambivalent Relationships', 24.
112 SCA, MC 2008/146, Sheffield Corporation, Licensing Justices, Minutes, Box 83, 19/11/1965–06/01/1970, 52.
113 The Crazy Daizy has been identified as an important space for alternative music in Sheffield through the 1970s and 1980s. See Matthew Worley, 'Past! Future! In Extreme!: Looking for Meaning in the "New Romantics", 1978– 82', *Journal of British Studies*, (2024, advanced online access), 9, https://doi.org/10.1017/jbr.2024.57; Haslam, *Life After Dark*, 263.
114 *Ibid.*, 173.
115 'Cavendish Opening', *The Stage*, 9 March 1967, 3.

3

Regulating youth after dark

In July of 1982, Sheffield's licensing magistrates were taken to court by Mecca Leisure Ltd over a refusal of structural alterations to their London Road venue, Tiffany's. Part of a larger chain of Mecca-owned nightclubs, the Tiffany's nightclub brand was well established by the 1980s and reflected changes to Mecca's entertainment provision in the post-war period. However, this court case exposed significant tensions between the national entertainment company and local authorities about the appropriate use of this leisure space, and it tells us much about the ongoing debates surrounding youth, leisure, and morality in the second half of the twentieth century. Accused of 'still living in the days of the veleta and the foxtrot', the licensing magistrates' concerns reflected the seismic shifts in late-night leisure over a few short decades.[1] In the same month as Sheffield's licensing magistrates were being taken to court over their plans to limit access to bar facilities, the House of Lords was discussing the role of alcohol in the lives of young offenders during a debate on the Criminal Justice Bill.[2] Later in the decade, the House of Commons began to debate the role of local authorities and the courts in response to the quick rise in unregulated 'acid house' parties.[3]

Debates about how best to regulate and control the leisure choices of young people have raged for well over a century, and the continuing concern over youth recreation can be traced in detail from the calls for rational recreation in the Victorian period, to the 'flapper vote folly' in the 1920s, to the panics over seaside clashes between mods and rockers in the 1960s. In the post-war period, various local authorities including police, health and safety inspectors, council officers, and licensing magistrates worked to mediate and regulate the public spaces of youth leisure, particularly those that were open until the early hours of the morning. These spaces, which had a transformative effect on the urban environment after dark, held clear potential to disrupt established ideas about appropriate leisure.

While Chapter 2 explored the ways in which an increasingly global leisure industry intersected with the national and the local to reshape the urban leisurescape, this chapter argues that this national picture can only

Regulating youth after dark

be fully understood when viewed through a local lens. The leisurescapes of individual towns and cities, while reflecting national trends in leisure and entertainment provision, were mediated and shaped by local concerns, and this had a significant effect on the way young people moved through their local environment, how they interacted with youth leisure, and the types of youth leisure they had access to. Licensing, as a central mechanism for the regulation of youth-oriented leisure, played out in a distinctly local arena. The first part of the chapter explores what Peter Baldwin termed the 'problem of modern night', considering why attempts to control and regulate youthful leisure were so often centred on the night.[4] The second part of the chapter considers how this desire to regulate youthful leisure played out at the local level. Focusing predominantly on the case of Sheffield, it demonstrates clearly how an increasingly shared youth experience was moulded by local contexts and concerns. In doing so, the chapter demonstrates that while the development of the night-time economy took place at a global scale, 'nightlife experiences for many remain largely rooted in specific localities'.[5] Far from signifying a period of growing homogeneity and uniformity, the latter half of the twentieth century demonstrates that the local remains a central way through which we can understand the youth experience.

'The moral dangers to which the young are exposed': youth leisure and the problem of the urban night

Commercial leisure was a cause for concern from its inception, and calls to control access to these spaces were driven by a desire to regulate people's use of public space as well as their morality. The growth of commercial and popular leisure through the early part of the twentieth century, and the changing contexts in which this growth took place – particularly in relation to the growth of mass media and the aftereffects of the First World War – meant that leisure was seen as simultaneously 'important to social renewal and a new civilised way of life' and 'counter-productive to a reconstruction of civic society'.[6] Nowhere were these anxieties more pronounced than in relation to young people's leisure and, as a result, they faced particular scrutiny over their leisure choices. However, as Carolyn Jackson and Penny Tinkler have astutely argued, there is a 'recurring amnesia' towards each new generation of young people and, as such, they are 'always perceived as shockingly different from those [young people] of yesteryear'.[7] In short, where, when, and how people were choosing to spend their leisure time mattered, and the potential for leisure to act as a corrupting or damaging force continued to cause significant anxiety in Britain.

98   *Youth and the changing urban environment*

It is therefore no surprise that the concerns first attached to commercial youth leisure in the late nineteenth and early twentieth centuries continued unabated in the post-war period. When considered alongside the stark transformation in access to youth leisure, both spatial and temporal, it becomes clear why the new spaces of youth leisure were at the heart of many calls for control and regulation. The drive to regulate these spaces of youth leisure often acted as proxy for the control of young people themselves. Public space is, as Gill Valentine has argued, 'often the only autonomous space many teenagers are able to carve out for themselves' in the modern city, and as such could be positioned as a threat to the established public order.[8] That threat almost always boiled down to two key issues: how and where young people were spending their time. Through the post-war period, it was the commercial spaces of youth leisure and, in particular, those spaces that provided late-night entertainments, that attracted the most concern. These new coffee bars, jazz clubs, discos, and late-night bars, it was argued, encouraged drunkenness, violence, disorder, and immoral sexual behaviour. That behaviour was only rendered more visible by the growing number of venues in urban centres that catered explicitly or solely to young consumers.

These anxieties, while attached to new spaces and increasingly unfamiliar lifestyle choices, were of course not new. The presence of young people in public had long been a cause for concern, and their use of public space contested. As Laura Harrison aptly demonstrates, frustration at crowds of young people outside leisure venues dates back as early as the 1870s.[9] In the interwar period, these anxieties became explicitly attached to new commercial forms of youth leisure such as dancing, in which fears about 'sexual impropriety' and 'changing gender boundaries' came to the fore of critical debate.[10] There were calls throughout the twentieth century to provide young people with adequate guidance to ensure their leisure and recreation time was spent productively, and the act of simply 'hanging around' on street corners was discouraged, as was spending time in the 'wrong' places.[11] In the post-war period, a time when urban redevelopment was accelerating the growth of commercially owned semi-public spaces, social workers, courts, politicians, journalists, and members of the public decried the 'gangs' of youths who were to be found at seaside resorts, outside shopping centres, cinemas, and coffee bars. Their presence was unwelcome, disrupting the established order of these public spaces. However, it was the liminality of many commercial youth leisure spaces – being neither wholly public or private, both visible and unknown to passers by – that encouraged and often required young people's movement through town and city centres. This movement and visibility were themselves a source of contestation, as were the gatherings of young people they created.

However, it was not simply the growing visibility of the new spaces of post-war youth leisure that were a cause for concern. Anxieties around these new spaces were most pronounced in relation to late-night leisure, against which longstanding concerns about the recreational activities of the young collided with anxieties about the urban environment after dark. The modern urban night, despite the advent of street lighting and a growing public presence, 'was not an extension of day; it was a liminal new world in which conflicting moral values mingled uneasily'.[12] Matt Houlbrook has demonstrated clearly how, in the interwar policing of London's queer public spaces, authorities introduced 'policing systems focused upon a venue's owner', the result of which was an enhanced 'ability to control public sociability'.[13] In post-war Britain, where urban centres after dark were increasingly dominated by the growing 'night-time economy', there were real and sustained fears about the dangerous potential of access to late-night leisure. These fears coalesced around several distinct but interconnected issues, but most notably violence, disorder, sexual immorality, and drunkenness. These concerns, as Houlbrook aptly shows, intersected with an increasingly ordered, observed, and regulated city, meaning that anxieties about youth leisure and youthful patterns of consumption showed themselves through regular calls for monitoring and control.

Responses to 'darkness' are culturally constructed, shaped by particular visions of what it is seen to represent. In the context of the urban night, these associations were shaped by longstanding fears of both the moral threat and temptation posed by the city after dark. Nick Dunn argues that 'urban dark places are notable in this regard through ongoing strategies to "deal" with them, typically through infrastructures, policies, and practices to control and manage them'.[14] The calls to 'deal' with urban dark places were driven by the need to minimise danger and disruption and, as such, the question of *who* could be found in urban spaces at night was of paramount importance. Peter Baldwin's study of the American urban night in the early twentieth century demonstrates clearly that anxieties about the dark were driven by class and race-based ideas about respectability, but also by a distinct vision of youth: one that was untainted by 'dark wisdom', 'unsuited to young people', that could be gained in urban spaces at night.[15] These fears spoke to the desire to protect young people – and particularly young women – from moral transgressions. As the night-time economy became ever more engrained in post-war towns and cities, the calls to regulate and control these spaces – and by extension the young people who frequented them – grew louder.

100   *Youth and the changing urban environment*

'Crackdown on the disco thugs': calls to regulate youthful leisure

As Chapter 1 showed, authorities did not shy away from the use of regulatory powers in attempts to control new spaces of youth leisure such as coffee bars and beat clubs and, indeed, were quick to recognise when existing regulations needed to be altered or updated. Commercial leisure venues themselves were also invested in balancing the provision of entertainment with their public image, and they played a significant role in local-level regulation. As such, institutional responses to the growth of late-night commercial leisure were often concerned with the practicalities of regulation: how, on what grounds, and in which contexts could these new leisure spaces – and the activities of those who moved within them – be brought under the jurisdiction of relevant authorities. The British media narrated these fears, making regular links to late-night violence and sexual permissiveness. These behaviours were by no means representative of the majority of young people who socialised in these spaces and young people were aware of and able to navigate the uneven landscape of leisure venues with varied reputations. Despite this, the public narratives created around new forms of late-night youth leisure in the late 1950s and 1960s were significant: they entrenched a clear link between the night-time economy and immorality, and were one of the key ways in which calls to regulate these spaces were circulated.

The press took particular interest in youth lifestyles in the post-war era, and showed ongoing concern about the threat posed by the new affluent teenager. This alarm about the 'state of youth' often presented itself by highlighting the dangers posed by youth consumption – considering both what young people consumed, and where they consumed it. In post-war Liverpool, Sam Caslin has demonstrated how the attraction of 'Beatle-land' for young girls was feared to 'corrupt the morally vulnerable due to the availability of sex, alcohol and indecent entertainment in urban environments'.[16] As Damien Phillips argued in his study of media responses to youth leisure, there was an oscillation between two stereotypes: the press 'accepted the legitimacy of the youthful enjoyment of leisure … Yet at the same time, it is censorious of the emergence of bohemian ideologies amongst the young.'[17] The press therefore approached new and unfamiliar forms of youth leisure with suspicion. As a result, national narratives about youth leisure were adopted at the local level resulting in an ongoing 'desire to police young people's informal use' of new commercial leisure spaces.[18]

The *Daily Mirror* told readers of 'screams of teenage girls' in Birmingham following a coffee-bar stabbing in April 1961, while warning of them about the 'big menace from the coffee-bar cowboys' in June.[19] Frustration about noise disruption was top of the agenda in reports about a coffee bar near London's Covent Garden in 1965, with one resident highlighting that 'the

Regulating youth after dark

primary cause of noise is the packs of youths and young women, I will not say maidens, who converge upon' the bar until the early hours.[20] Obvious anxieties about the 'state of youth' were at play in these stories – violence, permissiveness, public indecency, to name a few – and they were 'taken up with gusto' by the press.[21] These press stories drew on the fear of the night, on the connotations of violence and disorder that came with it, and on the unfamiliarity that many of its adult readers had with these new spaces of youth leisure.

In Manchester, which in the early 1960s was at the heart of the 'pep pill panic', local institutions worked quickly to respond to the growing number of commercial youth venues. A 'Drugs Squad' was established, alongside wider calls for greater powers to be given to the police and licensing magistrates to enable them to enter and inspect these clubs.[22] The membership-only status of these clubs initially made entrance by authorities difficult, and in the absence of alcohol, they were not subject to the same licensing requirements as public houses or nightclubs. In Brighton, a committee was similarly established to investigate the town's coffee bars and their links to drug use. Police were frustrated, it was reported, by the overcrowded nature of these bars, which hampered their investigations. At night, teenagers would 'overflow onto the pavement', making it 'difficult to obtain evidence as offenders are screened from observation and drugs are quickly disposed of'.[23] These complaints highlighted the increasingly contested nature of young people's use of public and semi-public space; their leisure was at once more visible and yet increasingly unknown to those on the outside. The fears concerning the dangerous potential of coffee clubs were certainly not unique to Manchester or Brighton, and there were soon additional calls for powers to regulate this new and fast-growing leisure space. As Charlie Lynch's study of moral panic in 1960s Falkirk shows, there were clear 'ideological commonalities between local concerns and then emerging national campaigns'.[24]

One iteration of this came from the Working Party on Juvenile Jazz and Dance Clubs in the West End of London, established by the Home Office in 1964. The working party was responding, in particular, to the 'growth of clubs providing music and dancing facilities at all hours for young persons in central areas of London'.[25] Soho and the surrounding areas of West London had long been associated with hedonism and vice and had a well-established network of late-night bars and clubs, but the presence of teenagers in these areas into the early hours of the morning renewed calls for greater control and regulation.[26] The working party placed great emphasis on the question of young people's morality, which was intimately tied to questions about when and where teenagers were socialising. Indeed, in reflecting on the group's central aims, members lamented that 'moral

102   *Youth and the changing urban environment*

problems were only incidental' to previous calls to regulate these new spaces of youth leisure, whereas the issue of morality would form 'the whole content' of their work.[27] The group's work raised a critical question – could morality be regulated in concrete terms and, if so, how could this be done? In preliminary discussions, it became clear that it was the temporal aspect of youth leisure that was one of the areas of greatest concern, and it was in this area that much of the group's work focused.

The working party's chair suggested that no club that provided music and dancing or 'entertainments of the like kind as a regular feature' for young people under 17 should be permitted to open past 11 p.m. without a licence which, it was made clear, would have particular requirements regarding opening hours and rights of entry attached.[28] Files for the group included details of areas where the temporal regulation of young people in public was already in play; in Chicago, for example, it was reported that those under the age of seventeen were not permitted on the street between 11.30 p.m. and 6 a.m. on weekends (and 10.30 p.m. on weekdays) unless working or accompanied by a relative or adult.[29] The curfews referenced in the group's research had a long history, particularly in North America, and reflected middle-class concerns about working-class and immigrant neighbourhoods.[30] The introduction of curfews such as these were 'intended to guard the boundaries of knowledge' by removing children from the 'moral diversity' encountered in urban areas at night.[31] Investigations into the jazz clubs of London's West End by the group indicated that they encouraged a 'general amoral attitude and a lack of responsibility' and their late-night opening acted, alongside the 'excitement readily available', as 'a further inducement to the young people to stay away from home'.[32] One concerned letter-writer to the group suggested that 'children who are out very late at night must get involved in some kind of trouble'.[33] In a meeting between representatives for the police, London County Council, and government departments including the Home Office, the Home Secretary Henry Brooke expressed his desire to keep in close touch with the question of commercial youth clubs, 'particularly in view of the moral dangers to which the young people were exposed'.[34]

The group's central focus was on the mechanics of regulating morality, and it was agreed that proposals should be put forward in line with other licensed venues: licensing magistrates, with evidence provided by the police, would be responsible for ensuring adherence to the conditions of any potential new licence. They were also clear to address the subject of clubs with no fixed abode – an increasingly popular format for leisure entrepreneurs in the late 1950s and early 1960s – by proposing to licence organisations, rather than venues, 'so as to include, e.g. the peripatetic club while excluding public halls hired to a number of different organisations'.[35] While the temporal

Regulating youth after dark 103

controls wished for by the working party were not fully realised, many of the issues raised by the working group were eventually incorporated into the Private Places of Entertainment Act in 1967. Upon introducing the Act for its second reading in the House of Lords, Lord Parker of Waddingham stated that the growth of unlicensed clubs 'is like a disease which is spreading at the moment all over the country'.[36] In reply, the Earl of Longford argued that 'considerable concern has been expressed in the last year or so about the growing dangers, moral as well as physical, to which young people in particular are exposed' in these clubs.[37] When introduced later in the year, the Private Places of Entertainment Act introduced the requirement for private clubs used for music, singing, and dancing to be subject to formal licensing and, by extension, to controls on capacities, safety, and opening hours. The controls on opening hours in particular brought clubs in line with other late-night licensed venues which, following the introduction of the 1964 Licensing Act, enabled them to open until 2 a.m. (or 3 a.m. in areas of central London).

What becomes apparent in public post-war discourse about commercial youth leisure is the perceived importance of preserving and protecting young people's 'morality'. The leisure time of adolescents was the subject of so much anxiety precisely because it exposed the liminality of youth; neither children nor adults, their access to leisure was a finely balanced negotiation between growing independence and a publicly acceptable framework for recreation. It is also clear that questions about morality were predicated on an overtly middle-class vision of youth that remained suspicious of the movement of young people through urban spaces late at night. As one councillor in Brighton exclaimed, late-night coffee bars are 'a natural outlet for drug pushers whose work amounts to what can only be termed as moral murder'.[38]

Commercial dance halls, while a more established and therefore familiar leisure venue, remained a site of anxiety – particularly in relation to young people. Some halls became linked with violence and gang conflict, while others were associated with the 'less violent but similarly serious' issue of rowdiness or public disorder.[39] The *Sunday Times* reported on plans for 'mobile squads' of police officers in 1959 to tackle the 'menace of gang warfare' afflicting dance halls and coffee bars across numerous large cities.[40] Others reported frequently on deaths and injuries as a result of violence in the vicinity of dance halls, making links to 'Teds' or roving groups of youths. These fears were undoubtedly exaggerated, and attitudes towards dance itself were shifting. As we saw in Chapter 1, numerous youth organisations sought to replicate the amusements provided by commercial dance halls and dance was, in the right settings, seen as a productive outlet for young people in the post-war period.[41] Indeed, in her study of young people living in Notting Hill, the social researcher Pearl Jephcott highlighted the lack of 'reputable' commercial leisure provision for adolescents in the area, leading to young people having 'many temptations to spend their free time drifting'. There was, Jephcott lamented, 'no big dance hall near at hand, no stylish cinema, and no smart-looking, popular café'.[42] However, Jephcott's focus on reputability was important. For every large and well-managed commercial leisure space, there were many more that were not viewed as favourably.

The associations between violence, delinquency, and commercial leisure space were firmly ingrained in the public imagination by the end of the 1960s, but it was during the 1970s that these reached a fever pitch. In the late 1970s, a new term entered the media's lexicon in discussions of new youth lifestyles: 'disco thugs'. Coined by the *Daily Mail* in response to their 1979 investigation into rising violence in dance halls and discotheques, the 'disco thug' panic called for increased curbs to be placed on late-night venues which, the *Mail* argued, had been given 'a special status, establishing the disco as a unique meeting place for young people' following the popularity of the 1977 film *Saturday Night Fever*.[43] The investigation was a reflection of the pace at which the urban centre at night had transformed; in a little over ten years, the number of late-night drinking venues in urban centres had exploded and Special Hours Certificates were commonly used to extend the opening hours of entertainment venues until the early hours of the morning. In many respects, the disco thug panic was a continuation of earlier fears attached to the jazz clubs of the 1920s and beat clubs of the 1950s and 1960s. The *Daily Mail*'s concerns about two girls under the age of 16 'dancing intimately with two men who look at least eight years older than them' easily mapped on to media reports from half a century earlier that exposed readers to the sexual threat posed to young women's morality in the nightclubs of London's West End.[44] It spoke clearly to the moral ambiguity of these spaces, and to the threat of the leisured night.

The disco thug panic of the 1970s was also, in many ways, an extension of wider concerns about societal violence in the 1970s. It was in this period that there was a growing preoccupation with crimes of violence amongst the young, which Stuart Hall et al. argued was positioned as 'the inevitable outcome of [a] weakening of moral authority'.[45] This was only heightened following the emergence of punk in the mid-1970s, the response to which was 'part of an engagement with what was perceived by many as a new set of social problems'.[46] The *Daily Mail*'s campaign worked to highlight generational difference in experiences of late-night leisure, telling parents that modern discos were not 'a cosy night out, like the ones the older generation had so regularly when dance halls were the place to go'.[47] The modern disco, they claimed, 'is a parade of potency' where competition between men for

Regulating youth after dark   105

'the respect of other males and the admiration of females' could easily boil over.[48]

The *Daily Mirror* also worked to 'expose' violence at discos, claiming that war had been declared on 'the discos of death' following a 'hard-hitting' campaign by the paper.[49] The 'war' in question was a meeting between owners of several nightspots in London and members from the Greater London Council (GLC), as going to the disco was 'often becoming an appointment with fear for unsuspecting teenagers'.[50] Following the recent deaths of eight people in London discotheques, the GLC announced a 'tough new code' for entrance to discos in November 1979, including weapons searches and a ban on people being admitted when clearly intoxicated. The language used by the campaigns of both the *Mail* and *Mirror* were typical of the hyperbole often deployed in relation to youth, and designed clearly to invoke public reaction. Phrases such as 'frenzied disco killings' and 'violent disco mania' served to build a very particular image of late-night leisure as dangerous and unpredictable.[51] For these papers, the issue was twofold: how to protect young people, and particularly young women, from rising levels of violence and moral impropriety, as well as tackle the wider public disturbances caused by large crowds of young people in cities late at night. While framed within the particular context of discussions about societal and youth violence in the 1970s, the 'disco panic' was a firm response to the growing proliferation of late-night leisure in Britain.

Beyond the violence and public disturbances associated with youth leisure, calls to regulate these spaces were increasingly centred around the relationship between late-night leisure establishments and alcohol. By the end of the twentieth century, this relationship was not only firmly established but was increasingly a source of serious concern, and the phenomenon of youth drinking 'binges' was a regular topic of public and political discussion.[52] However, it was in the 1970s and 1980s, several decades earlier, that alcohol consumption became a fundamental part of the late-night leisurescape for many young people. One implication of the Private Places of Entertainment Act, introduced in 1967 in the wake of the explosion of unlicensed late-night coffee clubs, was that many young people moved from unlicensed coffee bars and clubs into licensed nightclubs and discos. This is not, of course, to say that young people did not consume alcohol in their leisure time prior to this, simply that the spaces in which young people were socialising at night were now, more often than not, licensed to sell alcohol. This relationship, it was argued by temperance organisations and judges in the 1970s, was 'making nonsense of the licensing law' and creating 'one law for ordinary drinkers and another for teenagers at discotheques', whose use of Special Hours Certificates enabled them to extend their opening into the early hours.[53]

106   *Youth and the changing urban environment*

The question of alcohol consumption was, therefore, high on the agenda by the 1970s and 1980s. More broadly, this was a period of heightened alcohol consumption, though this increase was made more visible by the expansion of youth-oriented drinks such as lager. Per capita consumption of alcohol had almost doubled between 1950 and 1975, with the consumption of lager, spirits, and wine increasing dramatically.[54] As such, many of the concerns surrounding late-night youth leisure in the latter decades of the twentieth century coalesced around the dangers and disturbances posed by excessive alcohol consumption. In 1983, there were strong calls to implement stricter licensing conditions to limit instances of underage drinking, with *The Times* reporting that crimes by young people were often committed 'after they left licensed premises, with the public house and discotheque having taken the place for thousands of teenagers of the coffee bar and youth club'.[55] In 1986 the *Daily Mail* reported on the 'scandal' of teenage drinking, citing a recent study by the Institute of Alcohol Studies which showed that the number of young people convicted of drunkenness 'is rising at a record rate, and for the first time this century teenagers are now more at risk than the middle aged'.[56] The publication of a report into drunken violence by the Association of Chief Police Officers in 1988 led to 'a wave of public concern', during which the term 'lager lout' – synonymous with young, male, and typically working-class drunkenness – became a powerful narrative marker for youth drinking.[57] This renewed attention did not necessarily coincide with rising levels of public drunkenness, but a greater readiness by the police and popular press to report on it.

These shifts did not escape the attention of the government. In 1986, the Conservative government, under the leadership of Margaret Thatcher, established the Working Group on Young People and Alcohol. The Group, set up to deliver their findings to the 24 November 1987 Standing Conference on Crime Prevention, was one of three Working Groups tasked with exploring the relationship between young people and crime. Baroness Lady Masham of Ripon oversaw the group's work as chairperson and, over the course of six months, worked with a range of civil servants, youth workers, charity campaigners, and drinks-industry representatives to assess the shifting relationship between young people and alcohol. The group was set up alongside two others: juvenile crime and child molestation and abuse, and it undertook its work in a period of heightened anxiety about the relationship between young adults, alcohol, and late-night leisure. While the group's remit was broadly focused on establishing links between rising rates of youth drunkenness and adolescent crime, members were also concerned with the many ways in which alcohol consumption had become embedded in the social lives of adolescents and young adults in Britain.

Following public disturbances in several cities on New Year's Eve in 1986, Home Secretary Douglas Hurd ordered a report into 'mob violence'.[58] In a September 1987 letter from the Home Office, the group were reminded of the importance of exploring 'disorder as distinct from crime', with particular focus given to the need to consider public disorder as a distinct issue relating to youth drinking.[59] The group explored a number of possible options for regulating young people's access to alcohol, and highlighted inadequacies in existing approaches to the regulation of youth drinking. Underage drinking in particular was identified as a source of concern that required interventions in areas including education, advertising, and law reform and, in presenting their findings to the Standing Conference in 1987, the group argued that the 'law on underage drinking is no longer taken very seriously by many'. Critically, the link between alcohol consumption and late-night urban disturbances was firmly established by the group, who argued that there was a 'problem of drunkenness concentrated amongst young males, with considerable costs for the criminal justice system'.[60] These problems made themselves most apparent 'shortly after the end of permitted drinking hours, particularly on Friday and Saturday nights'.[61] The transformation to youth drinking cultures is explored in more depth in Chapter 4, but the work of the Working Group on Young People and Alcohol demonstrates clearly that, by the end of the 1980s, the concerns of many institutions and state officials focused on the behaviour of young people in public and semi-public spaces and, in particular, on the dangers caused by alcohol consumption.

The anxieties surrounding youth leisure in the post-war period were, in many respects, a continuation of longstanding discussions about the state of youth. While the spaces in which young people were socialising were changing, as was their temporal relationship to the urban environment, the ongoing calls to regulate youthful leisure space in the latter half of the twentieth century were driven by deep-seated anxieties about young people's susceptibility to moral transgression and delinquency. The desire to control the movement of young people was heightened by the introduction and spread of commercial leisure spaces into the urban environment, and only further compounded by their intersection with the modern night.

Licensing leisure: power, regulation, and the magistrate

One of the central institutional mechanisms for regulating leisure space was through the licence. While youth workers, educators, and social commentators worried about the actions, behaviours, and moral transgressions of young people in these new commercial spaces of leisure, these spaces did not sit entirely beyond the realm of formal regulation. As such, the remainder of

108   *Youth and the changing urban environment*

this chapter explores the role that licensing played as a core mechanism to regulate and manage young people's access to late-night leisure in post-war Britain.

In the sphere of late-night leisure, the implementation and monitoring of the alcohol licence acted as a crucial link between state and market, public and private. Mariana Valverde has argued 'that problematic consumption is better regulated through licensing than through direct governmental control measures ... is an assumption so thoroughly naturalized in contemporary regulatory practice as to be completely invisible'.[62] Valverde further posits:

> the legal technology of the licence allows governments to ensure that certain spaces, activities, and people are under constant surveillance and are subject to immediate disciplinary measures but without state officials (or centralized state knowledges) being involved in this micromanagement of those dimensions of everyday urban life that are regarded as problematic.[63]

Through the alcohol licence, the responsibility for regulating and controlling both the sale of alcohol and the behaviours of those who consume it is therefore passed onto the licensee, rather than being driven by official state mechanisms. Indeed, the very decision of who is granted an alcohol licence has historically been used as an important way of regulating minorities and deviance.[64] Alcohol licensing in Britain 'has been one of the central mechanisms for regulating the sale of alcohol' but, according to David Beckingham, 'the role that the licensing process has played in shaping the relationship between those drinkers and drinking spaces and between regulatory agencies and urban space remains under researched'.[65] That much of the literature has focused on national debates about alcohol regulation is surprising; from their establishment in the early modern period, licensing magistrates had a tendency to apply central regulation with 'considerable regional variation'.[66] In the context of youth leisure and the night-time economy, this omission has real significance. Youth drinking has historically been perceived as particularly troubling given that the public consumption of alcohol has long been associated with 'problematic' behaviour and social disruption, whilst fears over young people's morality and deviance in the twentieth century were considerable.

Licensing magistrates in Britain had the power to grant alcohol licences following the introduction of the Ale Houses Act of 1551, and their ongoing presence as a regulatory force through the twentieth century worked against the broader trends in state mechanics in this period.[67] John Davis has noted that, over the course of the twentieth century, local authorities became 'agents of the central welfare state', with many services becoming increasingly centralised.[68] One outlier to this general trend of centralisation was

Regulating youth after dark 109

the continued use of licensing magistrates to regulate the spaces of alcohol consumption in England, Wales, and Scotland, members of which remained volunteers throughout the twentieth century. Valverde has stated that the survival of 'middle and upper-class volunteers who have no legal training, and are neither bureaucrats nor experts, could simply be read as a continuation of Tory ways of life'.[69] Alternatively, she argues, it indicates that in a world 'where there has been a huge explosion of highly technical knowledges, there are still spaces – particularly within law or in the face of law – in which other knowledges manage to govern without much contestation'.[70] When extended to the licensing of youth leisure spaces, we can see that decisions about which spaces were granted new licences, alongside applications from older licensed venues to renovate and upgrade their leisure facilities, were often made by a generation entirely unfamiliar with, and often suspicious of, recent developments in youth leisure. Indeed, Arthur Marwick, in his survey of post-war British society, argued that 'the very pace of technological change, the very multiplicity of new inputs, meant the opening of a gulf between the proponents of the new culture and the older generation'.[71] As will be demonstrated, the micromanagement of leisure space by licensing magistrates led not only to clashes between market and state, but clear disagreements over the very form that youth leisure should take.

Despite calls to tighten restrictions on young people's access to alcohol, the post-war period has, more broadly, been recognised as a period of significant liberalisation in national alcohol licensing laws. The 1961 and 1964 Licensing Acts were used, for the first time, to make accessing alcohol easier. The introduction of exemption orders and Special Hours Certificates for late-night licensing gave licensed venues far more freedom to sell alcohol until late into the night, something that James Nicholls argues eventually led to the death of fixed opening hours.[72] Venues holding these licences could open until 2 a.m. (or 3 a.m. in areas of central London) between Monday and Saturday. At the same time, the development of supermarkets and expansion of off-licences fuelled the growth of home drinking. By the 1980s, national licensing policy was closely tied to the politics of market forces. As early as 1972, the report of the Erroll Committee, established to review licensing law in Britain, recommended a more liberal approach to licensing that sought to limit the powers of licensing magistrates. While its findings were not immediately implemented, many of its recommendations made its way into the 1988 Licensing Act. In particular, this Act removed the 'afternoon gap', meaning pubs could open throughout the day, and extended existing opening hours. This meant that, aside from Sundays, public houses in England could now open from 11 a.m. to 11 p.m.[73] Shane Butler et al. argue that Thatcher's 1989 'Beer Orders' – the decision to demonopolise the brewing industry's hold on licensed venues – led the way

110   *Youth and the changing urban environment*

for the establishment of pub chains and diversified the types of alcohol on offer in licensed venues.[74] The introduction of the 2003 Licensing Act, the final of three major periods of licensing reform in post-war England, has been positioned as 'arguably the most significant reform of alcohol laws since 1872', and marked the moment at which responsibility for licensing was transferred away from magistrates to local councils.[75] At a national level then, alcohol licensing in the latter half of the twentieth century served to entrench licensed spaces as central and accessible sites of leisure and sociability.

However, the mechanics of licensing in Britain intersected in critical ways with wider debates about order, decency, and forms of 'problematic' consumption. In discussing the findings of the Erroll Committee's 1972 report on alcohol licensing, one magistrate asked whether all Justices of the Peace were 'isolated from their social context when exercising functions other than purely judicial ones? Should they be?'[76] Licensing magistrates were, in their view, not only tasked with the granting and regulation of licences but with ensuring that the wider landscape of licensed venues was structured in what they considered to be a responsible way. As this chapter demonstrates, the difficulties of defining what constituted 'responsible' had numerous implications for the way that late-night leisure developed in Britain. The relationship between youth leisure and alcohol was, by its nature, positioned as problematic, and managing these complexities in an era of changing youth lifestyles was central to much of the licensing magistrates' work in this period.

The Intoxicating Liquor Act 1923 formally outlawed the purchase and consumption of alcohol in public houses by people under the age of 18, and this age limit remained in place through the twentieth century. In practice, however, this was difficult to enforce; politicians debated the feasibility of implementing age checks on younger drinkers well into the 1980s, and the Erroll Committee suggested in 1972 that given that this law was 'widely disregarded', the age limit should be dropped to 17.[77] In response, one frustrated magistrate penned a poem to the industry magazine *Justice of the Peace* decrying the ongoing 'problem' of youth drinking:

> Do they think this will settle the problem?
> For another will surely appear,
> As the age of the youngest defendants
> Will be, roughly, reduced by one year![78]

The shifting nature of young people's relationship with alcohol was one of the most significant developments in experiences of youth leisure in the post-war period, and licensing magistrates were tasked with responding to

Regulating youth after dark

this. Their work was shaped both by the emergent narratives surrounding youth drinking and their firm belief that they were, despite their relative distance from these spaces, best placed to make these decisions.

'City on the Move': licensing and the reimagination of the deindustrialising city

As this chapter has shown so far, youth lifestyles were the subject of persistent controversy and concern. The perceived need to regulate commercial youth leisure was driven both by the long-contested nature of young people's presence in public space and a desire to protect them from the potential dangers posed by commercial leisure and urban centres after dark. However, these discussions also took place in the context of fast-paced urban change and, as the post-war period progressed, a moment in which the very purpose of the urban centre was being questioned and reimagined. The remainder of this chapter focuses on two key issues: how the growing night-time economy was regulated at the local level and how this intersected with distinct and often conflicting visions of the post-industrial city. By the end of the twentieth century, the night-time economy was viewed in many cities as a driver of 'civic renewal, streets being brought back to life by large numbers of visitors, or – more accurately – consumers'.[79] However, in the midst of deindustrialisation, this process of transformation was messier and less clear cut, and exposed the contested uses of urban space at night. As dance floors replaced factory floors, the question of who, and how, the urban centre served was placed high on the agenda. In Sheffield, this question became increasingly critical as deindustrialisation picked up pace in the later decades of the twentieth century.

The release of the promotional film *Sheffield: City on the Move* in 1972 was part of Sheffield City Council's wider strategy to update the image of the city. Focusing on technology, retail, and leisure, the film promoted Sheffield as a thriving modern city and encapsulated the drive for urban renewal and regeneration in many towns and cities in this period. 'Sheffield of the seventies swings', the narrator informs us over images of dancing couples and flashing lights. Featured in the film was the newly opened Fiesta cabaret club, highlighted as the largest in Europe and designed to portray Sheffield as a centre of sophisticated and developed nightlife. The focus given to the city's nightlife in this film speaks both to the growing entertainment industry in the city and the cultural significance that a venue of this sort denoted. The film, and the concurrent redevelopment of Sheffield's shopping precincts, including the building of the new Castle Market and pedestrianisation of the main shopping street, Fargate, were a reflection of the wider burst of urban

112　　　　*Youth and the changing urban environment*

renewal in this period during which 'diverse, mixed use, urban districts' were replaced with 'new landscapes of affluence'.[80]

As the demand for leisure opportunities for the young increased from the 1950s, a growing number of purpose-built and repurposed buildings emerged in Sheffield that were designed to attract young people in their late teens and early 20s. As Chapters 1 and 2 demonstrated, the pace at which these spaces emerged to cater to this new market was remarkable. Entrepreneurs, local business owners, and large-scale commercial organisations showed a remarkable capacity to adapt to new tastes and often showed creativity and ingenuity in order to achieve this. Storage cellars became jazz bars, old dance studios became all-night beat clubs, and cinemas were transformed into dance halls. This ingenuity caused immediate problems for those responsible for the regulation and management of leisure space, not least because many of these early changes in the city's leisurescape were a result of temporary and ad-hoc arrangements that sat outside of the existing mechanisms for legislation and regulation. For the city's licensing magistrates, who were responsible for the granting of the necessary licences for entertainment venues, a swift response to these changes was required. This response, while informed by national concerns about the changing state of leisure provision, was mediated and enacted in ways that had distinctly local ramifications.

An area of significant concern in the city was the transformation of existing licensed venues in response to changing leisure appetites. In particular, the growing use of public houses for live music and dancing through the early 1960s provoked concern from the city's licensing magistrates. In the absence of venues dedicated to new forms of youth music, function rooms in public houses became a popular choice for local musicians and music promoters, as well as savvy publicans who welcomed the additional custom. That public houses were increasingly situated as a central site for youth-oriented leisure in the city was seen as a cause for concern for two key reasons: the venues were not designed with young patrons in mind, and they were seen to be contributing to a rise in the number of young people consuming alcohol underage and to excess. Such was the scale of growth in publicans applying for new licences to enable them to host live music and dancing, Sheffield's licensing committee felt it necessary to call a special meeting to discuss ways forward in December 1965.

The meeting was sparked by the application of four public houses, all on the outskirts of the city, for Music, Singing, and Dancing licences. At the time of the meeting, Sheffield had four existing public houses where dancing was permitted, and these new applications, it was felt, demonstrated a wider shift in the attitudes of publicans, who were increasingly 'looking for ways in which they could compete with the entertainment facilities' offered

Regulating youth after dark 113

elsewhere.[81] In discussing the granting of these licences to public houses, it was noted that 'at first licences were only granted where a floor area of at least 600 square feet was available if a room was to be used for dancing or 400 square feet for music only but that this rule had gradually disappeared with the introduction of music by mechanical means'. These additional applications were viewed with apprehension by the magistrates for a number of reasons, but in particular because it opened the door for publicans to apply for Special Hours Certificates which would allow them to open until 2 a.m. in line with other dancing establishments in the city. This development risked presenting difficulties of adequate supervision, public disturbances outside of the venue, and increased duties for the city's police 'at the worst possible time' of night.[82] As such, the magistrates committed to further research on whether a licensing policy was required that took into account the experiences of other large cities and that would look to the future to 'provide a policy designed to accord with the altering pattern of living at present indicated by pressure for entertainment of the sort provided by nightclubs'.[83]

The magistrates and local police were particularly concerned about the rise of drinking by young people and the implications of this for public disorder. The Chief Constable reminded magistrates that 'young people were attracted to dances', which served to act as a warning against the further spread of late-night dancing in licensed establishments.[84] Indeed, in his annual reports to the committee through the latter half of the 1960s, the Chief Constable showed ongoing concern about the rates of drunkenness amongst young people in the city and the difficulties of policing youth in this new environment. In 1965 it was reported that there had been an 'increase in drunkenness in the 14 to 20 age group', and that Sheffield stood 'fairly high' in the list of cities for which drunkenness statistics were available.[85] The following year, it was highlighted that the further spread of late-night dancing spots with 'discotheque lighting' was making the supervision of these spaces difficult, while in 1968 it was reported that there had been an 'alarming increase' in the number of people convicted of underage drinking.[86]

The growing attention given to youth drinking in the city was not driven solely, or even primarily, by concern about young people's wellbeing. With the growth in late-night leisure provision and the increasing centrality of alcohol and pop music to the leisure spaces frequented by young people, the issue of disruption to local residents became a recurring feature in the discussions of the licensing committee. These issues were first raised in the 1960s during opposition to the King Mojo nightclub in residential Pitsmoor explored in Chapter 1, but accelerated in the 1970s as growing numbers of venues in residential areas applied for licences. Particular attention was paid to two popular teenage haunts: Shades and Turn Ups, both of which were

114 *Youth and the changing urban environment*

located in the residential south west of the city. Discussions about Turn Ups were ongoing through the early years of the 1970s, and exemplified a much wider debate about the location of nightclubs in the city. The club was subject to repeated petitions by residents complaining of noise and disruption, and in 1976 the licensing magistrates revoked the venue's licence pending formal investigation. The magistrates commented that 'even in this day and age, people in a residential area are entitled to a reasonable level of peace and quiet. Equally, people are entitled to go to clubs and seek relaxation and enjoyment, and we recognise the part these play in the life of the city'.[87] Following further complaints, the owner of Turn Ups moved the premises to Commercial Street in the city centre, and agreed to surrender the licence for the Nether Edge venue.

The approach of the magistrates in the 1970s certainly seems to suggest that they weren't seeking to actively restrict young people's access to late-night leisure in this period. Indeed, their recognition of the social significance of licensed leisure spaces for both leisure and sociability indicated a clear shift from the morality-driven concerns of the early 1960s. This was driven in part by the recognition that young people's prominent position within the growing night-time economy represented a much wider and long-lasting transformation to youth lifestyles. However, while they recognised and accepted this shift, the licensing magistrates remained committed to licensing venues in a way that minimised wider social disruption. Rather than restrict access to late-night leisure, the magistrates embarked on a period of spatial regulation that sought to shape the very environment that young people moved through.

In the early 1980s, this period of spatial regulation brought the magistrates into direct conflict with the city council's wider policy of urban renewal and cultural regeneration. The dynamics of the city's local politics have been explored extensively elsewhere, but between the 1960s and 1980s, Sheffield's Labour-led council was committed to a programme of 'socially useful' economic and urban development that overlapped in important ways with the city's commercial leisure offerings.[88] Recognising in particular the ongoing effects of unemployment on the city's teenagers, the council spent significant sums of money on supporting cultural ventures that would benefit those who were marginalised from Sheffield's wider leisurescape. However, Sheffield was not alone in this commitment to providing accessible leisure spaces through this period. The left-wing Greater London Council (GLC) and a number of other local councils utilised various public funding streams, including Arts Council grants, the Urban Programme, and Youth Opportunity Programme, to support the local cultural scene by funding community centres, arts programmes, and theatre companies.[89] In Sheffield, the council prioritised arts and culture within their broader 'alternative social policy', defined by council leader David Blunkett as 'instead of goods and services being defined in money terms (their exchange value), they are defined by usefulness'.[90] It is this approach to municipal service provision which explains the emergence of various council-funded enterprises, including Red Tape Recording Studios, Anvil Cinema, and Sheffield Audio Visual Enterprise Centre, which by the late 1980s fell under the banner of the Cultural Industries Quarter.[91]

An early entry into this landscape of culture-driven urban development was an arts centre and nightclub, the Leadmill, which opened in May 1980. The opening of the Leadmill marked the beginning of a commitment to municipally led cultural renewal in the city, and it provides a fascinating example of the often complex relationship between youth culture, commerce, and local authorities.[92] The Leadmill opened on Leadmill Road in an area of abandoned industrial buildings, a short walk from the train station and city centre. The venue was developed by a team of volunteers in the hope of creating a cultural space for marginalised and unemployed people in the city, with the direct aim of providing an alternative to the commercially driven nightlife to be found elsewhere in the city. As well as the main venue, the space contained workshops and rehearsal space to support local musicians and artists and regularly held exhibitions to display the work produced. The main venue applied for an alcohol licence, but was refused by licensing magistrates in September 1980. The Leadmill's application for a licence was in order to 'subsidise a co-operative craft unit and natural food café', and the venue stressed that it would not get off the ground without the financial income from bar sales.[93] The visiting magistrates, 'whilst admiring the ideals of the organisers', denied the application on the grounds that there was an existing public house within fifty yards of the Leadmill, alongside wider concerns about the venue's suitability.[94] Unable to operate on a sound financial basis without a licence, the venue closed. A letter to the *Star* newspaper in October 1980, one month after its closure, demonstrated the social role that the venue played in its opening months: 'it provides a service much needed by local groups, and the best opportunity the kids of Sheffield have to see these groups in pleasant surroundings, at reasonable prices, and without worrying that there is a possibility of trouble'.[95] This response spoke clearly to the now-firmly established narratives about commercial youth leisure in the city, drawing on clear associations between late-night leisure and violence.

Following the refusal of its alcohol licence, the venue sought funding from local government grants to develop the building and meet the conditions set out by the licensing magistrates. A Traditional Urban Programme Capital Grant of £14,000 was awarded to the venue in March 1982 by Sheffield City Council, while an Urban Aid grant of £16,000 was provided by South Yorkshire County Council in June 1982.[96] The council's support of the Leadmill was part of its wider political initiative aimed at urban renewal;

in 1981 the council set up a Department for Employment and Economic Development (DEED), parts of which focused on the development of local cultural and media industries.[97] While a nightclub and arts centre may not have fit the traditional remit of local authority funding, the Leadmill was developed with clear social aims in mind: 'to encourage artistic activities, particularly those appealing to minority (non-profit making) cultural tastes'; 'to provide a venue for popular music at a price affordable by the unemployed'; and 'to encourage the use of the premises as a meeting place by the unemployed, ethnic minorities, and the general public'.[98] With unemployment in the city 250 per cent higher in 1989 than in 1979, and young school leavers being particularly badly hit by the contraction of local industries, the venue could make a clear case for its social value to the community.[99]

In a visit to the Leadmill as part of the venue's reapplication for a licence to sell alcohol in 1982, one licensing magistrate commented that 'a lot of work had been done and the premises were much improved since an application was refused two years ago'.[100] The magistrates commented on the need to ensure the separation from customers under the age of 18 from the licensed area, but they granted the licence in September 1982 and the venue reopened the same month. However, despite the licence being granted, the Leadmill's issues with the magistrates were not at an end. On a 1984 visit, one magistrate said 'he thought the standard of decor and finish existing

Figure 3.1 Sunday afternoon 'jazz for lunch' session at the Leadmill, Sheffield, 26 January 1986. © Damon Fairclough.

left little to be desired. In his opinion it was not good enough'.[101] However, as Figure 3.1 shows, the Leadmill's decor was minimalist, designed to be in keeping with the building's industrial heritage. These comments revealed the gap between the needs and desires of consumers and venue owners, and the attitudes of the licensing magistrates at this time.

Despite often being at odds with the licensing magistrates, the venue did have support from local organisations and the Leadmill quickly became a central part of Sheffield's cultural landscape. In July of 1983, Julian Spalding, then the Director of Arts for Sheffield City Council, noted that 'the Leadmill, in the space of ten months, has established itself as a major multi-purpose arts centre in the city ... they have successfully attracted a wide range of social groups, which is both culturally and socially desirable'.[102] In his concluding remarks on the venue, Spalding summarised what he felt to be the benefit of the Leadmill to the city:

> There is an urgent need for entertainment centres of this type which can cater specifically for the needs of the unemployed and the disadvantaged. This is not being provided for by the commercial sector, which tends to cater only for an 'identifiable' market. Commercial provision is often therefore socially isolating. Closures also tend to be dictated more by the financial needs of the owners rather than the financial needs of the public.

The initial refusal of the Leadmill's alcohol licence, alongside the magistrates' clear frustration at the venue's design and decor, existed in clear contradiction to the wider ambitions of the city to utilise arts, music, and the night-time economy as a form of cultural regeneration. Communicated in opposition to the 'dangers' of commercial leisure – here conceived both as potentially dangerous and culturally isolating – these tensions also demonstrate the power of commerce. The standards of the licensing magistrates regarding building suitability, and used clearly in their decision-making process, were shaped by commercial venues, many of which had significant capital to invest in renovation and redesign.

'We are satisfied that there is ... need to continue strict control over the availability of liquor': regulating the 'problem' of late-night leisure in post-war Sheffield

Through the post-war period, Sheffield's licensing magistrates maintained a commitment to reducing disruption and disorder, taking great care to consider the implications of their decisions for the city's residents. The magistrates repeatedly voiced their support of non-residential venues in the early 1970s, and worked closely with residents and the council to ensure that

118   *Youth and the changing urban environment*

nightclubs deemed to be a 'nuisance' were held to account. During the 1976 investigation into Nether Edge venue Turn Ups, the magistrates stated: 'we want to say now, with emphasis, that commercial interests seeking to come into residential areas with entertainment centres should recognise that they face the risk of losing a very great deal if their operation cannot be made congenial to local residents'.[103] This policy was one the magistrates enforced strictly, and the Turn Ups 'problem' was something that they wished to avoid in the future. Regarding an application in 1983 to open a venue in Beighton, on the outskirts of the city, the visiting magistrate commented that he 'could not recommend the application and envisioned another "Turn Ups" situation'.[104] The particular focus placed by the licensing magistrates on commercial interests is noteworthy, and suggests a recognition that commercial organisations formed an increasingly large part of the city's local economy and often wielded significant economic power. However, it also demonstrates the clear link being made between late-night leisure and disruption, something the magistrates felt strongly should be confined to the city centre and removed from residential areas of the city. This desire to spatially regulate commercial youth leisure was, alongside an attempt to protect public peace and minimise late-night disorder, a central aspect of the magistrates' approach in the period between the 1970s and 1980s. One central way that this was implemented was through the introduction of a policy of 'need'. The magistrates increasingly believed that the unfettered growth of licensed venues for young people in the city was to be avoided, and they remained concerned at the supposed 'problem' of youth drinking.

In reply to a 1981 appeal by the Fleur De Lys nightspot in the wealthy residential suburb of Totley, the licensing magistrates commented that:

> We also wish to refer to the increasing concern being widely expressed regarding the consumption of alcoholic drinks and the problems arising therefrom. We are sure that you will agree that this licensing committee must take heed of those sentiments and where appropriate they must influence our decisions. We are satisfied that there is, in this day and age, a need to continue strict control over the availability of liquor.[105]

The principle of need had first been introduced as a licensing technique in the eighteenth and nineteenth centuries. Indeed, James Nicholls argues that 'many of the fiercest political battles in the history of the drink question' were fought over this principle.[106] However, the policy of need – and, by extension, the local power of licensing magistrates – was increasingly questioned in the shifting post-war drinking landscape. Despite a number of reports outlining that young people's alcohol consumption in the post-war period was, on the whole, an 'unproblematic part of the lives of

Regulating youth after dark   119

the majority of British teenagers', calls to restrict the licensed leisurescape remained.[107]

The Erroll Committee report on licensing in 1972 suggested that the principle of need was out of date and should be abandoned. It was not, the committee felt, within the 'scope' of magistrates' duties to consider need and suggested 'that the way in which the justices exercise this discretion makes for inconsistencies and uncertainties in the administration of the law'.[108] However, responses to their findings from magistrates across the country were less than complimentary and were the topic of regular debate in the industry magazine *Justice of the Peace*. A 1986 article suggested that the committee's findings were 'coldly logical. Many licensing matters go hand in hand with local knowledge about bad behaviour resulting from excessive drinking and are therefore matters for the magistrates. This is a basic commonsense [*sic*] approach.'[109] At the local level, then, magistrates continued to exercise controls based on local contexts and concerns. In Nottingham, for example, the city's licensing magistrates were particularly concerned with the 'problem' of vagrancy and street drinking, despite a move towards public health models of excessive alcohol consumption in the 1970s.[110] Despite the Erroll Committee's recommendations, magistrates firmly believed that local knowledge was an essential component of the successful management and regulation of licensed spaces. In 1971, ahead of the publication of the Erroll Committee's report, Sheffield's licensing committee 'rejected any suggestion that duties should be taken from licensing justices'.[111] Their justification was:

1) Justices are an independent body not having any political or commercial axe to grind – unlike local authorities.
2) The Bench is accustomed, by reason of its centuries of history and years of experience, to applying a judicial approach to matters brought before it for decision. Any transfer of licensing responsibilities could only be to some body not possessing those qualifications.
3) Matters affecting licensing are local matters, and justices are best fitted to deal with them because of their position in the local community. If the present system of licensing control were to continue in some form it could not adequately be administered on a national footing.

Their claim that justices had no political or commercial axe to grind is certainly worthy of question given the voluntary nature of their position and the long history of magistrates using their platform for morality and temperance campaigns.[112] While their focus on local knowledges was positioned in relation to particular 'problem' areas and knowledge of the existing geography of licensed venues, it also acts as an important reminder that while young people across large swathes of Britain, Europe, and North America

120 *Youth and the changing urban environment*

were consuming within an increasingly global marketplace of leisure, this played out in the leisure landscape of their local town and city.

Having established the ongoing importance of local knowledges and, by extension, local enforcement of alcohol policy, Sheffield's committee set out their plan for the year at the beginning of 1980:

> We take regretful notice of the increase in convictions concerned with the purchasing or consuming of intoxicating liquor on licensed premises by persons under the age of 18. This represents an increase of 26½ percent ... the overall picture indicates a need to continue firm control over the availability of liquor.[113]

In discussing their response to increased convictions by underage teenagers, the magistrates made a direct link with city-centre venues:

> Members of this committee from their general observations have become aware that certain licensed premises, mainly situated in the city centre, seem to be mentioned too frequently in our courts generally, when cases in respect of a variety of offences are being heard.

The licensing magistrates released an addendum in 1983 detailing their new approach to licensing. In October, they released a formal statement of their policy:

> The increase of alcohol related problems which according to relevant indicators, has taken place over recent years, and of which the committee is aware from its own knowledge and experience, is considered to be due in some part to the great availability of alcoholic liquor. The committee therefore state as a matter of general policy that the question of need and undue proliferation of outlets are factors which are taken into account in the consideration of all applications for new Justices' licences.[114]

In November of the same year, this concern with issues arising from the city-centre were reiterated by the Chief Constable of the city's police force in his reply to the addendum:

> The proliferation of licensed premises, especially in the city centre, has undoubtedly been a contributory factor in the increase in cases of drunkenness and drink related offences dealt with by my officers. By adoption of more stringent criteria for the granting of a licence, the Justices will minimise any further increase in respect of licensed premises and their attendant problems.[115]

Regulating youth after dark 121

The Chief Constable went on to say:

> Unruliness and bad behaviour at night time can be attributed mostly to young people over indulging in intoxicants and … any curb on outlets for their re-sale will at the worst prevent the situation deteriorating and perhaps lead to the city centre becoming a more pleasant and safer place for the many law abiding people of Sheffield who transit through, and work in, the centre at night.

By 1983, the licensing committee and police were both in agreement that the proliferation of venues in the city centre, in part a result of the magistrates' policy to deny and revoke licences in the suburbs, had become problematic enough to require new licensing policy. This suggested a development in the approach of the licensing magistrates; the introduction of a clear and cohesive strategy, in coordination with the police, was a reflection of the swift pace at which the urban leisure landscape had transformed. By the 1980s, the magistrates had transformed the approach that had been utilised across the post-war period, moving from granting licences on an individual basis to one that considered the landscape of the licensed city as a whole.

This change culminated in the 1987 statement of policy. The magistrates' focus on 'need' was enveloped into a more moralistic approach encompassing fears about the dangers of alcohol alongside wider concerns about anti-social behaviour. The committee stated that two general propositions about the situation in 1987 emerged:

a) There is at present a very serious problem of alcohol misuse in our society. One publication refers to it as an 'endemic disorder of frightening magnitude'.
b) The ease with which alcohol can be obtained through the various types of outlet has a bearing upon the level of consumption. That is to say, the greater the availability of alcohol the greater the consumption will be.[116]

In developing this new policy, the licensing magistrates were advertising their intent to pursue a far firmer line of approach to decisions made about new and existing licences. This rhetoric of licensing for public benefit continued for the remainder of the decade. In 1988 the chair stated that it was 'the essential purpose of this committee so far as it is able to do so, to hold a proper balance between ordinary commercial considerations on the one hand and the general public interest as we perceive it, on the other'.[117] In 1989, the chair's comments again declared that 'close and careful control over the number (or proliferation) of outlets can only be for the greater public good'.[118]

Concerns around the harmful effects of alcohol consumption had been conspicuously absent in discussions of the licensing magistrates in the previous two decades despite the presence of public health approaches to alcohol at a national level, but as the proliferation of licensed venues made alcohol a central element of the lifestyles of young people, the attitude of alcohol as a 'problematic' form of consumption returned.[119] Occurring against a backdrop of wider anxieties about delinquency, youth violence, and rising crime, this move towards tighter regulation was influenced by wider concerns about young people's morality and what were deemed to be 'problematic' forms of consumption. The proliferation of late-night venues was not the only concern of the licensing magistrates. The standard of licensed venues and the changing ways in which young people used these spaces continued to be a topic of discussion for the licensing magistrates throughout this period. Concerns around respectability and expectations about what a licensed venue should look like, and whom it should serve, continued to attract debate. Long-serving magistrates who were increasingly unfamiliar with the changing leisurescape of the young repeatedly clashed with commercial leisure venues in this period.[120]

Of particular concern to the magistrates was the city centre rock club Rebels. At a meeting in June 1982, a licensing committee member 'felt he could no longer wait to pass comment on the Rebels night club.'[121] The committee member told the meeting of:

> the appalling state of the premises. Also that the premises were overcrowded, underage people were present and that there was a smell of hashish being smoked. The lighting was at a minimum level and the emergency exit could not be seen. On the entrance stairway there was some broken glass and the nosings on the steps were damaged and dangerous.[122]

Other magistrates who visited the premises:

> expressed themselves as utterly appalled and disgusted at the conditions and circumstances they encountered there. The dangerous condition of the long flight of stairs by which the premises are approached has long been a source of concern; there were many broken bottles and glasses about: the premises appeared to be grossly overcrowded: there were reports of 14/16 year olds being there in the early hours of the morning: the emergency exits were not discernible: the lighting was of an unacceptably low level: the toilets were in an atrocious state: there were pictures on the walls of an obscene or indecent nature: the visiting justices were generally alarmed by the type of clientele and their activities.

Following these complaints, the magistrates agreed to hold a special meeting to discuss the state of the city's nightclubs on 27 August 1982, at which the licensing magistrates were to meet with representatives of the police and fire brigade. At this meeting, a committee member 'spoke at length regarding his visit to Rebels and the deplorable state of the premises. The access stairway was littered with broken glass and he was certain the premises were overcrowded as the Magistrates could only just get past the entrance.'[123] The concerns of magistrates indicated an ongoing concern about the moral dangers that late-night clubs posed to young consumers, and demonstrate clearly the desire to adapt existing regulations as a way of extending their capacity to control young people's access to, and movement within, these spaces.

The need for stricter regulation of nightclubs was a matter of discussion for the remainder of the decade. The problem was deemed to be that the 'methods of operation of these night spots are such that inevitably incidents of disorder arise resulting in the police having to attend'.[124] As the number of the city's evening leisure spaces expanded, the licensing magistrates were forced to professionalise, developing coherent and coordinated strategies to hold venues to increasingly higher standards. Throughout the mid-1980s, the magistrates worked with the police to undertake comprehensive visits to nightclubs in the city to ensure that they were being run according to their licence conditions. In reply to the Chief Constable's annual report to the licensing committee in 1986, the chair told the meeting:

> Our experience was not uniformly satisfactory. In some cases we were concerned with the poor standard of cleanliness and the apparent inadequacy of supervision. In some, there appeared to be strong evidence of overcrowding; we have, in fact, one licensee before us this morning with a conviction for gross overcrowding contrary to the terms of his Entertainments licence. Some indeed were flagrantly in conflict with licensing requirements in that no food at all was available. We remind all licensees that they are not permitted just to run late-night public houses. The sale of intoxicating liquor is ancillary or secondary to the provision of music and dancing and substantial refreshment. We have asked the Police and other relevant Authorities to keep matters generally under review.[125]

The magistrates' comments about venues being run as 'late-night public houses' demonstrates how national licensing policy was increasingly out of step with the ways in which these venues were being used. The requirement for a late-night licence in this period included providing food, a restriction that did not reflect the activities being undertaken by young people at these venues, which were predominantly drinking and dancing. This was not

124 *Youth and the changing urban environment*

solely a concern in Sheffield; as early as 1974, opponents of Special Hours Certificates – the name given to the extension of licensed hours – noted that there was nothing in the licensing system to 'insist that people drinking in discotheques have to be served with food'.[126] The issues raised by the magistrates with regard to the changing use of evening leisure space in these venues show clearly that licence holders were reluctant to be beholden to the views and restrictions placed on them by an increasingly out-of-touch licensing committee.

While the mid-1980s have been positioned as a flashpoint of debates about youth drinking, fuelled by images of hooliganism and lager louts, this chapter demonstrates that licensing magistrates were taking affirmative action to address this issue at a local level almost a decade earlier. By the start of the 1980s, in response to increasing levels of alcohol consumption by young people in the city, the magistrates' previous concerns about disturbance and disruption were replaced by a much more specific concern about problematic consumption and immoral behaviour, a development that had a significant effect on the way that the city's licensed spaces were monitored and regulated.

'Living in the days of the veleta and the foxtrot': Sheffield licensing magistrates vs Mecca Leisure Ltd

Licensing magistrates, then, had significant power to shape policy, and they implemented this in ways that had a clear bearing on the leisure spaces that young people had access to. Their decisions often put them in conflict with commercial venues in the city, many of which, as we saw in Chapter 2, were owned by companies operating on a national or international scale. Using a case study of a prominent court case between Sheffield licensing magistrates and Mecca Leisure Ltd, this final section of the chapter argues that the spatial regulation of nightlife – both in the wider city and inside leisure venues themselves – reveals the contested nature of youth leisure in the late twentieth century. This affected not only how leisure developed in the urban environment, but what young people were permitted to do once inside these spaces.

In July 1982, the licensing magistrates were in legal conflict with Mecca Leisure Ltd over plans to change the layout of their London Road venue, Tiffany's. Earlier that year, Mecca submitted plans to the magistrates with the intention of increasing the dining area and removing the dance floor on the first floor to create a longer bar. Mecca wished to change the style and layout of the club because 'the simulation of a South Seas Island ... had become outdated'.[127] These initial plans were refused by the licensing magistrates, and a lengthy appeal process ensued. The licensing magistrates' reasons for refusing the proposed plans were twofold: that 'the sale of liquor must be ancillary to music and dancing (not music alone) and substantial refreshment', and that the proposed plans would reduce the amount of space available for dancing. Sheffield's licensing magistrates recommended that dance floors should provide six square feet of space per person. This calculation had been used for years to calculate the capacity of venues, and was in line with other decisions being made at the time in the city. The magistrates argued that by reducing the size of the dance floor, the venue would no longer be suitable to uphold the conditions of its Music, Singing and Dancing licence. The maximum capacity of eight hundred people was calculated on the presumption that 50 per cent of those inside would be using the dance floor, and by reducing the space available for dancing, people would instead be using the venue primarily for the bar facilities.

In providing evidence to support Mecca's appeal, an industry expert stated that he had 'never experienced the size of the dance floor being determined by the occupancy'.[128] Mecca's Director of Property and Estates, Mr Jones, told the appeals court that 'during the past twelve years Tiffany's has catered for both ballroom and disco-style dancing [but] … the style and habits and demands for dancing have changed'.[129] 'From the old time', he continued, 'we have passed through an era of jitterbug, be-bop, jive and twist. The biggest change … came in the early 1960s with the twist when dancers no longer needed space to twirl around.'[130] The appeals court recorded Mr Jones as concluding that 'dancing has become more static. The big demand for listening to the music came in. The emphasis has changed to static dancing and listening.'[131] These appeal documents are clear evidence of the changing use of space by young people in nightclubs, and of the commercial drive to adapt to the changing leisure demands of youth. The licensing magistrates' initial refusal of the plans, and Mecca's later appeal, further demonstrates the disparity between the use of this space by young people and the restrictions placed on it by the magistrates.

During the appeal, Mecca attacked the stance of Sheffield's licensing magistrates, arguing that 'the policy therein submitted is wholly arbitrary, unreasonable and capricious. It is submitted that throughout the country and in existing clubs in Sheffield this "crude and unrealistic yardstick is not applied, it is irrelevant."'[132] Legal counsel for Mecca further submitted that 'there is not a single whisper of evidence to suggest that if you took 50 per cent of capacity and multiplied it by 6 square feet you would magically arrive at a state where drinking would be ancillary to dancing'.[133] The appeal was refused by the Crown Court, and was eventually taken to the High Court. Following the initial refusal of the plans, Mecca sought a ruling that the policy implemented by Sheffield's licensing magistrates was

Figure 3.2 Tiffany's nightclub, formerly the Locarno Ballroom, London Road, Sheffield, 1977. © Sheffield Newspapers Ltd and Picture Sheffield.

'unlawful and irrelevant', despite the company having since sold the club to new owners.[134] Mecca felt that ruling in support of the six-foot yardstick was 'misconceived and would produce draconian, absurd and very damaging consequences'.[135] Further to this, Mecca submitted that the Crown Court 'erred in holding that the need to ensure that drinking should be ancillary to music and dancing was a relevant factor to be considered on an application for structural alterations'.[136]

Over a year after the appeal was first launched, the High Court ruled in favour of the licensing magistrates. The High Court, whilst agreeing that the Crown Court had 'overstepped the bounds of relevance' in linking the size of the dance floor to whether or not dancing was to remain the main activity, ruled that the six-foot yardstick applied by Sheffield's licensing magistrates was lawful. The Judge commented that 'their anxiety and diligence to ensure that observance of the conditions of licences granted by them is commendable and their formation of a "policy" to guide them in considering applications for renewals, transfers and new licences cannot, in my view, in principle, be criticised'.[137] Indeed, such an approach had subsequently been adopted in other areas of the country including Derbyshire and Avon and Somerset, and Mecca's decision to pursue the court case despite having sold the club was influenced in part by their 'apprehension' about the precedent this policy presented.[138]

This case reveals clearly the intersection between commerce and the regulation of youth leisure in the later twentieth century. The continued use of licensing magistrates in post-war Britain meant that national alcohol policy was implemented in clear response to local concerns, with important ramifications for the local leisure environment. The case of Mecca Leisure Ltd v Sheffield Licensing Justices had a tangible impact not only on the redevelopment of nightclubs in an era of significant commercial change for the company, but on the movement of young people through these spaces.

Conclusions

The development of the night-time economy in the mid to late twentieth century was arguably one of the biggest changes to the tapestry of cultural life for young people in Britain. By the turn of the twenty-first century, late-night bars and nightclubs could be found in every major town and city, and generations of young people found pleasure and escape within their walls. The liberalising effects of alcohol licensing in the 1960s and 1970s, alongside the commercial response to changing youth lifestyles, kick-started a leisure industry that was dominated by youth, and played a significant role in shaping national debates about alcohol consumption at the turn of the twenty-first century. When examined at the local level, however, we see that these leisure spaces were contested, and the implementation of national policy had distinctly local characteristics. This chapter has argued that licensing was a significant tool through which youth leisure could be regulated and managed. However, as a somewhat anomalous body – acting independently from the wider mechanisms of state regulation – their influence has rarely been acknowledged by historians of youth in modern Britain. While the work of the licensing magistrates was not always designed to restrict access to youth leisure, licensing nevertheless acted as a tool through which a desirable leisurescape could be moulded. What constituted desirable, however, was by no means static and was influenced by both national and local concerns, as well as a longstanding desire to regulate the modern urban night. The position of licensed venues such as pubs and nightclubs as spaces of youth leisure was contested, and responses to these venues were shaped as much by ideas about what constituted appropriate leisure as by the potential illegality of alcohol consumption by underage youths. Their emergence also raised questions about the place of young people in the modern city.

In Sheffield, the licensing magistrates developed clear policies to enable them to respond to the swift changes in the city's leisure provision in the 1960s. While public houses vied to attract younger patrons with music and dancing, dance halls rebranded themselves as late-night nightclubs. In the 1960s and 1970s, licensing policy was concerned predominantly with preventing late-night disruption to residents in the city; while the magistrates were clearly concerned at the growing number of underage teenagers entering licensed spaces, their policy was one of spatial regulation rather than restriction. However, following the continued rise of weekend violence and disruption at weekends – in part a product of earlier policy to consolidate licences in the relatively small city centre – justices became concerned not only with limiting anti-social behaviour, but with the micromanagement of youth drinking. As such, a moment of supposed liberalisation in alcohol policy was, when viewed at a local level, one of determined regulation. The approach of the city's licensing magistrates was best summed up in a 1986 meeting:

> We have to consider carefully each case and in doing so we face considerable commercial pressures, quite properly and naturally, but it is our endeavour to hold the balance with the public interest in mind and by so doing to promote the cause of sensible drinking ... Liquor licensing is but one element, though in our view a very important one, in a preventive approach to this problem. To some it may be irritating and irksome if seemingly attractive commercial opportunities are denied. We cannot please everyone and we have to act in what we perceive to be the broad public interest.[139]

In defending their actions in the 'broad public interest', the licensing magistrates made clear that they not only intended to ensure that licence holders behaved responsibility, but that they felt their role encompassed the wider management of public alcohol consumption. In this way, the licensing magistrates played a central role in shaping the city's leisure provision.

Perhaps most of all, this chapter acts as a stark reminder to historians of modern Britain that the local contexts in which new patterns of consumption

Regulating youth after dark

and sociability were developed are crucial. While scholars have rightly identified a transnational shift in youth lifestyles across large areas of Europe and North America in the post-war period, it is essential that we don't overlook the local as an analytical tool. It is through the local that we can see how the 'lifestyle revolutions' of the post-war period played out in the towns and cities of Britain, and it is through the local that we can better understand how young people moved through these new leisure environments.

Notes

1 'Council Move on Nightclubs Curb', *Star*, 23 February 1982, 7.
2 HL Deb 19 July 1982, vol 433, col 686.
3 HC Deb 8 November 1989, vol 159, col 979; HC Deb 4 December 1989, vol 163, col 135.
4 Peter Baldwin, '"Nocturnal Habits and Dark Wisdom": The American Response to Children in the Streets at Night, 1880–1930', *Journal of Social History*, 35:3 (2002), 594, https://doi.org/10.1353/jsk.2002.002. Also see Peter Baldwin, *In the Watches of the Night: Life in the Nocturnal City, 1820–1930* (Chicago, IL: University of Chicago Press, 2012).
5 Robert Hollands, 'Divisions in the Dark: Youth Cultures, Transitions and Segmented Consumption in the Night-Time Economy', *Journal of Youth Studies*, 5:2 (2002), 156, https://doi.org/10.1080/13676260220134421.
6 Snape and Pussard, 'Theorisations of Leisure in Inter-War Britain', 3.
7 Carolyn Jackson and Penny Tinkler, '"Ladettes" and "Modern Girls": "Troublesome" Young Femininities', *The Sociological Review*, 55:2 (2007), 252, https://doi.org/10.1111/j.1467-954X.2007.00704.x.
8 Gill Valentine, *Public Space and the Culture of Childhood* (London: Routledge, 2004), 85.
9 Harrison, *Dangerous Amusements*, 154–163.
10 Nott, *Going to the Palais*, 211. See Penny Tinkler, 'Cause for Concern: Young Women and Leisure, 1930–50', *Women's History Review*, 12:2 (2003), 233–262, https://doi.org/10.1080/09612020300200359.
11 For more on this see Valentine, *Public Space and the Culture of Childhood*, 83–96.
12 Baldwin, '"Nocturnal Habits and Dark Wisdom"', 597. For more on the conceptualisation of the dark, see Wolfgang Schivelbusch, *Disenchanted Night: Industrialization of Light in the Nineteenth Century* (Oakland, CA: University of California Press, 1998).
13 Matt Houlbrook, *Queer London: Pleasures and Perils in the Sexual Metropolis, 1918–1957* (Chicago, IL: University of Chicago Press, 2005), 80.
14 Nick Dunn, 'Place after Dark: Urban Peripheries as Alternative Futures' in Tim Edensor, Ares Kalandides, and Uma Kothari (eds), *The Routledge Handbook of Place* (London: Routledge, 2020), 156.

15 Baldwin, 'Nocturnal Habits', 593.
16 Caslin, *Save the Womanhood!*, 204.
17 Damien Phillips, 'The Press and Pop Festivals: Stereotypes of Youthful Leisure' in Stanley Cohen and Jack Young (eds), *The Manufacture of News: A Reader* (Beverly Hills, CA: Sage, 1973), 324.
18 Bradley, 'Rational Recreation', 78.
19 'The Big Menace from the Coffee-Bar Cowboys', *Daily Mirror*, 1 July 1960, 1; 'A Stab Death at the Coffee Bar', *Daily Mirror*, 17 April 1961, 7.
20 'Coffee Bar "Packs" Anger Sir Mortimer', *Daily Telegraph*, 22 September 1965, 17.
21 Carol Dyhouse, *Girl Trouble: Panic and Progress in the History of Young Women* (2nd edn, London: Zed Books, 2014), 145.
22 Jackson, 'Coffee Club Menace', 295.
23 'Police Curb on Coffee Bars Sought', *Daily Telegraph*, 18 September 1965, 9.
24 Charlie Lynch, 'Moral Panic in the Industrial Town: Teenage "Deviancy" and Religious Crisis in Central Scotland, c.1968–9', *Twentieth Century British History*, 32:3 (2021), 391, https://doi.org/10.1093/tcbh/hwaa017.
25 TNA, BN 29/1684, Causes of Juvenile Delinquency, Undesirable Clubs, Minutes of first meeting, 15 September 1964.
26 For the particulars of Soho's history as an entertainment centre, see Judith Walkowitz, *Nights Out: Life in Cosmopolitan London* (New Haven, CT: Yale University Press, 2012).
27 TNA, BN 29/1684, Causes of Juvenile Delinquency, Undesirable Clubs, Minutes of second meeting, 23 July 1965.
28 TNA, BN 29/1684, Causes of Juvenile Delinquency, Undesirable Clubs, Minutes of first meeting, 15 September 1964.
29 TNA, BN 29/1684, Causes of Juvenile Delinquency, Undesirable Clubs, 'Note for file', 30 September 1964.
30 Valentine, *Public Space and the Culture of Childhood*, 90.
31 Baldwin, 'Nocturnal Habits', 606.
32 TNA, BN 29/1684, Causes of Juvenile Delinquency, Undesirable Clubs, LCC Children's Department Report, 1964.
33 TNA, BN 29/1684, Causes of Juvenile Delinquency, Undesirable Clubs, Letter dated 23 May 1964.
34 TNA, BN 29/1684, Causes of Juvenile Delinquency, Undesirable Clubs, Minutes of first meeting, 15 September 1964.
35 TNA, BN 29/1684, Causes of Juvenile Delinquency, Undesirable Clubs, Minutes of second meeting, 23 July 1965.
36 HL Deb 3 February 1967, vol 279, col 1098.
37 HL Deb 3 February 1967, vol 279, col 1104.
38 'Police Curb on Coffee Bars Sought', *Daily Telegraph*, 18 September 1965, 9.
39 Nott, *Going to the Palais*, 287.
40 'Police Plan War on Teenage Gangs', *Sunday Times*, 1 March 1959, 31.
41 Nott, *Going to the Palais*, 296.

42 Pearl Jephcott, *A Troubled Area: Notes on Notting Hill* (London: Faber and Faber, 1964), 111.
43 'The Deadly Disco Night Fever', *Daily Mail*, 4 June 1979, 18.
44 *Ibid.*, 18.
45 Stuart Hall, Chas Critcher, Tony Jefferson, John Clarke, and Brian Roberts, *Policing the Crisis: Mugging, the State, and Law and Order* (2nd edn, Basingstoke: Palgrave Macmillan, 2013), 37.
46 Gildart, 'The Antithesis of Humankind', 132.
47 'How Can We Stop This Dance of Death?', *Daily Mail*, 7 June 1979, 23.
48 *Ibid.*, 23.
49 'Triumph for Mirror Campaigns', *Daily Mirror*, 26 June 1979, 2.
50 '"Dance of Death" Peril at the Disco', *Daily Mirror*, 2 May 1979, 15.
51 'Disco Death Crackdown', *Daily Mirror*, 16 November 1979, 15.
52 For more on this, see Virginia Berridge, Rachel Herring, and Betsy Thom, 'Binge Drinking: A Confused Concept and Its Contemporary History', *Social History of Medicine*, 22:3 (2009), 597–607, https://doi.org/10.1093/shm/hkp053.
53 'Late Night Drinking at Discos under Attack', *Daily Telegraph*, 14 August 1974, 17.
54 James Nicholls, *The Politics of Alcohol: A History of the Drink Question in England* (Manchester: Manchester University Press, 2011), 341.
55 'Stricter Legislation Against Under-Age Drinking Demanded by JPs' Clerks', *The Times*, 25 April 1983, 3.
56 'Scandal of "Rampant" Teenage Drinking', *Daily Mail*, 3 December 1986, 9.
57 Nicholls, *The Politics of Alcohol*, 216.
58 'Hurd Orders Report on New Year Mobs', *Daily Telegraph*, 3 January 1987, 1.
59 TNA, HO 295/118, Letter to Anthony Townsend, 1 September 1987.
60 TNA, HO 295/118, Alcohol and Crime: Standing Conference on Crime Prevention, Working Group on Young People and Alcohol Report, 17.
61 *Ibid.*, 18.
62 Mariana Valverde, *Law's Dream of a Common Knowledge* (Princeton, NJ: Princeton University Press, 2003), 125.
63 *Ibid.*, 144.
64 There is a significant body of work that explores the role licensing plays in social and moral regulation. For examples of this, see Phil Hubbard, *Cities and Sexualities* (Abingdon: Routledge, 2011); Nicholas Dorn, *Alcohol, Youth and the State* (London: Croom Helm, 1983); David Beckingham, *The Licensed City: Regulating Drink in Liverpool, 1830–1920* (Liverpool: Liverpool University Press, 2017).
65 David Beckingham, 'Gender, Space, and Drunkenness: Liverpool's Licensed Premises, 1860–1914', *Annals of the Association of American Geographers*, 102:3 (2012), 648, https://doi.org/10.1080/00045608.2011.652850.
66 Shane Butler, Karen Elmeland, James Nicholls, and Betsy Thom, *Alcohol, Power and Public Health: A Comparative Study of Alcohol Policy* (London: Routledge, 2017), 95.
67 Valverde, *Law's Dream*, 130.

68 John Davis, 'Central Government and the Towns' in Martin Daunton (ed.), *The Cambridge Urban History of Britain: Volume III* (Cambridge: Cambridge University Press, 2001), 286.

69 Valverde, *Law's Dream*, 139.

70 *Ibid.*, 139.

71 Marwick, *British Society Since 1945*, 98.

72 Nicholls, *The Politics of Alcohol*, 195.

73 Henry Yeomans, *Alcohol and Moral Regulation: Public Attitudes, Spirited Measures and Victorian Hangovers* (Bristol: Policy Press, 2014), 172.

74 Butler, Elmeland, Nicholls, and Thom, *Alcohol, Power, and Public Health*, 135.

75 Yeomans, *Alcohol and Moral Regulation*, 176.

76 'Local Authorities and J.P.s: A Matter of Licensing Jurisdiction', *Justice of the Peace and Local Government Review*, 137:13 (1973), 198.

77 *Justice of the Peace and Local Government Review*, 136:53 (1972), 833.

78 'Notice', *Justice of the Peace and Local Government Review*, 237:2 (1973), 26.

79 Phil Hadfield, *Bar Wars: Contesting the Night in Contemporary British Cities* (Oxford: Oxford University Press, 2006), 45.

80 Alistair Kefford, *The Life and Death of the Shopping City: Public Planning and Private Redevelopment in Britain since 1945* (Cambridge: Cambridge University Press, 2022), 200. These themes are also explored in Sam Wetherell, *Foundations: How the Built Environment Made Twentieth-Century Britain* (Princeton, NJ: Princeton University Press, 2020) and Saumarez Smith, *Boom Cities*.

81 SCA, MC 2008/146, Sheffield Corporation, Licensing Justices, Minutes, Box 83, 19/11/1965–06/01/1970, 14.

82 *Ibid.*

83 *Ibid.*

84 *Ibid.*

85 *Ibid.*, 30.

86 *Ibid.*, 116; 286.

87 SCA, MC 2008/146, Sheffield Corporation, Licensing Justices, Minutes Box 81, 13/01/1976–06/12/1977, 222.

88 Payling, *Socialist Republic*.

89 For a productive summary of work on the question of regeneration and the 'inner city' in this period, see Aaron Andrews, Alistair Kefford, and Daniel Warner, 'Community, Culture, Crisis: The Inner City in England, c. 1960–1990', *Urban History*, 50:2 (2023), 202–213, https://doi.org/10.1017/S0963926821000729.

90 David Blunkett and Geoff Green, *Building from the Bottom: The Sheffield Experience*, Fabian Society No. 491 (London: Fabian Society, 1983).

91 Nick Oatley and Cath Mackie, 'Sheffield's Cultural Industries Quarter', *Local Economy*, 11:2 (1996), 172–179, https://doi.org/10.1080 /02690949608726324.

92 For more on the city's commitment to cultural renewal in this period, see Kenny, 'A "Radical Project"'.

Regulating youth after dark

133

93 SCA, MC 2008/146, Sheffield Corporation, Licensing Justices, Minutes, Box 83, 05/02/1980–17/12/1980, 127.

94 *Ibid.*, 127.

95 'Leadmill's Service', *Star*, 22 October 1980, 12.

96 SCA, SYCC CB/1526, The Leadmill Association, funding received to date (November 1980–February 1983).

97 Astrid Winkler, 'Sheffield City Report', *CASE Report* 45 (2007), 15, via http://eprints.lse.ac.uk/5133/1/CASEreport45.pdf [last accessed 22 May 2023].

98 SCA, SYCC CB/1526, Employment Programme Committee Application, July 1983.

99 Paul Lawless and Peter Ramsden, 'Sheffield in the 1980s: From Radical Intervention to Partnership', *Cities*, 7:3 (1990), 208, https://doi.org/10.1016/0264-2751(90)90048-C.

100 SCA, MC 2008/146, Sheffield Corporation, Licensing Justices, Minutes, Box 85, 07/02/1984–18/12/1984, 243.

101 *Ibid.*, 243.

102 SCA, SYCC CB/1526, Letter from Julian Spalding to the Community Arts Panel, July 1983.

103 SCA, MC 2008/146, Sheffield Corporation, Licensing Justices, Minutes, Box 81, 13/01/1976–06/12/1977, 222.

104 SCA, MC 2008/146, Sheffield Corporation, Licensing Justices, Minutes, Box 85, 08/02/1983–17/01/1984, 511.

105 SCA, MC 2008/146, Sheffield Corporation, Licensing Justices, Minutes, Box 84, 06/01/1981–16/12/1981, 3.

106 Nicholls, *The Politics of Alcohol*, 221.

107 Deborah Lister Sharp, 'Underage Drinking in the United Kingdom since 1970: Public Policy, the Law and Adolescent Drinking Behaviour', *Alcohol and Alcoholism*, 29:5 (1994), 555–563, https://doi.org/10.1093/oxfordjournals.alcalc.a045584.

108 *Justice of the Peace and Local Government Review*, 136:53 (1972), 833.

109 'People Who Live in Glass Houses', *Justice of the Peace*, 150:34 (1986), 537.

110 Virginia Berridge and Jane McGregor, 'Local and National Policy Making for Alcohol: Nottingham, UK, 1950–2007', *Social History of Alcohol and Drugs*, 25:1–2 (2011), 148–164, https://doi.org/10.1086/SHAD25010148.

111 SCA, MC 2008/146, Sheffield Corporation, Licensing Justices, Minutes, Box 83, 10/02/1970–17/01/1971, 315.

112 Valverde, *Law's Dream*, 150–156.

113 SCA, MC 2008/146, Sheffield Corporation, Licensing Justices, Minutes, Box 84, 05/02/1980–17/12/1980 [loose insert].

114 SCA, MC 2008/146, Sheffield Corporation, Licensing Justices, Minutes, Box 85, 08/02/1983–17/01/1984, 540.

115 *Ibid.* [loose insert].

116 SCA, MC 2008/146, Sheffield Corporation, Licensing Justices, Minutes, Box 87, 09/01/1987–15/12/1987 [loose insert].

134   *Youth and the changing urban environment*

117 SCA, MC 2008/146, Sheffield Corporation, Licensing Justices, Minutes, Box 86, 08/01/1988 – 08/11/1988 [loose insert].

118 SCA, MC 2008/146, Sheffield Corporation, Licensing Justices, Minutes, Box 86, 06/01/1989 – 24/11/1989 [loose insert].

119 There is an extensive literature which deals with alcohol and morality. See Nicholls, *The Politics of Alcohol*; Yeomans, *Alcohol and Moral Regulation*; David Gutzke, *Women Drinking Out in Britain Since the Early Twentieth Century* (Manchester: Manchester University Press, 2014).

120 During discussions about the importance of licensing magistrates, Sheffield's committee agreed that longer service of members was favourable. In November 1980, of the membership of fourteen, eight had served between seven and fifteen years. SCA, MC 2008/146, Sheffield Corporation, Licensing Justices, Minutes, Box 83, 05/02/1980–17/12/1980 [loose insert].

121 SCA, MC 2008/146, Sheffield Corporation, Licensing Justices, Minutes, Box 85, 18/01/1982–04/01/1983, 121.

122 *Ibid.*

123 *Ibid.*, 181.

124 SCA, MC 2008/146, Sheffield Corporation, Licensing Justices, Minutes, Box 86, 08/01/1988–08/11/1988, 45.

125 SCA, MC 2008/146, Sheffield Corporation, Licensing Justices, Minutes, Box 87, 16/01/1986–19/12/1986 [loose insert].

126 'Late Night Drinking at Discos under Attack', *Daily Telegraph*, 14 August 1974, 17.

127 SCA, MC 2008/146, Sheffield Corporation, Licensing Justices, Minutes, Box 85, 08/02/1983–17/01/1984, 4.

128 SCA, MC 2008/146, Sheffield Corporation, Licensing Justices, Minutes, Box 85, 18/01/1982–04/01/1983, 4.

129 *Ibid.*, 1.

130 *Ibid.*

131 *Ibid.*

132 *Ibid.*, 4.

133 *Ibid.*

134 'Judge Endorses 6ft Rule for Dances', *Morning Telegraph*, 4 November 1983. Insert in SCA, MC 2008/146, Sheffield Corporation, Licensing Justices, Minutes, Box 85, 08/02/1983–17/01/1984.

135 *Ibid.*

136 SCA, MC 2008/146, Sheffield Corporation, Licensing Justices, Minutes, Box 85, 08/02/1983–17/01/1984, 2.

137 *Ibid.*, 9.

138 'Queen's Bench Division', *Justice of the Peace*, 148:17 (1984), 228.

139 SCA, MC 2008/146, Sheffield Corporation, Licensing Justices, Minutes, Box 85, 10/01/1986–02/12/1986 [loose insert].

Part II

Youth, lived experience, and identity

4

Gymslip drinkers

In 1987, the Home Office produced the Masham Report on underage drinking, finding that 20 per cent of all young men were drinking regularly in pubs and clubs by the age of 15. The drinking habits of young women, it was noted, were also a cause for grave concern. The report concluded that the current rate of alcohol consumption by teenagers was a major problem in Britain, and 'that the law regulating the consumption of alcohol by those under 18 is complicated, anomalous, and widely flouted'.[1] The report, drawn from research by the Working Group on Young People and Alcohol, made clear that rates of underage drinking were on the rise across Britain. Baroness Masham, chairperson of the working group, explained the group's findings in a November 1987 sitting of the House of Lords and suggested that 'there are not enough attractive youth facilities to draw young people away from the alcohol/pub culture'.[2] The Masham Report laid bare the growing concerns about underage drinking in post-war Britain, and sparked a national discussion about the role of alcohol in the leisure pursuits of teenagers and young adults. In highlighting a growing youth pub culture, Baroness Masham clearly pointed to the licensed spaces of youth leisure as a causal factor in these behavioural shifts.

This chapter explores the role that alcohol consumption played in the lives of British youth across the latter half of the twentieth century. In doing so it argues that alcohol consumption by teenagers and young adults is an indicator of the ordinary spectacle of post-war youth – one of the many ways in which forms of consumption practiced by adults become extraordinary when performed by young people – and reveals a particular attitude to youth consumption that prioritises narratives of risk and disruption. In particular, this chapter demonstrates that the youth-driven transformation of the urban leisurescape explored in Part I of the book went hand-in-hand with a transformed drinking culture. This transformation was temporal as well as spatial, enabled by changes in licensing laws and the stratospheric growth of commercial late-night leisure spaces. As the previous chapters have shown, both formal and informal attempts to regulate and control these spaces were rooted firmly in the recognition that they were central to

138 *Youth, lived experience, and identity*

the post-war youth experience. There was ongoing concern about the potential danger that these spaces posed to young people, and to young women in particular. These fears were particularly heightened in venues that were licensed to sell alcohol into the early hours.

The majority of academic work on teenagers and intoxication has focused extensively on teenage intoxication as a form of 'deviant' behaviour in youth cultures of the post-war period, or instead has explored the rise of teenage hedonism through drug use.[3] Where scholars have considered the relationship between young people and alcohol, much of this work is concentrated on the binge drinking panics of the 1990s and 2000s. Much less has been said, however, about the role of alcohol consumption in the leisure experiences of young people in the years before the 1990s. Indeed, it has been suggested that the 'limited quantity and variety of studies of alcohol within a leisure context stands at odds with the central position that alcohol often occupies both directly and indirectly within the leisure experience'.[4] Yet many young people regularly consumed alcohol through the post-war period and the growth, from the 1960s onwards, of youth-oriented leisure spaces that were licensed until the early hours meant that socialising in licensed bars and clubs became commonplace for many young people aged 15 and above.

While Part I of *Growing Up and Going Out* considered the spatial transformation of youth leisure in Britain, Part II turns to questions of behaviour, consumption, and identity. As such, this chapter is interested in how and why young people's relationship with alcohol shifted in the post-war period and how far alcohol consumption was built into new forms of sociability. The first part of this chapter explores the changing relationship between young people and alcohol across the second half of the twentieth century, demonstrating the extent to which alcohol became firmly engrained in the leisure choices of many adolescents and young adults. The second half of the chapter draws on oral history testimony from young people who grew up in Sheffield between the 1960s and 1980s. It considers the increasing frequency with which young people socialised in licensed venues in the city centre and what this meant for their relationship to this space. The city centre became, over this period, a central site for late-night youth leisure, and young people often navigated this in ways that provided both a spatial and temporal distance from the wider city leisurescape.

'Few people would dispute that the drinking behaviour of most adolescents has changed during the last decade': the changing shape of youthful drinking in twentieth-century Britain

While alcohol consumption has long been established as a central aspect of many forms of sociability in Britain, the relationship between youth and alcohol remained, by its very nature, problematic. The consumption of alcohol sits at the nexus of debates about harm, responsible consumption, and morality, all of which become heightened in relation to adolescence. Despite the increasing proliferation of licensed venues aimed at young consumers in the years after the 1960s, and clear evidence of a changing relationship with alcohol, historians of post-war youth have tended to overlook the role that alcohol played in young people's leisure time and sociability. There are likely several reasons for this, but I suspect the primary causes of alcohol's exemption from much youth-oriented scholarship are twofold: its position through the majority of the twentieth century as a substance legally restricted to those over the age of 18, and the relative 'ordinariness' of alcohol consumption when compared with illegal drug use. This propensity to overlook alcohol consumption obscures the fact that many young people under the age of 18 purchased, consumed, and socialised in spaces licensed to sell alcohol through the second half of the twentieth century. What is clear, however, is that the drinking patterns of young people were broadly underexplored in this earlier post-war period, even by contemporaries. Louise Jackson and Angela Bartie argue that while various anxieties about underage alcohol consumption emerged across the post-war period, 'these concerns rarely withstood detailed investigation'.[5]

Young people's drinking and, more commonly, their very proximity to alcohol has – despite often being overlooked in favour of more spectacular forms of youthful consumption – long been a cause for concern. Hogarth's infamous 1751 engraving *Gin Lane* featured, amongst wider scenes of debauchery and disarray, a drunken mother and abandoned child. Reformers in this period highlighted the gin-drinking mother 'in part because the bodily dependence between mother and child offer[ed] a way to conceptualize the harm gin causes to bodies beyond the drinker's own'.[6] Fears about maternal drinking, both highly classed and gendered, similarly occupied the concerns of moral reformers at the end of the nineteenth century. This was positioned as a 'national curse' that was causing 'domestic chaos'.[7] Fears about the harm caused to infants as a result of intoxication continued to be voiced by temperance organisations and moral reformers through the nineteenth and early twentieth centuries. The temperance group the Band of Hope, established in Leeds in 1847, encouraged children to sign a teetotal pledge and outlined the dangers – economic, moral, and bodily – of alcohol consumption.[8] Victorian and Edwardian temperance campaigners considered young people's presence in public houses 'not only morally reprehensible, but a cause of social ruin'.[9] Public houses, it was felt, exposed children and young people to loose morals and sexual impropriety, and demonstrated the worst vices of men and women. In turn, this exposure ran the risk of cementing the alehouse, tavern, or public house as a site of sociability and conviviality when young people entered adulthood, thereby repeating the cycle for a future generation.

At the turn of the twentieth century, the dangers of young people's relationship with alcohol, and their proximity to intoxication, was communicated most often in terms of the moral potential and future citizenship of youth rather than in relation to risk or public disorder.[10] This was cemented with the introduction of the 1908 Children Act, which prohibited children under the age of 14 from entering the public bars of licensed premises. While the act was unevenly applied and often flouted, its introduction 'provoked sustained controversy' in relation to young people's proximity to drunkenness.[11] While drink was positioned as an inherently public problem, one that spoke to concerns about national health, public disorder, the family, and British morality, the specific concerns attached to alcohol and youth differed in important ways in the late nineteenth and early twentieth centuries.[12] Children and young people were more likely to be identified as in need of protection from adult drinkers, or as early advocates for temperance, than they were to be the primary concern of alcohol campaigners.

In England, Wales, and Scotland, the Intoxicating Liquor Act 1923 first outlawed the purchase and consumption of alcohol in public houses to people under the age of 18, extending the 1886 ban on those under the age of 13 consuming liquor on premises licensed to sell alcohol.[13] While licensing recommendations and regulations changed across the twentieth century, and debates ensued about the dangers of 'hard' spirits versus beer and the relationship between food and alcohol consumption, the consensus that young people's access to alcohol should be controlled remained steadfast. This was, however, difficult to enforce in practice; politicians debated the feasibility of enforcing age checks on younger drinkers well into the 1980s, and the changing appearance of adolescents, coupled with significant shifts in their lifestyle choices, made ascertaining who should, and should not, be purchasing and consuming alcohol increasingly difficult through the postwar period. The rise of so-called 'gymslip drinkers' posed a serious challenge to licence holders through the second half of the twentieth century.[14]

It was in the mid-twentieth century when the drinking habits of young people themselves were placed more firmly under the microscope. Rumblings about the growing 'problem' of underage drinking can be charted through the 1940s and 1950s. The British Temperance League, for example, commissioned Mass Observation to produce a report on juvenile drinking, which found that 'the proportion of young people in pubs has increased very considerably since the outbreak of war'.[15] However the report made clear that while pub attendance by young people was on the increase, media reports about juvenile drunkenness were overexaggerated.[16] A study by the Economic Research Council in 1954 explored rising rates of drunkenness

Gymslip drinkers 141

amongst young adults, with the *Daily Mirror* decrying the 'problem of the teen-age drunks' as a result.[17] The following year, a report published by the temperance organisation United Kingdom Alliance was said to provide 'evidence of a scandal and a headache for the nation's social reformers', while in a 1958 meeting of the Chester Christian Temperance society it was reported that 'teenage tippling' was a growing threat to the nation.[18] While the relationship between young people and alcohol did not attract the same moral outrages as illicit drug use, and convictions for drunkenness amongst young people remained low, the associations made between drunkenness, violence, and promiscuity ensured that it remained a contested topic through the period.

In the 1960s and 1970s, in the wake of growing attention being given to youth lifestyles, social scientists turned their attention more directly towards the drinking habits of adolescents and young adults in Britain. A series of studies and surveys were undertaken to establish the everyday drinking habits of young people, and reflected a growing concern about the lifestyles and consumption habits of young people in this period. This was, in some regards, an attempt to provide context for sensationalist headlines of the period, many of which painted a distinct image of teenagers as driven by hedonism and undergoing a crisis of discipline. There were concerns about a wave of crime and violence driven by youth, heightened in the mid-1960s due to concerns about 'pep' pills, rising arrest and prosecution rates for young people, and youth 'mobs' descending on seaside towns and holiday destinations. Of course, much of this was a visceral reaction to the increasing visibility of youth in the 1960s, driven by rising levels of disposable income and more freedom in young people's leisure time, with the *Daily Mail* conceding that there was 'a greater readiness to report rowdy teenage behaviour'.[19] Young people themselves were keen to refute the image often painted of youth in this period as undisciplined and lacking morals. One young writer to teenage magazine *Petticoat* lamented in 1969 that 'I feel like I'm going to explode! We are constantly fed with plays on television, radio, and stage and books about teenagers. What's wrong with that? Only that they're a load of untrue rubbish!' while another declared 'I'm sure there are thousands of teenagers who want to show the world just how responsible they are'.[20] It was in this climate of contradictions and heightened passion about the image of youth that researchers sought to explore the changing consumption habits of young drinkers.

It was not, however, until the late 1960s and 1970s that large-scale research into the relationship between young people and alcohol was conducted, and many early studies were interested in the construction of the young as 'problem drinkers'. Alcohol consumption was linked to rising levels of youth violence, delinquency, and public disorder and young people,

142   *Youth, lived experience, and identity*

it was increasingly felt, were more likely to drink in ways that encouraged risky behaviours such as criminality and promiscuity. One 1970 survey of research into the question of 'problem' drinking concluded, however, that 'the evidence does not support the notion that teenagers as a group consume alcohol in an uncontrolled manner; and no simple correspondence between "permissiveness" and problem drinking, or "disapproval" and lack of problem drinking, has been demonstrated'.[21] The 'problem' of the young drinker, then, was as much a response to a constructed crisis of youth as it was a reflection of the changing consumption habits of underage drinkers.

In the early 1970s, a series of publications was produced by researchers at the University of Strathclyde working under the banner of the Social Survey Division, which sought to explore the relationship between young people and alcohol. The studies were part of a growing body of work dedicated to young people's relationship with alcohol, and were conducted against the backdrop of rising rates of alcoholism and alcohol-related illness in England and Scotland. 'Alcohol', it was argued, 'forms part of the environment of the vast majority of children in our society', and with a lack of formal teaching about alcohol consumption, children and young people's consumption of alcohol was therefore 'mostly derived from the behaviour of other people'.[22] Published in two volumes, *Children and Alcohol* (Volume I, 1972) and *Teenagers and Alcohol* (Volume II, 1972) sought to consider the implications of alcohol research for health education, arguing that this could 'encourage moderation in the use of alcohol by young people'.[23] It was also in this period that a new model of public health emerged in which 'alcohol as an issue did not just comprise concern about the "disease" of "alcoholism" ... it was potentially a matter for everyone'.[24] As Alex Mold has shown, the question of responsible alcohol consumption was high on the agenda for public health officials by the 1970s.[25] This heightened concern about responsible consumption, the rising per-capita consumption of alcohol, and associated public health implications was therefore a prevalent feature of many studies of adolescent and underage drinking in the 1970s.

In *Teenagers and Alcohol*, volume II of the study that was based on a survey of 1,321 girls and boys in Glasgow between the ages of 14 and 17, John Davies and Barrie Stacey argued that while adolescent alcohol consumption lacked 'the notoriety of drugs', there was ample evidence to demonstrate that underage drinking was 'extremely widespread'.[26] In particular, their research pointed to several key findings: that drinking in the home, or the home of a friend, was very common in younger age groups but declined as young men and women approached the age of majority; drinking habits shifted when young men and women were in the company of peers, rather than adults, with young women far more likely to drink spirits when with friends; and, by the age of 17, the public house and dance hall were the most likely venues of alcohol consumption for young men and women respectively. Over 65 per cent of those surveyed consumed alcohol outside of the home, and for those aged 16 and 17 this was increasingly likely to be in licensed spaces such as public houses or youth-oriented venues such as dance halls.[27] Davies and Stacey's research pointed clearly to a culture of underage drinking that began in the home, often initiated by 'special occasions', and moved to a more 'clandestine' culture of open-air drinking for younger adolescents, and leisure-based drinking for older adolescents and young adults.[28]

In 1978, Ann Hawker, an alcohol researcher based at the Medical Council on Alcoholism, London, argued that 'few people would dispute that the drinking behaviour of most adolescents has changed during the last decade'.[29] Hawker's study was one of the first large-scale attempts to measure the drinking habits of English youth in the post-war period, utilising a far bigger sample than Davies and Stacey at 7,306 young men and women between the ages of 13 and 18. Hawker similarly found that the majority of young people were frequent drinkers, with the frequency and location of alcohol consumption shifting according to age. Of the 17- and 18-year-olds that were surveyed, almost three-quarters described drinking once a week or more, while 65 per cent of young men and 64 per cent of young women stated that the pub was the most common place to drink.[30] Hawker's research recorded a similar shift in the patterns of underage drinking that moved into licensed spaces as the age of majority drew nearer.

The patterns established through the 1970s continued into the 1980s and, in this period, the altered drinking habits of youth were subject to far more scrutiny. Baroness Masham's 1987 report into underage drinking, sponsored by the Home Office and based on research undertaken by the Working Group on Young People and Alcohol, outlined clearly that underage drinking was firmly established in the leisure practices of young people across Britain. The story of young people's alcohol use was, the Working Group concluded, 'one chapter in the much longer tale of our society's failure to come to terms with alcohol abuse'.[31] Data from the Office of Population Census and Surveys about the drinking habits of 4,862 13- to 17-year-olds in England, Wales, and Scotland found that by the age of 17, 60 per cent of young men and 47 per cent of young women in England and Wales self-reported as regularly consuming alcohol at least once a week.[32] Of those young people who consumed alcohol by the age of 17, 68 per cent of young men and 57 per cent of young women did so in a public house or bar.[33] The Working Group, which had primarily been tasked with exploring the relationship between underage drinking and crime, concluded that 'there is evidence of regular, often illegal, drinking of alcohol by adolescents'.[34]

144   *Youth, lived experience, and identity*

Cohort study data also demonstrates clearly that alcohol consumption was a significant part of young people's lives in the latter part of the twentieth century. The National Child Development Survey (NCDS) asked respondents, all of whom were born in March 1958, about their drinking at ages 16 and 23, with data for participants across both surveys available from 9,337 individuals.[35] At age 16, participants were asked when and where they had last consumed an alcoholic drink, and at 23 about their 'usual pattern' of drinking. Results from these questions confirmed 'high levels of drinking amongst young adults', with a clear correlation between drinking behaviours established in adolescence and those undertaken in young adulthood.[36] The 1970 British Cohort Study (BCS70) ran a cohort sweep of participants at age 16 in 1986, under the name of Youthscan, and obtained data from 11,622 of the cohort. Within this, a number of questionnaires tackled issues including education, health, lifestyle, and family and friends. Several questions touched on alcohol consumption, and offered young people the opportunity to discuss their drinking habits. This study found that 45 per cent of boys and 36 per cent of girls began consuming alcohol before the age of 15, and 29 per cent of boys and 25 per cent of girls drank in 'moderate' frequency on two or three days of the week.[37]

The prevalence of underage drinking in Britain was firmly established by the 1970s and 1980s, and contemporary data demonstrated clearly that this was something young people frequently did in the company of their peers. This fact became a topic of low-level concern through the 1970s and 1980s and, as Chapter 3 showed, was tied in to wider anxieties about the 'state' of youth through this period and the dangers of irresponsible forms of consumption. In their study of young people's risk-taking behaviour, Martin and Moira Plant found that 'the majority of young people in Britain do consume alcohol and that most during their teenage years experience intoxication and other mild adverse consequences associated with drinking'.[38] What also became apparent to researchers was the role that licensed leisure spaces played in the development of young people's drinking habits, particularly for those aged 15 and above.

Hawker's 1978 study on adolescent drinking found that, for a majority of young people, pubs with attached dances were an attractive place to socialise and drink. Hawker's research hinted at a growing generational divide in people's use of public houses, suggesting that youth-oriented public houses were 'a comparatively new invention', and that 'introducing discotheques into pubs has provided young people with a combination of music and alcohol in an atmosphere which many adults do not enjoy'.[39] Further, and most importantly, Hawker argued that for those young people who chose to consume alcohol in pubs, in clubs, or at dances, they viewed 'the place where they drink as important as the drink itself'.[40] In other words, the

Gymslip drinkers

growing centrality of alcohol to young people's leisure and sociability was driven as much by the rising number of late-night venues catering to young consumers as it was by any particular desire for intoxication. Baroness Masham's Working Group similarly found that 'licensed premises appear to be an important source of alcohol to a large proportion of adolescents under 18'.[41] The growing number of young people entering and consuming alcohol in licensed spaces simultaneously increased calls to ensure their access to these spaces was restricted while exposing the difficulties of identifying underage drinkers. Judging the age of young people was becoming 'notoriously difficult', an issue which was only compounded by licensees needing to prove that they were *knowingly* selling alcohol to minors.[42] Indeed, studies on adolescent drinking from the 1980s showed that 'only a minority of teenagers reported ever having been refused alcohol in licensed premises or retail outlets because of their age'.[43]

While the spread of licensed late-night venues played a central role in the alcohol consumption of many young people in post-war Britain, growing attention was also given to the role of the off-licence in the 1970s and 1980s. Hawker's sample, for example, found that only 33 per cent of boys and 19 per cent of girls between the ages of 13 and 18 had been refused the sale of alcohol in pubs and off-licences, with the rest of the sample either reporting as non-drinkers or able to access alcohol at home.[44] The Licensing Act of 1961 extended the opening hours of off-licences, meaning they could open during the day, paving the way for the introduction of alcohol onto supermarket shelves.[45] During a debate on Licensing Reform and Alcohol Abuse in February 1987, Allan Stewart, MP for Eastwood (now East Renfrewshire) noted that a 'main area of concern is under-age drinking'.[46] Stewart highlighted that the Scottish Council on Alcohol had 'expressed considerable concern about the problem [of underage drinking]. It is worth recording that the Council attributed the problem to the spread of off-licences' and had not considered 'the relaxation of licensing hours as the source of the problem'.[47] Despite evidence showing that more young people were entering and consuming alcohol in licensed premises, the off-licence presented a particular problem as within a group of young people 'there will be one who can enter an off-licence legally to purchase alcohol for the consumption of the other members of the group'. The Working Group on Young People and Alcohol were so concerned about the role of the off-licence in encouraging public and underage drinking that they explored the potential of implementing a total ban on young people drinking in public. This suggestion was quickly rejected on the grounds of unenforceability and a reluctance to contribute to the further criminalisation of youth, but indicated clearly the apprehensions surrounding the changing landscape of youthful drinking.[48] Anxiety about youthful consumption of alcohol, then, was particularly

146 *Youth, lived experience, and identity*

conspicuous in relation to those in the transition years between adolescence and adulthood, whose proximity to intoxication held the potential to harm and disrupt both the body and body politic.

Breweries, drinks producers, and business owners recognised the growing youth market, both in the products that were sold and the operation of licensed venues. The drinking habits of young men and women in Britain were diverging quickly from the wider population, and the market embraced this wholeheartedly. Traditional public houses in towns and city centres were increasingly replaced with themed bars and refurbished pubs that sought to attract young drinkers. Competition from off-licences and supermarkets was driving up sales of alcohol for domestic consumption, and 'young drinkers of wine and lager chiefly reshaped' the public landscape of alcohol consumption.[49] Lager, in particular, emerged as the drink of choice for young men in the 1970s and 1980s. As David Gutzke aptly demonstrates, lager's explosive rise 'underlined this transformation' of young drinking habits; comprising only 4 per cent of the market in the early 1960s, lager accounted for 40 per cent of beer drunk by men under 35 by the 1980s.[50] Young women who grew up in the same period reported drinking shandy and cider, before 'progressing to drinking spirits with sweet mixers'.[51] Into the later 1980s and 1990s, young people's relationship with alcohol and its position in their pursuit of late-night leisure was transformed not only by the spaces they were drinking in, but in terms of the types of alcohol they were consuming. Young drinkers were offered an increasingly vast array of drinks with distinct marketing and packaging that spoke to their preferences for sweeter alcoholic beverages. Strong ciders and lagers, fortified wines, aperitifs, and alcopops quickly came to dominate the youth market.[52] All of this culminated in what became termed as 'sessional drinking': a distinct youth-dominated drinking binge typified by intake of often high alcohol-by-volume (ABV) drinks in a concentrated window, most often during the evening and, specifically, on weekends.[53]

Public discussion about underage drinking reached its zenith at the end of the twentieth century. Through the late 1980s and 1990s, and particularly in the run-up to the 2003 Licensing Act, anxiety about youth drinking focused not only on the growing frequency of underage drinking but on a distinct form of youth drinking: the drinking binge. While it is beyond the scope of this chapter to explore the ways that binge drinking was narrated into the twenty-first century, it is worth highlighting that concerns about drinking binges were in force several decades earlier.[54] In 1988, the Viscount of Falkland pointed to rising levels of disposable income, particularly in the south of England, as a potential cause of the disorder that was increasingly associated with town and city centres on weekends. It was, the Viscount suggested, 'a sad commentary on British life that a section of British youth

Gymslip drinkers 147

seems determined to use a large proportion of its disposable income in buying alcohol not simply for eventual consumption but for immediate consumption'.[55] He continued, 'I do not know whether this is a commentary on the dark side of our new prosperity, which has brought a great deal of affluence to young people, who are unfortunately using it in this way.' The Home Secretary under Margaret Thatcher, Douglas Hurd, characterised this disorder as caused by young drinkers with 'too much beer in their bellies, and too much money in their pockets'.[56] Such affluence, of course, tended to be concentrated very significantly in parts of London and the south east, and did not solely explain the more general rise in alcohol consumption among the young. Other contemporary research, however, also indicated a move towards drinking 'binges', with the National Youth Bureau reporting to the Working Group on Young People and Alcohol that:

> It is seen as common practice for some young people to receive the dole cheque and then have a 'binge' that weekend, living quite poorly therefore for the next two weeks. This is seen as an alleviation of their difficulties.[57]

Indeed, a group of friends who grew up in Sheffield during the heightened years of youth unemployment in the 1980s quipped: 'we were all on the dole … we'd get our £30 in one building and move on and spend it in the next one!'[58] However, as noted by various police forces and local authorities, and as demonstrated in Chapter 3, the weekend disorder identified here was present across many parts of the United Kingdom and was linked directly to both the growing number of licensed venues aimed at young consumers and the extension of opening hours until the early hours of the morning. That anxiety at the youth drinking 'binge' was simultaneously laid at the door of both affluence and unemployment, however, suggests a more wholesale change in youth behaviours. The material difference in this behavioural change was the perceived meaning attached to it: young people's alcohol consumption was positioned as either a symptom of unbridled celebration or desperate escapism.

While there was growing concern about the increasingly spectacular nature of youth drinking, many commentators also highlighted the dangers of drunkenness becoming an ordinary part of young people's leisured landscape. In the first meeting of the Working Group on Young People and Alcohol, one headteacher and member of the Teachers' Advisory Council on Alcohol and Drug Education felt it was important that one of the group's primary aims should be to 'reassert the priority of alcohol education'.[59] It was, they felt, wrong that 'alcohol education took second place to education about drugs'. The focus on education was carried through the Working Group's research, and their final recommendations pointed clearly to the

148   *Youth, lived experience, and identity*

importance of education as a tool in tackling both underage drinking and alcohol misuse amongst the young. The Masham Report stated that the law alone was not enough to 'explain the reasons why alcohol consumption needs to be regulated for the good of society and the individual'.[60] It was clear the members of the Group were concerned about the lack of general education available around alcohol use, both in formal settings such as schools and informal settings such as the home. In a rather damning summary of the situation, the report argued that:

> alcohol abuse is often seen as secondary to, and in some cases preferable to, other forms of drug abuse: this is not the case. Alcohol abuse accounts for ten times the number of young people's deaths caused by illicit drug use. For that reason, alcohol education should form part of a broad approach to drug education.[61]

It is clear that, by the end of the 1980s, it was felt by some that the nature of young people's drinking required a more critical intervention in the fields of public health and health education. It was no longer enough, many commentators felt, to assume that illicit drug use was necessarily more dangerous or harmful than alcohol consumption for young people in Britain. This concern was only compounded in the following decades as the alcoholic products marketed at young drinkers diversified in both flavour and strength.[62]

While a lack of centralised data makes it difficult to chart the drinking practices of British youth, surveys, cohort data, and contemporary studies do show clearly the presence of alcohol consumption during young people's leisure time across the post-war period. This demonstrates in marked terms the central role that intoxication played in the lives of British youth and suggests that, by the end of the twentieth century, young people's consumption of alcohol was part of a much broader lifestyle shift towards late-night leisure that had, for many, the spaces of drinking at its core.

Late-night leisure and the transformation of youthful sociability

Contemporary data indicates a clear shift in the frequency and amount of alcohol that young people were consuming and, as they reached the ages of 15 and above, that much of this consumption was happening outside of the home, often in licensed venues. This is borne out in oral history interviews conducted with those who grew up in Sheffield between the 1960s and 1980s. Oral history testimony, unlike quantitative survey data, offers crucial insights into how young people understood the relationship between

Gymslip drinkers 149

alcohol and their teenage sociability and, just as importantly, how alcohol consumption may have shaped their movements through the urban leisurescape. Valentine et al. argued that for people who reached young adulthood between the 1960s and 1980s, alcohol consumption 'was an important means of joining in or participating in social networks'.[63] The remainder of this chapter explores the experiences of young people who grew up in Sheffield between the 1960s and 1980s, a period in which the city's leisure landscape changed dramatically, as did the lifestyles of the young people who moved through it. It argues that while the leisure spaces available to young people in the city were increasingly oriented around the consumption of alcohol, young people's experience of these spaces often remained explicitly gendered. For young women in the 1960s in particular, their presence in these spaces was often part of a complex negotiation between autonomy and expectation. It also demonstrates that while the spaces in which alcohol was consumed were increasingly important to the youth leisurescape, sociability remained the primary draw.

For young people growing up and going out in the city in the 1960s, the opportunities for late-night leisure were limited. As Chapter 1 demonstrated, the first late-night clubs and purpose-built nightclubs in Sheffield didn't open until the second half of the decade, while the city's unlicensed beat clubs came under regular fire from both police and licensing authorities. Despite this, Sheffield's teenagers saw the city and its licensed leisure spaces as important sites of sociability. When asked how often she socialised Trish, a teenager in the mid-1960s, responded: 'I'd go out Friday, Saturday, possibly Sunday, erm, then eventually Thursday … it was just socialising, and just to be out, not to be in.' Trish's statement that 'it was … just to be out' demonstrates clearly the importance of space outside of the home for many young people in post-war Britain. Over the course of the post-war period, the act of going 'down town' became an established and recognised part of many young people's lifestyles, and the weakening of wider social and gender conventions that had dictated much of the pre-war and immediate post-war landscape of young people's social lives offered new opportunities for young people, and for young women in particular.

Trish's testimony revealed that the majority of her socialising with friends occurred outside of the house. After detailing how often she socialised away from the home, she went on to say: 'we had, me and my friends had a pub run, and we'd have a big gang of friends and you'd meet them in … the Cossack'. Trish went on to list the venues her and her friends would move between: all were public houses and all were in the city centre. Another interviewee, David, portrayed a similar lifestyle. David recalled spending a lot of his time in Sheffield's rock pubs: 'Well we all used to meet up in the various rock pubs in Sheffield. The Albert, the Nelson, the Buccaneer, all

150   *Youth, lived experience, and identity*

those. We were regulars in those places.' It was, of course, in this period that many public houses sought to appeal to a younger demographic; by introducing live performances and recorded music, a number of the city's public houses were effectively reoriented towards a younger customer base. As Chapter 3 showed, public houses became an important part of the live music scene for young people. In the Derbyshire town of Staveley, for example, one landlady's 20-year-old son ran beat sessions through the mid-1960s that attracted young people from across the South Yorkshire region.[64] David recalled how City Hall would host big name acts, but the city's public houses were an important site for smaller bands and local music.

One key development was the emergence of Sheffield's folk scene which, by the mid-1960s, was firmly established on the city's cultural circuit. David was heavily involved in Sheffield's folk scene throughout the 1960s and 1970s, and his experiences of folk music in the city's public houses over the course of the 1960s resonated with other interviewees of the period. Folk was a particularly influential scene in Sheffield in the 1960s, with two pubs, the Highcliffe and the Three Cranes, at its centre. Of the people interviewed about their youth in the 1960s, three spoke at length about the city's folk clubs. Trish explained she 'didn't go to the [night]clubs ... so mainly it was sort of going to pubs'. She went on to tell me about her music tastes and said there were:

> Two strands. A bit of folk music, there was the folk club at the Three Cranes which was a big folk club and Sheffield has still got a bit folk scene and that's probably the bit that's stayed with me the most.

The folk club at the Three Cranes was called the Barley Mow, and it was established in 1964. Sheffield-born J. P. Bean, author of *Singing From the Floor: A History of British Folk Clubs*, recalled his first ventures to the Barley Mow at 16 'as a marvellous place to be'.[65] Bean described how 'the L-shaped room held about forty people comfortably, but up to 140 crammed in – sitting, squatting, standing, wedged against the walls and perched on the piano'. The British folk revival began in the mid-1950s, but it was in the 1960s when Sheffield's folk scene took off. David explained that the folk scene 'was a big one ... I used to go to folk clubs on Saturday night. Thursday nights, Friday nights. There was an awful lot of folk music in Sheffield'. The Highcliffe folk club began in 1967, and clubs like this were described by Bean as an early form of 'mini-concert venues'. It was host to the early gigs of well-known musicians such as Billy Connolly and Gerry Rafferty's Humblebums, Barbara Dickinson, and John Martyn. Sue, a student at the Sheffield School of Art in the mid-to-late 1960s, remembered that there were 'all sorts of the, the best of the best in contemporary

Gymslip drinkers 151

folk and blues played at our local pub which was just amazing'. She continued:

> I loved the music there because it was blues and contemporary folk, and it was always something new. And also, it was very fashionable at the time. It was the era of Bob Dylan, Simon and Garfunkel, all of these sort of, contemporary folk type people. So the fact that it was one of the best folk clubs in England … I came to some of the other ones, I went to the Beehive, and the Grapes, but the Highcliffe was the best. I was just lucky I think.

Sheffield's folk clubs provided a space for young people to converge and express their cultural interests outside of the home. Michael Brocken explored the divides in the folk revival movement of the 1950s and 1960s and argued that by the early 1960s, there was a 'clearly defined generation gap' between the traditional and contemporary folk movements, with the contemporary folk movement appealing primarily to younger fans.[66] By allowing contemporary folk clubs to be held in their venues, the landlords of these pubs were actively trying to attract a younger audience, and in turn this cemented the public house as a site of both leisure and sociability for young music fans.

Sue had a distinct experience as a teenager in the city as her social life was focused principally around the epicentre of the art college, which was within walking distance of her family home. Unlike David and Trish, who socialised primarily in the city centre, the key sites of Sue's social life were based away from the city centre and relatively close to her neighbourhood in the south west of the city. However, as Sue's social group was made up predominantly of art students rather than local residents, she was offered a relative level of separation from the traditional neighbourhood social scene despite its close proximity to her familial home. Sue's interview again demonstrates the frequency with which she socialised outside of the home. Sue said:

> I went out every night except Sunday night when I was at art college. Every Wednesday was the Shades, and every Friday was the, no no no, every Saturday was the Shades. Every Friday was the Highcliffe … and then the other nights I would be in the Banner [Cross] … I would go there straight from art college and then it was walking distance from home so I'd walk home every evening.

The experiences of Sue, David, and Trish demonstrate that young people were carving out spaces for themselves in Sheffield's licensed leisurescape in the 1960s, often aided by the city's landlords. While the city's night-time economy remained in its relative infancy, publicans that embraced the new

Figure 4.1 Entrance to Shades nightclub, Ecclesall Road, Sheffield, est 1968. © Ray Brightman and Picture Sheffield.

young consumer by staging live music and singing offered the chance for new forms of youthful sociability that placed the public house at its heart.

However, not all young people took the opportunity to socialise away from home throughout the week. Pat, a teenager in the late 1960s, tended to go out once or twice a week, and generally at weekends. She described finishing her Saturday job and heading into town: 'we'd go for a coffee, we might go to the Top Rank'. Similarly Kevin, who was married at 19, said:

> I had a Saturday job ... on the Moor [central Sheffield] when I was going out with my wife before we were married and I got £1.25 a day for it. I'd bank 25p of it and spend the rest. And that lasted me all week including going out. It'd usually be Friday, Saturday nights we'd go out.

Kevin also limited his going out to the weekends when he was at school. When asked how often he went out he said 'oh only once, maybe twice a week'. Marian, a teenager in the late 1960s and early 1970s, told a similar story: 'I would say we probably went out every Friday and some Saturdays, but in the holidays it would be more daytimes because we didn't live close to each other.' Marian, whose grammar school friends came from a large

Gymslip drinkers   153

catchment area across the city, explained that 'our parents were very much involved until we were eighteen. It would take half the night to get there on the bus so one father would bring us back one week and one father the other week.' For Marian and her friends, who did not live close to each other, location was one of the primary factors in their lifestyle choices; the centrality and increasing consolidation of leisure spaces in the immediate city centre was a central factor in her decision to socialise there at weekends. Indeed, Marian recalled taking advantage of study time during her A-levels in the early 1970s: 'we used to go in the library when we were studying for A-levels then go to the Buccaneer afterwards in school uniform!' The Buccaneer, an underground rock pub housed under the Grand Hotel in the city centre and a short walk from the Central Library, was utilised as a convivial and convenient space by Marian and her friends during their period of study leave; their usually disparate locations, and the logistical difficulties of arranging travel at night, ensured they took advantage of leisure opportunities when they could.

The amount of time that young people spent away from the family home varied amongst different types of groups, and by location, but research interviews indicate that for many young people by the 1960s and early 1970s, the act of socialising with friends away from the home, predominately in licensed leisure spaces, was becoming a common lifestyle choice. Of the interviews conducted with participants who were teenagers in the 1960s, only a minority would regularly stay out later than the closing time of pubs; this was due as much to logistics – being able to get the last bus, access, and the suburban location of many of the clubs in Sheffield at the time – as it was about desire. These external factors serve as an important reminder that many young people's experiences of evening leisure were limited by structural factors such as location, family commitments, and access to adequate disposable income. However, these experiences show clearly that the public house was becoming a key site of sociability for many young men and women through the 1960s, and that being of school age did not preclude their entrance into these spaces.

By the 1970s, the frequency with which young people were socialising in the city's evening leisure venues was increasing; the introduction of late-night venues onto Sheffield's licensed scene ensured not only that the city's young people continued to socialise in the city-centre, but that they were increasingly socialising into the early hours of the morning. The city's burgeoning student population helped fuel this further, bringing with them the introduction of mid-week 'student' nights where drinks deals were plentiful.[67] Gillian, a teenager in the mid-to-late 1970s, recalled going out regularly during the middle of the week because it was cheaper. She said: 'we used to be clubbing in the middle of the week. You'd get in at two or three

154   *Youth, lived experience, and identity*

[am] and get up for work the next day.' Similarly Helen, who moved into Sheffield city centre from the outskirts of the city to study at the nursing college in the late 1970s, said: 'I was living in the Nurses' Home, it was a bit of a culture change. I'd got a bit of a wage coming in and we would come out into town quite frequently into the student places where drinks were cheaper.'

As the number of late-night venues available for young people increased through the 1970s and 1980s, so did the frequency with which young people were accessing them. Juan, a student and teenager in the late 1970s and early 1980s, recalled:

> When I was off on my hols [from University] it probably would have been three, four nights, I mean I was out all the time. Yeah … I definitely did R&Js [Romeo's and Juliet's] definitely did Tuesdays and I definitely did Thursdays and Saturdays it was switching between the different clubs.

Similarly, Jacqueline recalled: 'It got to the point where I'd go out three, four times a week. But for different places.' When asked how often she socialised outside of the home, Debbie, a teenager in the late 1970s, explained:

> *D:* I went out, I would say, a good three or four, five times a week.
> *S:* Every week?
> *D:* Every week! Staying in? [shakes head]

By the late 1970s and early 1980s, going out multiple times during the week and at weekends to socialise in the city's late-night leisure spaces was not uncommon for many of Sheffield's teenagers. Adrian, who grew up in the late 1980s, explained:

> But I think that's maybe one reason why nightclubs at that time had such a hold on, they had such a vital place in people's lives because if you weren't going home at half ten they were the only place you could be.

The late closing hours of 2 a.m. for many nightclubs was three and a half hours after the closing time of the city's pubs. As such, the city centre was frequented predominantly by young people during these late hours, creating a temporal separation between young and 'traditional' drinkers.

This temporal shift had significant logistical implications for young people, particularly those with limited disposable income. Walking home at night was, for many young people, whether by reason of distance or safety, simply not viable, while a private taxi cab was often prohibitively expensive. As such, public transport acted as a key tool that enabled young people to

Gymslip drinkers

155

navigate the city after dark. Following the Local Government Act of 1974, Sheffield's buses were run by South Yorkshire Passenger Transport Executive (SYPTE).[68] Throughout the 1970s, and until the deregulation of SYPTE in 1986, a 2 a.m. night bus would run from the city centre after the 'last bus' of the night which, depending on the route, usually departed between 11 p.m. and 11.30 p.m.[69] The introduction of subsidised travel by the city's Labour council in the 1970s, a central policy in their 'locally useful' socialism, meant that children and teenagers could travel for 2p and adults for 10p and, as such, the buses in Sheffield were accessible to young people with limited disposable income, enabling them to move through the city with ease. Indeed, a significant number of those interviewed who were teenagers and young adults in the 1970s and 1980s discussed the importance of the late-night bus, indicating the central role it played in the nights out of many young people in the city. This policy was particularly transformative for young people receiving unemployment benefit, who were able to travel across the city regularly to see friends and socialise. The low cost of the night bus when compared to the taxi reinforces the importance of public transport to many young people; it provided them with low-cost mobility, enabling them to access to evening leisure without relying on parental transport or significant levels of disposable income.

Juan recalled: 'So you ended up two o'clock bus or whatever … luckily the bus that I got was the 75 route [and that] just came out at two o'clock.' Similarly, Jackie, a teenager in the early 1980s, relied on the late-night bus as part of her cheap weeknights out:

> There were other nights you came into town [on the bus], 2p, and you'd go clubbing, like Isabella's, it was a nurses' night on a Tuesday … so you'd catch the night bus back, there used to be a night bus back, so our taxis even then used to be £5 … so you'd have to catch a night bus.

Tamar, a teenager in the mid-to-late 1980s, also recalled that after her nights out 'the way home was the night buses, the quarter past two night buses. And that was sort of where everybody converged.' Darren, also a teenager in the mid-1980s, recalled the scenes in the city centre following the departure of the last bus:

> A taxi rank used to be in there [Fitzalan Square, city centre] as well, black cabs would be queueing, on the top side. And at two o'clock, quarter-past two, there'd be a massive queue there, because the last buses had gone.

The departure of the last bus of the night acts as a powerful image of the changing landscape of the post-war city after dark: where night buses were once the mainstay of shift workers in Sheffield's heavy industry, they were now utilised by young consumers of the city's nightlife.

The later opening hours of nightclubs, paired with the option to socialise until 2 a.m., introduced a temporal separation between the cultural experiences of young adults and wider society in the city. Following the departure of the 11 p.m. bus, and with it the departure of the 'traditional' drinker, the city centre at night had become, by the 1970s and 1980s, a place dedicated to the hedonistic pursuits of youth. Young people's capacity to navigate this, though, often remained dependent on their proximity to public transportation.

'Mum and dad didn't like me going into pubs. You'll meet the wrong sort of people I was told': gender and generational difference in drinking experiences

While access to an increasing variety of leisure options left its mark on the majority of young people's lifestyles, it was arguably young women who experienced the greatest level of change. Between the 1960s and 1980s, it was becoming socially acceptable, and relatively common, for groups of young, unmarried women to socialise until the early hours, providing them with greater autonomy and more varied opportunities for leisure than their pre-war counterparts. However, the experiences of these young women were mediated through the lens of contemporary society. Despite the increasing number of leisure options available to young women, important differences remained, both in terms of how men and women used the licensed spaces of youth leisure and how men and women experienced these spaces.

Perhaps one of the biggest shifts over the period was the frequency with which young women were socialising in drinking establishments. Women's entry into the male-dominated world of public houses was a lengthy process and by no means confined to the years after the Second World War. Following gains during and after the First World War, David Gutzke suggests that 'the emergence of companionate marriage offered wives and courting women the chance to share with the men in their lives' wider leisure activities'.[70] However, the post-war years increasingly saw women socialising in licensed leisure spaces without men, and the rise of the 'girls' night out' as an important part of many young women's social landscape is an important manifestation of this change. Laura Fenton has argued that access to alcohol, and the spaces in which it was consumed, acted as 'a means of laying claim to a young adult subjectivity' for young women in post-war Britain.[71] Societal stigma towards women in pubs was lifting by the 1970s, no doubt helped by the rise of youth-oriented drinking establishments. Indeed, Gutzke notes that in 1970, pub avoidance by women in the 18–24 range was only 17 per

Gymslip drinkers

cent compared with their mothers' generation at 36 per cent, suggesting that social boundaries were shifting and it was no longer seen as inappropriate for young women to socialise in drinking establishments.[72] This is borne out in data from contemporary studies, with one 1976 study suggesting that women's presence in youth-oriented bars was a central part of their appeal for young men.[73] Pearl Jephcott similarly noted, several decades earlier, that 'social habits are changing' and it was 'the recognised custom at many dances to go in and out of the [dance] hall to the pub opposite'.[74]

However, whilst the presence of young women in drinking establishments was becoming more common, women made clear distinctions between different types of establishments and their decisions about which ones to socialise in were carefully considered. Gutzke argues that 'drinking etiquette powerfully sustained masculine culture and dominance, discouraging most unescorted women from encroaching on men's leisure space well into the 1980s'.[75] Phil Hadfield similarly demonstrates that, for those traditional drinking venues which remained 'physically and/or culturally and aesthetically removed from the main drinking circuits', informal methods of social and moral governance that deterred unaccompanied women from entering continued.[76] As such, women were not regularly entering pubs dominated by 'traditional' drinkers; instead, they took advantage of the increasing number of city-centre bars and clubs designed with the young drinker in mind, and where the determining factors of 'masculine culture and dominance' were replaced by age.

The gendered experience of pub-going was particularly pronounced in the 1960s. Of the women who grew up in the 1960s, socialising in public houses was often presented as a somewhat transgressive act. Their experiences suggest that young women's leisure choices, which had historically been far more limited than their male counterpoints by means of family and domestic responsibilities, remained curtailed in the post-war period.[77] One interviewee, Pat, explained that she 'didn't go into pubs, because mum and dad didn't like me going into pubs. You'll meet the wrong sort of people I was told.' The attitude of Pat's parents was not uncommon. In a wider conversation about parental expectations, Sue explained that her parents were

> Very working class, and strode very hard to be respectable and my dad especially was very restrictive with times I had to be in by and what I could be seen to do and what I could not be seen to do. So most of the time I had to be careful not to be seen to do! ... They believed in the 1950s version of respectability, and so, I did have a fight on my hands.

She went on to explain that how this attitude affected her behaviour in public houses:

158 *Youth, lived experience, and identity*

> There was a struggle there, yes ... There was a way that you needed to behave, you couldn't be seen to be drunk because then you would be throwing away your right. You would be proving the 1950s attitude right. So to some extent you were fighting for your freedom, but you were also fighting for your dignity. You were fighting to be taken seriously ... and women, especially bearing in mind we'd only just grabbed the right to go into pubs on our own, if we then acted like we couldn't take it, we would have been proving the point of the older generation.

Sue's belief in the need to be taken seriously by other drinkers suggests that her decision to drink in public houses held a more significant meaning to her than as simply being somewhere to socialise; she felt that her existence in that space was part of a delicate societal negotiation, and perceived this change as something that was hard won, but precarious. Helena Mills has argued that the 1960s was witness to 'new opportunities for British young women', and that they were encouraged 'to pursue self-fulfilment and self-expression. However, these new possibilities often conflicted with older values and expectations that privileged duty, self-sacrifice, marriage and motherhood'.[78] Sue's discussion of the '1950s attitude' of her parents speaks clearly to Mills's argument, suggesting that Sue's lifestyle was in conflict with the expectations placed on her by her family. Valentine et al. suggest that a 'moral hangover' continued through the post-war period, in which women drinking in public were 'expected to retain self-control and manage their performance of the self when doing so'.[79] Sue hid her pub-going from her parents as she knew they wouldn't approve. She recalled:

> I do remember my dad finding out that I was spending my lunchtimes in the Banner [Cross] when I was sixteen, because his cousin worked in the pork shop across the road and had seen me! Erm, but it didn't seem to be as bad going in at lunchtime. But at night time, well of course I went in every night as well! But some things, there were some things he just couldn't fight.

Sue's recollection that frequenting the pub during the day 'didn't seem to be as bad' sits parallel to Trish's memory of attending the late-opening coffee bar La Favourita, explored in Chapter 1, as 'very daring'. This belief also speaks to the liminal world of the modern urban night, in which the same neighbourhoods and venues had the potential to be transformed into spaces of transgression after dark.

Pat, while not socialising in pubs, was going to nightclubs such as the Top Rank Suite from the age of 15. However, she also explained how her leisure choices were curtailed by what her father would allow her to do. She recalled:

Gymslip drinkers 159

As soon as I started working, dad said well if you're old enough to start doing that you're old enough to go but I had to either get the last bus home or he'd come into town to fetch me. We'd finished at 11 [p.m.]. We had to be back home.

Despite working and having her own disposable income, Pat's cultural experiences were determined by what her father felt was acceptable. Socialising late at night therefore remained a transgressive act for many young women in the 1960s. Mills has further argued that 'young women were subject to stricter parental control than their brothers'.[80] Indeed, Sue recalled how her brother used this fact to keep the city's evening leisure spaces for himself. She said:

My brother was three years older and he went to the Mojo and the Esquire, and saw Dave Berry and all the, all the blues singers over from America you know your Long John Baldry's and people like that. Er, but he made damn sure that I didn't, he made it all sound so serious that I couldn't possibly be allowed to go so I didn't get to go to any of those places for which Sheffield was very famous for at the time.

The experiences of Pat and Sue suggest that the position of women in public spaces, particularly spaces such as the traditionally masculine pub, were being renegotiated in this period. Whilst Pat was simply not allowed in to pubs, and did not seek to challenge her parents on this, Sue positioned her presence in this space as a complex negotiation between her own desires and what she perceived to be her precariously won rights as a young woman in this space.

Of the women who grew up in the 1970s and 1980s, however, few referred to public houses and bars as places that were out of bounds to them. Indeed, for many young women, the public house and bar became a central part of the 'girls' night out'. While there had been a significant cultural shift in the previous decade that had given many women the opportunity to pursue new forms of late-night leisure, young women still exercised clear choices over which type of licensed venue they would socialise in. However, these choices were often incorporated into a distinctly gendered pattern of late-night drinking. Jacqueline recalled:

There used to be some nights where all the boys would come into town and it was quite sex divided. So the boys would go out on their own, and the girls would go out on their own. And on a Friday night there was a set pub routine and then you'd meet at certain points if you'd got a boyfriend to go home.

160 *Youth, lived experience, and identity*

She continued:

> If you were on a proper night out with like the girls you'd come into town on a Friday and you'd go to the Stone House which is near to where TK Maxx is now and then you'd go down by the Cathedral on Trippett Lane, all of those, and Dove and Rainbow and then you'd go to a club.

Similarly, Helen recalled visiting certain city-centre pubs when she went out with her female nursing friends:

> Used to be the Museum ... there was the Stone House, that was very smart back in the day ... there was the Mulberry Tavern, there was the Dove and Rainbow.

Gillian drew a distinction between going out with a big group and just going 'out with the girls', suggesting that the 'girls' night' was becoming a more important part of young women's sociability. She recalled going to

> Romeo's and Juliet's and places like that when it was the girls ... but you see when I went to the more rock ones, [that] was when I was seeing someone who was more into that type of music.

When the experiences of women who grew up in the 1970s and 1980s are compared to the responses of interviewees from the 1960s such as Pat and Sue, it is possible to suggest that over the course of the 1960s and 1970s, a subtle but significant culture shift had occurred in which regularly socialising and drinking alcohol in city centre venues was no longer viewed as off-limits to groups of young women. Indeed, the 'girls' night out' formed a central part of young women's sociability in the latter decades of the twentieth century and, as Robert Hollands argued, socialising with friends was for many women 'the single most important reason for having nights out'.[81]

The lives of young women changed in important ways between the 1960s and 1970s. While the behaviour and lifestyles of young women growing up in the 1960s were still subject to ongoing criticism and control, particularly by family members, the rise of youth-oriented spaces provided an alternative to the continuing dominance of traditional masculinity that had previously excluded young women from many licensed leisure spaces. By the 1970s, these spaces had been established as key sites of sociability, and were built into new gendered patterns of leisure.

Figure 4.2 Promotional image for the opening of the Stone House, Sheffield, 1971. © Sheffield Newspapers Ltd and Picture Sheffield.

'Going out and copping off was just a bit of fun': evening leisure spaces as sites for sexual encounters

The development of evening leisure space for young people provided heterosexual adolescents with new ways to meet and engage with members of the opposite sex. Commercial leisure space had, through the nineteenth and twentieth centuries, acted as a central site for courtship, romance, and

162   *Youth, lived experience, and identity*

sexual excitement.[82] Dance floors in particular had functioned as a fundamental and, on the whole, socially accepted site for multiple generations of courting youths to seize brief moments of close contact. However, as Part I of this book demonstrates, associations between the urban night and sexual or moral transgression did not necessarily diminish in the twentieth century, and the developments of the second half of the century in the sphere of late-night leisure did nothing to dispel these fears. For young people themselves, however, new opportunities for courtship and, increasingly, casual moments of sexual connection, could be found.

Accessing the sexual behaviour of adolescents and young adults poses significant challenges, and often comes with severe limitations. Hannah Charnock asserts that sexuality is a 'dimension of young people's lived experiences that we know much less about' in comparison to the wider transformation of sexuality in the post-war period.[83] The personal nature of sexual relations often predicates its absence in the archives, forcing historians to rely on sporadic, and often limited, contemporary studies into sexuality.[84] Indeed, studies into the sexual behaviour of heterosexual adolescents in the post-war period are scarce, and the majority of this work is focused on the 1960s, forcing Lesley Hall to conclude that 'at the end of the seventies, once again the picture is ambiguous'.[85] Studies conducted at the time do offer a glimpse into the changing attitudes and behaviours of young people with regards to sexuality and sexual activity. Michael Schofield's now influential study *The Sexual Behaviour of Young People* found that of 415 girls under the age of 16, only 6 per cent had any sexual experience, and this number rose to 16 per cent when girls over the age of 16 were asked.[86] However, by 1980, figures suggest that this had changed significantly or, at the very least, that young women were more openly discussing sexual activity. In April 1980, *19* magazine published the results of a survey of ten thousand women. The magazine stated that 'taking all girls under 21 ... 26% claimed to have had their first sexual experience before the age of 16. Of all sexually experienced girls ... 39% claimed to have had sexual experience at under 16 years of age.'[87] This was also a period in which sexual knowledge was made more readily available to young people through books and magazines; a new sexual morality was constructed that recognised young people's sexual agency, while maintaining clear boundaries around acceptable performances of sexuality.[88]

While there was by no means a complete sexual revolution in terms of attitudes and behaviours, there was in this period a move towards cohabitation, increased likelihood of pre-marital sex and 'heavy petting', all of which changed the ways in which young people communicated, expressed, and experienced their sexuality. Claire Langhamer suggests that disparities in the naming of courtship practices indicates 'a potential instability and

Gymslip drinkers

re-working of established models within the intimate personal relations of youth across the central years of the twentieth century'.[89] These trends, first identified in the mid-twentieth century, continued into the 1970s and 1980s and signified important changes to the sexual behaviours and courtship rituals of young people. Oral testimony certainly suggests that events such as the 2 a.m. dance at the end of an alcohol-fuelled night at the discotheque or nightclub were part of a widening casualisation of courtship practices amongst heterosexual youth. These behaviours developed in tandem with the spaces young people moved through: the anonymity provided by the dance floor, dark corners, and flashing lights of the nightclub, alongside its relative separation from the outside world, allowed young people to engage in more casual and overtly sexual forms of courtship. The experiences explored in the following pages support Charnock's claim that 'sexual behaviour changed in accordance with emerging social codes that positioned sexual knowledge and experience as components of social status and reputation'.[90] Engaging in sexual activity and, critically, being seen to do so, comprised an important part of both young men and women's sexual encounters and their homosocial relationships.

The developing night-time economy was, by the 1970s and 1980s, increasingly geared towards facilitating sexual encounters between heterosexual youths. Hollands and Chatterton argue that the urban nightscape was subject to an increasing feminisation in the late twentieth century, one that was tied in closely with the process of gentrification. This nightlife 'feminisation' was not solely structured around sexual opportunity; young professional women were a growing and important part of the night-time economy, and the new spaces of youth leisure competed to attract young women on their own terms.[91] However, Phil Hadfield notes that these new venues served a distinct social function, in which 'the sociability of neighbourhood and work gives way to the search for excitement, sexual encounter, and spectacle'.[92] These developments were not unique to Britain, and Jerald Cloyd identified the emergence of 'market-place bars' in the United States that catered 'specifically to young and usually single persons interested in meeting and possibly having sexual encounters with persons of a similar orientation'.[93] The prioritisation or pursuit of sexual experience was not driven solely by young people, however. This was built into the very fabric of mainstream nightclubs by the 1970s and 1980s, both in the built environment of the club – a dance floor surrounded by space to watch – and in its economic model.[94] As Mecca's Ivor Rabin explained in 1974, modern dance halls explicitly sought to offer the 'boy meets girl thing'.[95]

This economic model capitalised on a much longer history of dance floors as sites for sexual encounter and excitement and, as Jon Stratton argues, it was only in the 1950s that the strict conventions of white

164 *Youth, lived experience, and identity*

heterosexual dancing in Britain began to change.[96] In Britain's queer leisure venues – many advertised clearly, and many others which survived as long as they 'fell below the radar' – alternative spaces of social and sexual interaction were increasingly carved out away from the growing 'straight' scene.[97] As Daryl Leeworthy has argued, 'discos and dances were an essential part of the culture of queer liberation' in post-war Britain and 'the experience of going out and coming together helped to build individual and collective understandings of queerness'.[98] The desire for alternative spaces were driven by a range of factors, including seeking safety, acceptance, sociability, and community, and was further exacerbated by the privileging of heterosexual encounters in mainstream commercial leisure venues. Door policies managed the ratio of customers to ensure an equal split between men and women, while the management of dance floors ensured that dancers toed the fine line between sexual opportunity and sexual transgression.

While the formal partnered dancing found in dance halls in the nineteenth and early twentieth centuries had gradually been replaced by solo and group dancing, the dance floor continued to offer the possibility of romantic (or sexual) exchange for heterosexual teenagers and young adults. Both Tony and Debbie, teenagers in the late 1970s, recalled the ritual of the last dance, a slow song geared towards couples, many of whom may have met that night. Debbie said:

> And at the end they always used to play something like the Blue Danube so if you'd copped off with a lad, you'd always have the last dance, like a snoggy dance with him. But if you didn't cop off with anybody you'd go and get your coat!

Both Tony and Debbie saw this element of their weekends as casual encounters. Debbie said that:

> If you wanted to see them again you'd arrange to meet somewhere ... but often you didn't want to see them next Saturday because you wanted to meet somebody else do you know what I mean! And then you'd let him buy you a couple of drinks, you'd have a dance, you'd have a snog with him. And then you'd think, oh beer goggles. I don't think so!

Tony talked at length about meeting women on nights out with his friends, and unlike Debbie, this activity was built into the homosocial rituals of the night out. Tony recalled frequenting the Wig and Pen, a public house in the city centre, because 'all the solicitors would go there – and the solicitors' secretaries!' He also explained that he and his friends:

Gymslip drinkers

were a group of lads from what most people would say was the rougher end of town, so we used to come through to Abbeydale and Fulwood and the posher end, and it's very, very laddish, and I suppose a sign of the times, but that's where all the posh girls were. We were always on the lookout, should you say.

This 'laddish' behaviour continued into the weekend, when Tony and his friends would compete to spend the evening with the most attractive girl.

> They'd all have their handbags, dancing round their handbags sort of thing – and we'd all be nodding and voting sort of thing, and when it got to the New York, New York at the end of the night and you'd done the two o'clock dance and had a smooch and changed phone numbers – always got a fake phone number to give them – and then it got to New York and lights would go up and that was it really. We'd all go and queue up for a taxi. But the guy who'd won would be going out on the following Saturday night for free. We would cover his drinks. So there was a real element of competition to win. A real prize for next week if you went out the following week on a free night out so there was a real, yeah it got very competitive.

Darren explained: 'I don't really like nightclubs. I've never really been into them. I used to go because it was the thing to do and it was where all the girls were basically. But that's the only reason.' This attitude was mirrored in an article in Sheffield's local newspaper the *Star* about the city's nightlife, where it was reported that 'as far as meeting new friends is concerned, the lads are … enthusiastic'.[99] A study from 1990 similarly noted that sex and courtship were 'major attractions' for young men on nights out. 'The sociability of working men' it was observed, 'has given way to the "on the town" package of "posing"'.[100] For Jon Stratton, this points to the fact that these environments were 'fundamentally heterosexual' in their nature.[101]

However, for the women attending these nightclubs, male attention was not always welcome. Indeed, Gillian recalled that the sexualised nature of many commercial nightclubs and bars often made her feel uncomfortable. Of the Stone House – one example of the new 'branded' pubs aimed at young drinkers in Sheffield – she said:

> I never liked places like that though because it was always girls dancing round their handbags, you'd got to dress up, and all the lads just leering round the sides which is why I preferred places that were a bit more down to earth.

Gillian's preference for venues with a less explicitly sexualised dynamic supports Chatterton and Hollands' assertion that many young women consciously chose 'nightlife spaces that they perceived were more "women friendly" or at least safer'.[102] While attention from men was not always desired, and often avoided, many women did view the bar and nightclub as providing an opportunity for casual sexual encounters. When she discussed her trips to town, Debbie highlighted the spontaneous nature of these relationships:

> But you could meet a different boy every week and spend the night with him, or whatever. I don't mean at home, I mean in the club … I mean that's why you went to Romeo's and Juliet's. To meet your friends but also to see who you could cop off with. But they didn't tend to last long those relationships … going out and copping off was just a bit of fun.

Jacqueline also spoke about the casual nature of meeting men on a night out. She explained: 'sometimes if you were seeing somebody you'd meet them as part of the night, but also if you met somebody you met somebody'. Both Jacqueline and Debbie recognised that these encounters were unlikely to lead to anything serious, suggesting that the expectations and desires of young women regarding their romantic and sexual encounters were changing in the 1970s and 1980s.

The nightclub became an increasingly important space to meet members of the opposite sex in the latter decades of the twentieth century. Several of my interviewees referred to the door policy of 'mainstream' nightclubs promoting an equal balance of men and women. Darren recalled:

> It depends how busy they [were] and it depends who's in. If they [didn't] like the look of you for one particular night or if there's loads of lads and not enough girls in they'd start turning lads away … It's in their interests to try and keep it balanced.

Tamar recalled: 'having that whole sort of equal measure of girls and boys … was just really odd like, people are counting? That was just, it was also known as a meat market to us as well. People only went out to cop off.' Similarly, Adrian recalled one of the reasons why he avoided the Roxy nightclub: 'it was a meat market as well. It was the kind of place where they had "Grab a Granny" nights and it was just a bit, no I wasn't really down for that really.'[103] Indeed, the new 'Disco Code' introduced by the Greater London Council in response to a wave of violence at discos in the late 1970s actively encouraged venues to try and maintain an equal gender balance in clubs.[104] While the sexualised nature of nights out was not appealing to all young people and, in many cases represented continuing inequalities in the way that young men and women were able to occupy public space, the evidence suggests that the nightclub was, by the 1970s and 1980s, cemented as a space in which young people could meet and experiment with casual and fleeting sexual encounters.

The extent to which this is indicative of a wider move towards 'permissiveness' in the post-war period is unclear. Ultimately, marriage or extended cohabitation remained the eventual goal for many young people in this period, although the route was now much less clear-cut. However, it is plausible to suggest that the 1970s and 1980s saw a loosening of pre-marriage courtship behaviours and a more casual form of dating that was less bound by strict gender and societal conventions. Young people had long engaged in sexual acts with partners before marriage, but the space of the nightclub provided a very public place to do this. Indeed, the public nature of these new rituals of courting and sexual experimentation may well have been a central part of their appeal. As Hannah Charnock demonstrates, the potential to be 'spotted by one's peers' and for 'heterosexuality to be recorded within the broader social consciousness' was a central facet of the developing landscape of post-war youth sexuality.[105] I would also argue that the changing nature of youthful sociability in this period is critical to understanding these behaviours. The increasing popularity of licensed nightclubs as a leisure space for the majority of young people in the years between the late 1960s and 1980s marked a distinct break from the supervised dances of previous decades, and the anonymity of the dance floor, often fuelled by intoxication, served as a space where more sexualised forms of behaviour – though mediated through social expectation and peer observance – could be performed. The changing nature of the nightclub through the 1970s and 1980s – disco-style, with low lights and loud music – and the increasing frequency with which young people attended these venues provided a space for young people to interact with each other away from, and in ways that began to challenge, traditional notions of courtship.

Conclusions

This chapter has demonstrated the extent to which licensed leisure spaces were incorporated into young people's leisure and sociability in post-war Britain. The rise of late-night leisure, charted in Part I of this book, paved the way for a new culture of youth drinking that had a significant impact on young people's leisured landscapes. However, the perceived shift in young people's relationship with alcohol led, as both Chapters 3 and 4 have shown, to numerous attempts to control, manage, and restrict their consumption of alcohol and the spaces in which they consumed it. Social scientists, temperance campaigners, and government organisations watched the transformation of the urban city at night with trepidation. The problem of underage drinking, in particular, was highlighted as a threat to both young people's morality and their health. In many ways, these anxieties demonstrate how

168 *Youth, lived experience, and identity*

so-called 'ordinary' forms of consumption were rendered extraordinary and spectacular when performed by young people.

Yet, when explored at the local level, this ordinary spectacle also reveals the often complex negotiations between family and societal expectations that many young people navigated. As the second half of this chapter has shown, the role that alcohol – and the licensed spaces of youth leisure that it was consumed in – played in young people's lives remained gendered through the post-war period. Spaces of traditional masculinity such as the public house were, in many ways, remade in youth's image, yet women's entry into them was precarious. The dance floor retained its place as a site of potential romance and sexual encounter, offering both men and women opportunity for casual relations with the opposite sex. For some, though, this new culture of sexuality was an unwelcome distraction from the sociability and comradery of a night out with girlfriends. While the nature of young people's relationship to alcohol was undoubtedly shifting in this period, driven both by the growing spatial and temporal divisions between youth leisurescapes and the wider city, the pursuit of drunkenness or intoxication did not supersede sociability as the primary draw of youthful leisure.

Notes

1 TNA, HO 287/4375, Alcohol and Crime: Standing Conference on Crime Prevention, Working Group on Young People and Alcohol Report, 23.
2 HL Deb 25 November 1987, vol 490, col 659.
3 An important exception to this is Martin Plant and Moira Plant, *Risk Takers: Alcohol, Drugs, Sex and Youth* (London: Routledge, 1992), which explicitly considers alcohol use alongside illicit drug use.
4 Neil Carr, 'Editorial: Positioning Alcohol in the Leisure Experience', *Annals of Leisure Research*, 11:3–4 (2008), 265, https://doi.org/10.1080/11745398 .2008.9686797.
5 Jackson and Bartie, *Policing Youth*, 176.
6 Nicholas Allred, 'Mother Gin and the Bad Examples: Figuring a Drug Crisis, 1736–51', *Eighteenth Century Fiction*, 33:3 (2021), 376, https://doi.org/10 .3138/ecf.33.3.369.
7 Mariana Valverde, *Diseases of the Will: Alcohol and the Dilemmas of Freedom* (Cambridge: Cambridge University Press, 1998), 54.
8 Annemarie McAllister, '"Giant Alcohol": A Worthy Opponent for the Children of the Band of Hope', *Drugs: Education, Prevention and Policy*, 22:2 (2014), 106, https://doi.org/10.3109/09687637.2014.977227.
9 Stella Moss, '"A Grave Question": The Children Act and Public House Regulation, c. 1908–1939', *Crimes and Misdemeanours: Deviance and the Law in Historical Perspective*, 3:2 (2009), 99.

Gymslip drinkers

10 McAllister, '"Giant Alcohol"', 105
11 Moss, '"A Grave Question"', 101.
12 James Kneale, 'The Place of Drink: Temperance and the Public, 1856–1914', *Social & Cultural Geography*, 2:1 (2001), 44, https://doi.org/10.1080/14649360020028267.
13 Mari Takayanagi, 'Astor the Fairy Godmother: The Intoxicating Liquor Act 1923', *Open Library of Medical Humanities*, 6:2 (2020), 13, https://doi.org/10.16995/olh.567.
14 'Now It's Schoolgirl Deborah … and Guess Her Age Again!', *Star*, 26 August 1974, 7. See also 'Licensees Defeated by Teenagers' Dress', *Guardian*, 29 April 1970, 7.
15 Mass Observation, FR 1837–7A, 'Juvenile Drinking', June 1947, v.
16 Claire Langhamer, '"A Public House Is for All Classes, Men and Women Alike": Women, Leisure and Drink in Second World War England', *Women's History Review*, 12:3 (2003), 435, https://doi.org/10.1080/09612020300200367.
17 'The Problem of the Teen-Age Drunks', *Daily Mirror*, 3 June 1954, 8.
18 'The Scandal of the Under Twenty-Ones', *Daily Mirror*, 21 July 1955, 1; 'Teenage Tippling a Growing Threat to the Nation', *Chester Chronicle*, 1 March 1958, 9.
19 'You can Blame Respectability for the Punch-Up Figures', *Daily Mail*, 21 November 1963, 14.
20 'Write In', *Petticoat*, 1 March 1969, 29.
21 Barrie Stacey and John Davies, 'Drinking Behaviour in Childhood and Adolescence: An Evaluative Review', *Journal of Alcohol and Drug Education*, 17:3 (1972), 2. The article was reprinted in 1972 from *The British Journal of Addiction* 65 (1970).
22 Gustav Jahoda and Joyce Cramond, *Children and Alcohol: A Developmental Study in Glasgow: Volume I* (London: HMSO, 1972), xi.
23 *Ibid.*, xv.
24 Virginia Berridge, *Demons: Our Changing Attitudes to Alcohol, Tobacco, and Drugs* (Oxford: Oxford University Press, 2013), 191. There is an extensive literature on the rise of new models of public health in relation to alcohol policy. See for example John Greenaway, *Drink and British Politics since 1830: A Study in Policy-Making* (Basingstoke: Palgrave Macmillan, 2003), 158–165; Alex Mold, 'From the Alcoholic to the Sensible Drinker: Alcohol Health Education Campaigns in England' in Mark Jackson and Martin D. Moore (eds), *Balancing the Self: Medicine, Politics and the Regulation of Health in the Twentieth Century* (Manchester: Manchester University Press, 2020), 64–94; Betsy Thom, *Dealing with Drink: Alcohol and Social Policy in Contemporary England* (London: Free Association Books, 1999); Ryosuke Yokoe, *Alcohol and Liver Cirrhosis in Twentieth-Century Britain* (London: Palgrave Macmillan, 2023), 155–208.
25 Alex Mold, '"Everybody Likes a Drink. Nobody Likes a Drunk": Alcohol, Health Education and the Public in 1970s Britain', *Social History of Medicine*, 30:3 (2017), 612–636, https://doi.org/10.1093/shm/hkw094.

170   *Youth, lived experience, and identity*

26 Davies and Stacey, 'Drinking Behaviour', 2–4.
27 *Ibid.*, 25.
28 *Ibid.*, 39.
29 Ann Hawker, *Adolescents and Alcohol* (London: B. Edsall & Co Ltd, 1978), 7.
30 *Ibid.*, Appendix II, iii.
31 TNA, HO 287/4375, Alcohol and Crime: Standing Conference on Crime Prevention, Working Group on Young People and Alcohol Report, 7.
32 *Ibid.*, 9.
33 *Ibid.*, 10. Note: there were variations in the drinking habits of youth in Scotland when compared to those in England and Wales, with Scottish youth reporting lower levels of underage drinking. These discrepancies may indicate behavioural differences or reflect either greater hesitance amongst Scottish youth or over exaggeration by English and Welsh youth in self-reporting their alcohol consumption.
34 TNA, HO 287/4375, Alcohol and Crime: Standing Conference on Crime Prevention, Working Group on Young People and Alcohol Report, 2.
35 M. Ghodsian and C. Power, 'Alcohol Consumption between the Ages of 16 and 23 in Britain: A Longitudinal Study', *British Journal of Addiction*, 82 (1987), 176.
36 *Ibid.*, 179.
37 Holly Blake, Jacqueline Collier, Leon Polnay, and Sarah Armstrong, 'Drinking Habits of 16 Year Olds: Secondary Analysis of the 1970 British Cohort Study', Short Accessible Report May 2001, Academic Division of Child Health, University of Nottingham, via https://nottingham-repository.worktribe.com /index.php/preview/702962/AERC_FinalReport_0007.pdf [last accessed 9 April 2023].
38 Plant and Plant, *Risk Takers*, 61.
39 Hawker, *Adolescents and Alcohol*, 14.
40 *Ibid.*, 14.
41 TNA, HO 287/4375, Alcohol and Crime: Standing Conference on Crime Prevention, Working Group on Young People and Alcohol Report, 10.
42 *Ibid.*, 21.
43 Plant and Plant, *Risk Takers*, 27. This was also reported by those who grew up in the 1960s. See Gill Valentine, Sarah Holloway, and Mark Jayne, 'Generational Patterns of Alcohol Consumption: Continuity and Change', *Health and Place*, 16:5 (2010), 918, https://doi.org/10.1016/j.healthplace.2010.05.003.
44 Hawker, *Adolescents and Alcohol*, 41.
45 Nicholls, *The Politics of Alcohol*, 194. Stella Moss considers the implications of this for the growing levels of wine consumption in 1970s Britain. See Stella Moss, '"Continental Connotations": European Wine Consumption in 1970s Britain', *Contemporary European History*, 29:4 (2020), 431–450, https://doi .org/10.1017/S0960777320000417.
46 HC Deb 27 February 1987, vol 111, col 531.
47 HC Deb 27 February 1987, vol 111, col 531.

48 TNA, HO 287/4375, Alcohol and Crime, Letter from R. E. Hawkes to Mr Townsend, 9 September 1987.
49 Gutzke, *Women Drinking Out in Britain*, 194.
50 *Ibid.*, 194–195.
51 Valentine, Holloway, and Jayne, 'Generational Patterns', 918.
52 Judith Aldridge, Fiona Measham, and Lisa Williams, *Illegal Leisure Revisited: Changing Patterns of Alcohol and Drug Use in Adolescents and Young Adults* (London: Routledge, 2011), 59.
53 Fiona Measham, 'The "Big Bang" Approach to Sessional Drinking: Changing Patterns of Alcohol Consumption Amongst Young People in North West England', *Addiction Research*, 4:3 (1996), 283–299, https://doi.org/10.3109/16066359609005573.
54 There is an extensive literature on young people's changing drinking habits from the late 1990s into the 2000s. These themes are explored at length in Hadfield, *Bar Wars*. See also Marjana Martinic and Fiona Measham, *Swimming with Crocodiles: The Culture of Extreme Drinking* (London: Routledge, 2008); Aldridge, Measham, and Williams, *Illegal Leisure Revisited*.
55 HL Deb 16 June 1988, vol 498, col 439.
56 Quoted in Les Gofton, 'On the Town: Drink and the "New Lawlessness"', *Youth and Policy*, 29 (1990), 33.
57 TNA, HO 295/118, Alcohol and Crime: Standing Conference on Crime Prevention, Report from National Youth Bureau, 1987.
58 Simon Dagnall, Andrew Flude, and Sally Flude, Witness Oral History Project (2012).
59 TNA, HO 287/4331, Home Office Standing Conference on Crime Prevention, Working Group on Young People and Alcohol, Minutes of first meeting, 26 February 1987.
60 TNA, HO 287/4375, Alcohol and Crime: Standing Conference on Crime Prevention, Working Group on Young People and Alcohol Report, 25.
61 *Ibid.*, 25.
62 Aldridge, Measham, and Williams, *Illegal Leisure Revisited*, 57–61.
63 Valentine, Holloway, and Jayne, 'Generational Patterns', 920.
64 *Top Star Special*, December 1966, 4.
65 J. P. Bean, *Singing from the Floor: A History of British Folk Clubs* (London: Faber and Faber, 2014).
66 Michael Brocken, *The British Folk Revival: 1944–2002* (Aldershot: Ashgate, 2003), 87.
67 The city's student population grew significantly in the years after the Second World War. Until 1955, the population of full-time students at the University of Sheffield had not risen above two thousand. By 1980, however, it had reached eight thousand. See sheffield.ac.uk/about/history [last accessed 22 May 2023]. Following expansion from both the University of Sheffield and Sheffield City Polytechnic (now Sheffield Hallam University) in the 1980s and 1990s, the city had an estimated student population of forty-five thousand by the 2000s.

68 Karen Evans, Ian Taylor, and Penny Fraser, *A Tale of Two Cities: Global Change, Local Feeling, and Everyday Life in the North of England* (London: Routledge, 2002), 112.

69 Following the deregulation of buses in 1986, private bus companies took over operation. By 1994, some sixty-six bus operators were servicing Sheffield. While some night buses continued after deregulation, the timetables and routes were far less cohesive than under the SYPTE system, and fares jumped to £1, making taxis a more viable option for larger groups. Statistics from Evans, Taylor, and Fraser, *A Tale of Two Cities*, 103. For more on the political importance of Sheffield's low bus-fare policy, see Payling, *Socialist Republic*, 37–39.

70 Gutzke, *Women Drinking Out in Britain*, 2.

71 Laura Fenton, 'Practices of Learning, Earning and Intimacy in Women's Drinking Biographies' (Unpublished PhD, University of Manchester, 2017), 90.

72 *Ibid.*, 64.

73 Jerald Cloyd, 'The Market-Place Bar: The Interrelation Between Sex, Situation, and Strategies in the Pairing Ritual of *Homo Ludens*', *Urban Life*, 5:3 (1976), 267–396.

74 Pearl Jephcott, *Rising Twenty: Notes on Some Ordinary Girls* (London: Faber and Faber, 1948), 147–148.

75 Gutzke, *Women Drinking Out in Britain*, 92.

76 Hadfield, *Bar Wars*, 86.

77 See Langhamer, *Women's Leisure*.

78 Mills, 'Using the Personal to Critique the Popular', 466.

79 Valentine, Holloway, and Jayne, 'Generational Patterns', 921.

80 Mills, 'Using the Personal to Critique the Popular', 466.

81 Robert Hollands, *Friday Night, Saturday Night: Youth Cultural Identification in the Post-Industrial City* (Newcastle: Newcastle University, 1995), 66, via https://research.ncl.ac.uk/youthnightlife/hollands.pdf [accessed 12 April 2023].

82 These themes are explored in Part I of this book. See in particular Jackson, 'Coffee Club Menace'; Harrison, *Dangerous Amusements*; Charnock, 'Teenage Girls'.

83 Charnock, 'Teenage Girls', 1033. Recently published work is beginning to offer us greater insights. See for example Caroline Rusterholz, *Responsible Pleasure: The Brook Advisory Centres and Youth Sexuality in Postwar Britain* (Oxford: Oxford University Press, 2024).

84 This issue is addressed by a number of historians of sexuality. On sexuality and youth in particular, see Lutz D. H. Sauerteig and Roger Davidson (eds), *Shaping Sexual Knowledge: A Cultural History of Sex Education in Twentieth Century Europe* (London: Routledge, 2009).

85 Lesley A. Hall, *Sex, Gender and Social Change in Britain Since 1880* (London: Macmillan, 2000), 164.

86 Michael Schofield, *The Sexual Behaviour of Young People* (London: Longmans, 1965), 252.

87 Marwick, *British Society Since 1945*, 209.

Gymslip drinkers

88 Sarah Kenny, 'We Are No Longer Certain, Any of Us, What Is "Right" and What Is "Wrong": Honey, Petticoat, and the Construction of Young Women's Sexuality in 1960s Britain' in The Subcultures Network (eds), *Let's Spend the Night Together: Sex, Pop Music and British Youth Culture, 1950s–80s* (Manchester: Manchester University Press, 2023), 76–93. See also Tinkler, 'Are You Really Living?'.

89 Claire Langhamer, 'Love and Courtship in Mid-Twentieth Century England', *The Historical Journal*, 50:1 (2007), 181, https://doi.org/10.1017/S0018246X06005966.

90 Charnock, 'Teenage Girls', 1036.

91 Chatterton and Hollands, *Urban Nightscapes*, 151.

92 Hadfield, *Bar Wars*, 90.

93 Cloyd, 'The Market-Place Bar', 293.

94 Stratton, *Spectacle, Fashion and the Dancing Experience*, 199.

95 'Facing Mecca', *The Stage*, 24 January 1974, 8.

96 Stratton, *Spectacle, Fashion and the Dancing Experience*, 218.

97 Matt Cook, 'Local Matters: Queer Scenes in 1960s Manchester, Plymouth, and Brighton', *Journal of British Studies*, 59:1 (2020), 46, https://doi.org/10.1017/jbr.2019.244.

98 Daryl Leeworthy, 'Singing Elton's Song: Queer Sexualities and Youth Cultures in England and Wales, 1967–85' in The Subcultures Network (eds), *Let's Spend the Night Together*, 153.

99 'Sheffield's Theatre of Light and Sound', *Star*, 28 December 1977, 10.

100 Gofton, 'On the Town', 36.

101 Stratton, *Spectacle, Fashion and the Dancing Experience*, 199.

102 Chatterton and Hollands, *Urban Nightscapes*, 154. See also Fiona Hutton, *Risky Pleasures: Club Cultures and Feminine Identities* (London: Routledge, 2006).

103 Note: 'Grab a Granny' was a term used to denote club nights with discounted entry for older women, usually over the age of 25.

104 The introduction of this code was reported in the local press, including 'Stay Cool on the Disco-Beat Council Warns', *Acton Gazette* and *Hammersmith & Shepherds Bush Gazette,* both 29 November 1979, 17 and 'Disco Deaths Prompt GLC Advisory Code', *The Stage*, 29 November 1979, 4.

105 Charnock, 'Teenage Girls', 1047.

5

Leisure, consumption, and identity

Having charted the development of urban evening leisure spaces for young people in post-war Britain, as well as the ways in which these spaces shaped and influenced the leisure choices and lifestyles of Britain's teenagers and young adults, this final chapter asks: what do these transformations in youth leisure mean for our historical understanding of youth culture and the youth experience in modern Britain?[1] In particular, it seeks to locate the youth experience at the level of the local and the everyday. Historical and contemporary discourse on young people in post-war Britain has overwhelmingly focused on the experiences of subcultural youth; these cultural movements have, through the outrage, admiration, and attention sparked by them, forged a clear archival trail, and have left the most visible mark on society. Indeed, that visibility is the clearest way for historians to engage with histories of youth. As Bart van der Steen and Thierry Verburgh have argued, the myths of subculture 'are retold by subcultural actors and observers alike, through various channels of communication' and as such are able to 'significantly influence popular understandings of what youth subcultures are and how they develop'.[2] From their fashion and clothing, publications and music, to their presence on street corners and in shopping arcades, it is the visibility of post-war youth, marked apart by their consumption and lifestyle choices, that has so often drawn the attention of commentators and academics.

But what of those aspects of the youth experience that are less visible? What, for example, does it mean to build an identity and to create connection with others? How do structural factors such as access to disposable income shape young people's relationship with commercial youth culture? What meanings do young people attach to their leisure choices? Using oral testimony drawn from interviews with people who grew up in Sheffield between the 1960s and 1980s, this final chapter suggests that, by situating young people's interactions with commercial youth culture within the local and the everyday, it is possible to gain essential insight into the transformations of youth lifestyles in the second half of the twentieth century. In

Leisure, consumption, and identity 175

doing so, it contributes to the growing calls from historians who argue that it is only by placing young lives within their local context that it is possible to access a fuller account of the experience of growing up in a period of rapid and substantial social and cultural change. Felix Fuhg's study of working-class London youth in the long 1960s argued that 'the making of the modern metropolis and modern working-class culture were intertwined', while Laura Harrison's study of youth in the late nineteenth and early twentieth centuries suggested that 'exploring the relationship between the young working class and urban space allows for a more comprehensive and nuanced understanding of the lives of young people'.[3] Keith Gildart, meanwhile, has argued that 'not only [did] popular music mentally and physically transport performers and consumers from the drudgery of their everyday lives but provided them with new ways of looking at their position within their own localities in particular and English society more generally'.[4]

Exploring interviewees' use of space, their broader cultural practices, and their own engagement with wider narratives of youth culture suggests that while the popular narrative of a creative and active 'alternative' culture existing in diametric opposition to a passive and commercialised 'mainstream' is one that some of my participants engaged with, their cultural experiences were fluid and their decision-making process with regards to their lifestyle choices extended far beyond the limits suggested by this binary paradigm. Further, the extracts presented through this chapter highlight the individuality of the youth experience; while several patterns emerge, it is clear that young people's engagements with youth culture were formulated through a wide range of experiences that make the application of strict cultural frameworks difficult, if not untenable.

At various points in the interview process, the process of reframing and recontextualising of youthful subjectivities by interviewees was clear. Their memories were viewed through the lens of adulthood, and this was reflected in the stories they chose to tell and the way they chose to tell them. At various points, interviewees actively reflected on their experiences, and tried to provide explanations for their teenage thoughts and actions. For example, Tamar, who grew up in the late 1980s, reflected on her identity as a teenager, saying:

> But I think that's, I think a lot of teenage life is about just, let me try this persona for a bit and see if that fits and all of mine was in some alternative to what was mainstream at the time.

While a teenage Tamar may not have viewed her cultural experimentation as 'trying on new personas', as an adult she considered this part of a

176   *Youth, lived experience, and identity*

broader journey of self discovery. Similarly Jeff, who grew up in the mid-1980s, recalled moving through a number of styles as a teenager, before quipping 'Yeah, it was cultural, personal capital. It was, I don't know, who knows what was going on in one's teenage mind. It was about, it was kind of a self-esteem thing really.' Jeff spoke at length in his interview about the ways he pursued and curated his identity, discussing the desire for external validation from his peers. By interrupting his narrative with the reflective comment of 'who knows what was going on in one's teenage mind', Jeff was tempering his youthful experience through the lens of adulthood. In some ways, both Jeff and Tamar played down the significance of their association with alternative youth cultures as a product of adolescent experimentation.

The extracts presented here should not be read as attempts to retrospectively uncover the realities of youthful experience; instead, oral testimony provides a way of understanding how people engage with and narrate their experiences of youth, and how they negotiate established and dominant cultural frameworks in the construction of their youthful selves. Critically, it broadens our understanding of young lives by moving beyond the solely spectacular and beyond the metropole. For young people growing up and going out in Sheffield between the 1960s and the 1990s, their relationship to leisure space, and to the products of an increasingly global youth culture, were mediated at the level of the individual and the local. Family circumstance, access to disposable income, friendship group preferences, the local leisure landscape, and a desire to discover oneself were commanding factors in their everyday engagements with youth culture.

This chapter is arranged in four parts, each of which explores a different facet of young people's engagement within the realm of commercial leisure. The first two sections consider the role that sociability played in young people's leisure choices and in their transition through the life cycle. The third explores how interview participants constructed and narrated their engagement with popular youth culture as teenagers, while the fourth turns to the broader topic of youth consumption to ask how working-class youth navigated the consumer landscape to construct and present a coherent sense of self. The testimonies presented through this chapter demonstrate that young people's engagement with youth culture at the level of their town, neighbourhood, and street rarely mapped on to bounded cultural frameworks. Instead, they moved between leisure spaces, social groups, and cultural products, constructing identities that were shaped as much by their local environment as they were by the wider commercial landscape. In particular, they consider how changes to the built environment transformed not only young people's experience of leisure, but the meaning and significance they attached to it.

'A lot of them got married and moved away': changing understandings of 'youth' in post-war Britain

Youth is a complex concept, one that is malleable and unfixed. Defining what constitutes youth is, therefore, a question that has occupied many historians, social scientists, politicians, and social commentators through the years. Indeed Bill Osgerby argues that 'it may be inevitable that conceptions of "youth" and chronological age will prominently feature in attempts to make sense of social change'.[5] Those scholars interested in the study of the life course have, in recent decades, identified that the traditional markers of adulthood – leaving education, entrance into full-time employment, marriage, and often parenthood – become less stable into the later twentieth century.[6] As a result, determining the point at which 'youth' ended and the transition into adulthood was complete became more difficult. For Jeffrey Arnett, this transformation is indicative of what has been termed 'emerging adulthood': the years between the end of adolescence at 18 and the start of 'stable adult roles in love and work', often in the late 20s.[7] The growth of 'emerging adulthood' is, Arnett argues, a representation of significant transformations in the way that young adults move through the world and was defined by 'longer and more widespread education, later entry to marriage and parenthood, and a prolonged and erratic transition to stable work'.[8]

As the oral testimonies presented here demonstrate, that transition was further complicated by the growing availability of youth-oriented leisure. In the 1960s and 1970s movement in and out of the new spaces of youth leisure offered a visible indication of the transition away from youth and into adulthood, in which household finances and family commitments took precedence over late-night visits to clubs and pubs with friends. However, this model was complicated by the late 1980s: youth experiences often continued further into adulthood, with many people continuing to build youth-oriented leisure patterns well into their 20s and 30s. Critically, the traditional markers of marriage and parenthood no longer acted as an obstacle to youth-oriented leisure for those reaching young adulthood in the late 1980s and 1990s.

Through much of the twentieth century, entering into long-term relationships and marriage, particularly for young women, signalled an end to youth-oriented forms of leisure. As Claire Langhamer observed, the 'flight of women from the dance floor' is just 'one example of the disruptive effect of courtship on long established leisure practices and social networks'.[9] This marker is particularly significant given that the average age of first marriage for both men and women dropped over the course of the mid-twentieth century, from 27 to 24 for men between 1931 and 1971 and from 25 to 22 for women in the same time period.[10] Of my interviewees who reached

178 *Youth, lived experience, and identity*

adulthood in the 1960s and 1970s, many spoke about the impact of marriage on both their own social habits and their wider social group. One interviewee, Helen, who grew up in the mid-to-late 1970s, explained: 'I was married at twenty-three so I suppose, I mean that's quite young now isn't it, but most of my friends were married sort of early to mid-twenties and started having families shortly after that.' She went on to explain that she stopped attending pubs and nightclubs after she was married because:

> The money went in the bank rather than on going out drinking and clubbing and what have you ... Start saving up you know, trying to put a bit of money away. This was back in the days when you could get a mortgage relatively easily as long as you'd got a bit of money in the bank, a deposit, you were ok really.

Another interviewee, Debbie, who grew up in the late 1970s, recalled: 'By the time I was twenty-one and I'd got married and I'd stopped going down town ... Not that your husband wouldn't let you, it's just that you led a different kind of life then.' Gillian, who also grew up in the mid–late 1970s, similarly recalled: 'I was twenty-three. I bought my first house because we had low mortgages ... [I was] struggling to pay the mortgage and eat', meaning she had little spare income to spend on going out. Owen, who grew up in the mid-1970s and was in his mid-30s when he married, explained how his social group changed when many of them started to settle down: 'a lot of them got married and moved away. But the ones that lived local, they never seemed to come out without their wives'. For many young people, marriage marked an important turning point in their lives; as well as being the point at which many left the parental home, financial priorities shifted as thoughts turned towards raising a family or buying a home.

However, using marriage as a traditional marker for the end of 'youth' becomes more difficult by the late 1980s. By the late 1980s and 1990s, the average age of marriage was rising once again, continuing a trend that was first identified in the late 1970s, while the overall rate of marriage was dropping. By 1990, the average age of first marriage was 27 for men and 25 for women, rising to 30 and 28 respectively by the end of the twentieth century.[11] Similarly, the rate of marriage itself was declining at an astonishing rate. In 1980, almost 88 per cent of men and 94 per cent of women were married by the age of 34. By 2000, this had lowered to 61 per cent and 72 per cent respectively. While marriage remained the intended outcome for many, it no longer acted as a stable milestone that signified entrance into 'full' adulthood.[12] Of those interviewed who were teenagers in the 1980s, their entrance into adulthood in the 1990s was not always marked by a move away from or out of their established patterns of leisure and

Leisure, consumption, and identity

179

sociability. Damon, for example, explained how he and his wife began clubbing again after moving to Liverpool. He said:

> I held fast until the mid-nineties when me and ... my wife, just got massively back into it again. It was when we moved to Liverpool and Liverpool had a different atmosphere and we just really got back into it again. I was hitting thirty by this point so you know, that was the power, to me that was the power of dance music and the legacy of acid house was you could carry on doing this stuff when you were, what I would previously have considered as, middle aged!

Similarly another interviewee, Jeff, explained the legacy of rave and club culture on his social life. After completing his postgraduate degree and starting work he explained:

> I eased off punishing myself a bit by having this austere approach to life and being very sensible, or trying to be. So then I started getting back into clubbing a bit and yeah, then the nineties came along and I got into rave culture, wholeheartedly.

The cultural impact and ongoing aftershocks of rave and acid house come through clearly here. While scholars have presented varying theories about how, and the extent to which, rave was able to transcend traditional barriers of class, gender, and race in ways that other leisure spaces were simply unable to, it is clear that the rise of rave culture and acid house presented a space in which age became less important.[13] These transformations permeated the wider leisure landscape, and a growing number of 'aspirational' pubs and late-night bars opened in the 1990s and 2000s to cater to this new demographic of leisure seekers.[14]

This loosening of age-related barriers to nightclubs and the club scene can also be seen in relation to parenthood. Tamar, who had her first child as she finished her studies, began clubbing again when her children were old enough. She recalled:

> There was a point where it slowed down for me and that's because I got pregnant in '93 so I graduated in, I finished my degree in the summer '94, and had my baby in the summer '94 ... So I stopped for a good period of time and then I had my daughter as well and then, I suppose I got back into clubbing yeah, when my daughter was about three or four and going out.

Similarly Mark, who had his first child at the age of 19, recalled going out more in his 30s. He explained: 'I wanted to get out there, and my eldest he was growing up, well, he'd just turned eleven. And I just wanted a bit of a

180   *Youth, lived experience, and identity*

break. And that's when I started drinking again, erm, and coming back into town.' For Tara Brabazon, these experiences are indicative of the leisured lifestyles of the 'first (post) youth culture', retrospectively titled 'Generation X'.[15] The experiences of people growing up and going out in Britain in the 1980s and 1990s presented here support Brabazon's argument that 'age and ageing are socially inscribed and dynamic'.[16] As such, being a parent and/or married in your mid-to-late 20s or early 30s at the end of the twentieth century presented a different set of social and cultural scripts when compared with those available some 50, or even 15, years earlier. While the lives of many young people were undoubtedly changed by marriage or the arrival of children, it is possible to suggest that the moment at which youth turned into adulthood extended, and to some extent became blurred, over the second half of the twentieth century. This transformation was made visible by the growth of the youth-oriented night-time economy. A 'night out' for people such as Damon, Jeff, Tamar, and Mark in the mid-1990s was markedly different from their parents' generation in the mid-1960s and 1970s. A visit to a nightclub took the place of a night at the cabaret club, and signified a continuation of patterns of leisure and sociability that had been established much earlier in the life course.[17]

A study of people's engagement with commercial youth leisure, then, offers us new ways to think about how we chart people's movement across the life course. As Andy Bennett and Paul Hodgkinson argued, the very concept of 'youth culture' appeared 'increasingly ambiguous and open to interpretation' by the start of the twenty-first century.[18] Over the course of the second half of the twentieth century the leisure-oriented lifestyles of youth became an ever-more porous category, often extending beyond what was once considered the start of 'adulthood'. It offers a way of charting social and cultural change, as well as a way of considering whether the definitions of leisure-oriented 'teenagers', first established in the 1950s and 1960s, remained relevant for those people who came of age towards the end of the twentieth century. Commercial leisure remained at the heart of many young people's lived engagement with transnational youth cultures but, arguably, was no longer the sole preserve of youth itself.

'You wanted to go where you would feel comfortable': social groups and social spaces

As the previous chapters of this book have demonstrated, evening leisure spaces became central to new patterns of youthful sociability in the post-war period and their presence reshaped both the spatial and temporal

Leisure, consumption, and identity

181

relationship between young people and the urban environment. However, these spaces are often presented – both in academic scholarship on youth and in popular discourse on the night-time economy – as part of a landscape of 'resistance' against cultural hegemony, focusing on a select number of culturally influential and celebrated venues.[19] While the new late-night leisurescapes of the post-war period acted as a core nexus around which countless music and fashion-based leisure scenes developed, it was also a critical component of young people's lived engagement with youth culture. As such, it is a central means through which we can understand the transformation of young people's sociability in the second half of the twentieth century. Their presence in, and movement between, these spaces was informed by their own cultural interests and identities, but was also driven by established patterns of sociability and the particulars of the local urban landscape. Who young people socialised with, how they spent their time as a group, and what they sought from their time together played a central role in their interactions with youth-oriented leisure space.

Sociologists and ethnographers of youth have long recognised the importance of sociability and group dynamic in young people's lives.[20] For young people growing up and going out in Sheffield between the 1960s and 1990s, established cultural scripts loaded with value judgements about the city's various late-night venues intersected with young people's own desired social outcomes from their leisure time. While discussing her involvement with a local theatre group, Jacqueline, who grew up in the late 1970s, described the different circles she moved within. She recalled:

> so if I went out with them [theatre group] that was a very different conversation to if you went out with like my friends from school who were quite, let's get dressed up, let's go for a drink let's go clubbing. And then there were other friends who it was about, you know they were the ones who'd all gone to school together so you just went for a chat.

Jacqueline had a varied social circle, and her leisure activities reflected this fact. She further recalled:

> Friday night was always dressed up. Sunday night was casual. But again, depending on the group of friends you were with, like there were some groups of friends that really liked to dress up, even if you were just going round the village, you'd dress up on a Friday and Saturday and we even used to go out on a Sunday night until late, but if you were out on Thursday night that was jeans … you know it was casual.

Tamar, who grew up in the late 1980s, similarly explained:

182 *Youth, lived experience, and identity*

and I was quite lucky in that I had a diverse set of friends. So it wasn't necessarily that you only did one thing. I moved in between depending on who was going where and what I fancied doing.

Juan, who grew up in the late 1970s, similarly transitioned between a range of social groups from different areas of his life. He explained:

One of the things I noticed was various groups of people I could hang out, and hung out with. So there was one group which was maybe Afro-Caribbean ... So that was one group of mates, and that also crossed over, some went to school, some went to different schools, some went to the youth club, so there was people from the youth club so there was that lot, school mates. And that was a mixture of boys, girls. And as we started going out and there were people that you would meet along the way.

Juan's position as a Black teenager growing up in a predominantly white area of Sheffield – he recalled 'there were hardly any Black people, as I say, on my road' – shaped his social circles in important ways. He moved in a diverse group of friends, many of whom also came from minoritised backgrounds, that increasingly reflected the different facets of his social life. His testimony outlined clearly the evolving nature of many young people's social circles, which expanded and developed as people moved through the life cycle.

My interviewees moved between a wide range of different social groups, giving them access to a range of options for leisure and sociability. Frank Coffield et al. found during their study of young men and women growing up in the north east of England in the mid-1980s that there were five major types of friendship groups – all male, all female, mixed sex, best friends, and partners – and that 'at any one time a young person was likely to belong to more than one'.[21] Different groups of friends fulfilled different social needs, while also reflecting the different stages of young people's transition through the life cycle; from school friends to those who met at youth clubs and on nights out, friendship and sociability remained a central component of young people's engagement with youth leisure through the twentieth century.

Young people exercised a significant degree of agency in their engagement with evening leisure spaces. Based on a learned knowledge of the local leisurescape, adolescents and young adults moved through these spaces with a distinct idea about what each space offered them. Jacqueline recalled attending a variety of venues for different purposes. She explained:

Leisure, consumption, and identity

> The Limit was really important. If you wanted music you went to the Limit ... And then there was the Top Rank. The Top Rank was one of those ... if you liked dancing you could go and dance and really lose it. But at the same time you'd go the next week to see if your photos were on the wall, because there was also the balcony where you can stand and watch. But that was good for like, losing yourself music ... Erm, so again it depended on who you were out with how important the music was. So, I had a group of friends who we went to Battle of the Bands because we loved music. I'd got another group of friends I went clubbing with, they didn't care about that, they just wanted it to be part of their Friday, Saturday night. And they just wanted it to be good to dance to.

Jacqueline moved between a variety of the city's late-night leisure venues depending on what she wanted from her evening and who she was with; her social circle was varied and thus so were her social interactions and movement through the local leisurescape. Juan also navigated the local leisurescape with sociability and friendship in mind:

> I mean it depended really what you want, what type of music you're into or what sort of feeling you wanted. You're pushing your way through or if you want something quiet. And it really depended on that what you wanted to do.

He continued:

> You've got so many different places that you could go to. So it depended on what you actually felt like, or whether the group of people you were going to meet or wanted to meet, hung out mainly in, if that was their favourite place ... if the place was buzzing, I'd be, if it was a case of going there it would be because it was like a group decision. But by choice it would have been anywhere where there was good music and you could dance. I loved dancing.

Juan's own cultural interests were driven by his enjoyment of jazz funk and dancing, but his interview highlighted the often overlooked factor of the group dynamic. Gillian similarly highlighted the importance of the wider social group in her interview:

> I like a wide range of music. But I suppose stuff you can dance to. Disco stuff is fabulous, that's what you need there ... you just tend to go along with what everybody else wants to do.

Music, venue choice, or the pursuit of intoxication often came second to the simple desire to go on a night out with friends. Juan explained:

184 *Youth, lived experience, and identity*

> Our lot, I'm not a drinker, so we used to go on a pub crawl but it was like, we
> played it light in comparison to some other people. You know, it was a case
> of yes let's meet up have a chat, have a laugh, get to the club sort of thing. I
> wanted to catch up with what's going down.

Jacqueline similarly explained that while there was 'lots of drinking':

> There were other nights like the Battle of the Bands that drink wasn't even a
> part of it. Erm, or when I went out on a Sunday night, with [friends], it was
> more about just sitting, chatting. And that's where you did it, in the pub. So
> yeah, it was about fun.

Many young people's interactions with the commercial spaces of late-night
leisure were built into wider patterns of leisured sociability. As such, their
engagement with their local leisurescape was driven not only by their interest in particular bands, events, or scenes, but by their social circles.

A developed knowledge of the urban leisurescape enabled young people
to make clear and informed choices about where they wanted to spend their
time. Much like the adolescents in Pearl Jephcott's research some 30 years
earlier, the social reputation, company, and ambience of a venue remained
important. Jephcott's girls were 'knowledgeable about the sort of company
they will find at the local halls', and navigated the landscape of dance halls
accordingly.[22] While, for many, the concern about reputation was no longer
driven by a desire to avoid being connected with spaces associated with
immorality and sexual impropriety, a measured reading of what was on
offer in different venues remained. Juan stated:

> I mean the thing is with deviation or trying to deviate [between different ven-
> ues], it was I suppose you wanted to go where you would feel comfortable.
> You know, there were certain clubs where you know where you're not going
> to feel comfortable because it's not your genre. Other places you'd feel ok but
> it wasn't your genre.

Juan's experience as a young Black man in Sheffield shaped his interactions
with the city's leisurescape in important ways. He recalled that there were:

> some clubs that you were … more wary of going to than others. One of them
> for me was Josephines. Josephines wanted to push the sophisticated clientele
> feel so you had the bouncers and it was like a nightmare for certain people
> to get in. Once inside the club, I mean from what I remember they played
> really good music, that was the reason why you wanted to go. But, you had
> to get past the bouncers. And they would say you know, they'd come up with

Leisure, consumption, and identity

Leisure, consumption, and identity   185

everything. You're not dressed correctly, blah blah blah, just not letting you in and whatever.

He continued, 'Sheffield itself was actually quite a tolerant place, but there were still bits of intolerance'. This intolerance, in the form of racist and often aggressive door policies and encounters with bouncers and security, was an important factor for Juan and his friendship group when encountering the city's commercial late-night leisure spaces.

Similarly, Auriel, a mixed race teenager in the early-to-mid 1980s, recalled the city's mainstream clubs operating an informal 'quota' for clubbers, which explicitly sought to minimise the racial diversity of those present in the city's clubs. She stated:

> when I used to go out with Black friends, or in a mixed group ... the bouncers on the door would say things like 'oh sorry lads, no hats' or 'oh we're full up tonight' ... they'd go 'you girls can come in, you lads can't come in – we've got too many lads in' ... you'd walk in and it'd just be full of white men.[23]

For Auriel, this meant eschewing the city's mainstream venues in favour of Jive Turkey, a club night held across the mid-to-late 1980s in various locations – including monthly parties at the City Hall – and which quickly became well known as an early adopter of house music. Jive Turkey's reputation for playing the latest in funk and house meant it quickly became popular with many young Black people in the city and, as Jon Savage reported on a trip to City Hall in November 1988, acted as 'the perfect antidote to Sheffield's brusque and rough nightlife'.[24] As Dave Haslam argued: 'if you found a discotheque where you knew there wouldn't be a fight, you'd definitely go back'.[25]

The importance of atmosphere and comfort was a significant factor for many other young people moving through commercial leisure spaces. Debbie, in discussing her favoured late-night leisure spots, recalled:

> I used to go in the Black Swan. I used to go to nightclubs. Josephine's, and Romeo's and Juliet's. That was my favourite haunt ... And the Romeo's and Juliet's was just over the road from the Black Swan so that was very convenient.

Debbie's music and fashion tastes as a teenager in the late 1970s and early 1980s were primarily influenced by ska but she preferred frequenting larger 'mainstream' venues, many of which were run by large commercial organisations such as the Rank Organisation and Mecca. Romeo's and Juliet's, Debbie's favourite nightspot, was owned by EMI Leisure and operated in locations across the country. She explained:

186 *Youth, lived experience, and identity*

> They'd play the same kinds of music throughout the night. Mainly chart music, but if you wanted specialist music you'd go to the smaller type places, the spit and sawdust types. I mean I sometimes went to the smaller nightclubs but I didn't feel as comfortable. I didn't feel as though there was any point in getting dressed up because they were so shabby some of the places.

Despite Debbie's personal interest in ska music, she gravitated towards the city's larger nightclubs because they offered the opportunity to dress up. Similarly, these were spaces that felt comfortable and where she felt confident she would fit in. Adrian, who grew up in the late 1980s and early 1990s and gravitated towards the house and rave scene, recalled visits to Manchester's famous Haçienda club:

> I went to the Haçienda a couple of times, but it was very much after the glory days I would say. People talk about it with very rose tinted, but I found it quite a, quite scary to be honest with you. A bit moody.

Damon, who was also a teenager in the late 1980s, explained the importance of feeling comfortable in the pubs and nightclubs he and his friends socialised in as teenagers. As a self-defined member of the city's 'alternative scene', he explained 'you would pick and choose the ones where you could get served and where you felt comfortable in what you were wearing'.

The development of the 'night out' as a leisure pastime positioned the public house and nightclub as important to many young people's cultural landscapes in the post-war period, and was central to the development of new patterns of sociability. However, young people's relationship with these spaces and their movements through them were complex, and they constructed a detailed and knowledgeable picture of the leisurescape available to them. Their engagement with these spaces was driven in part by their own preferences regarding decor, music style, and fashion choices, but prioritised belonging, sociability, and atmosphere. It highlights, in particular, Doreen Massey's vision of place as being 'always unfixed, contested and multiple'.[26] For the young people moving through these spaces, the meanings they attached to them reflected the multiplicities of their social relations and their intersections with the built environment.

'Against the mainstream people': subculture, the 'mainstream', and narrating identity

Since its implementation at the University of Birmingham's Centre for Contemporary Cultural Studies in the 1970s, subcultural studies has

Leisure, consumption, and identity

remained at the heart of many studies of youth culture. While contested, their belief in the importance of taking youth styles seriously remains a foundational pillar upon which historians of youth seek to understand the youth experience. Scholars have discussed, debated, and disagreed over how, and to what extent, youth cultures and styles can be conceived of as coherent, active, or resistant. For Dick Hebdige, young people's 'deviation' from the dominant culture 'ends in the construction of a style, in a gesture of defiance or contempt, in a smile or a sneer'.[27] The centre's foundational text, *Resistance Through Rituals*, suggested that subcultural styles constituted a 'transformation and rearrangement of what is given (and "borrowed") into a pattern which carries a new meaning'.[28] This reading of youth styles has been challenged on a range of grounds: for overlooking the role of girls and young women, for failing to adequately acknowledge non-class-based explanations for young people's consumption choices, and for relying on an overly structured reading of youth lifestyles.[29] For those working on youth cultures at the end of the twentieth century, the emergence of post-subcultural theory suggested that 'the structurally grounded concept of subculture, if always problematic' had become 'increasingly redundant in relation to contemporary youth culture', in which youth styles, consumption choices, and lifestyles had become more fractured and individualised.[30] While given less attention, the mainstream has existed as a somewhat porous concept, often posed in 'antithetical relation' to a more worthy and authentic cultural form, and broadly seen as 'having little cultural value'.[31]

This oppositional narrative, of a tightly defined alternative culture and a loosely defined mainstream culture, is pervasive. Despite many attempts by academics to move away from or broaden conceptual approaches to youth cultures, the oppositional binary of mainstream and alternative remains a central framework through which questions of culture and identity are filtered. For J. P. Williams, the continued relevance of subculture lies 'at least partly in the creation and circulation of myths about its authenticity'.[32] This circulation and wider consideration of questions about authenticity and identity is not only apparent in academic scholarship on youth, but is widely utilised as a tool through which people are able to conceive of their own youthful experiences. For my interviewees, utilising an oppositional cultural binary was central to the subjective construction and narration of their youthful identities.

Constructing a sense of self was an important part of many young people's engagement with commercial youth culture in post-war Britain, and many of my interviewees referred to the factional nature of youth culture through this period. However, despite displaying a tendency towards visual and bounded descriptors of youth styles, indicating sharp divisions and oppositions between groups, the language used by interviewees when they

188   *Youth, lived experience, and identity*

described their own approach to identity was often much less defined. When asked about her relationship with music, Tamar said: 'Were clothes and music linked? Yes, yeah. The music I was listening to and the scenes I wanted to be involved in. Yeah, definitely.' While Tamar indicated a clear cultural preference, the 'scenes' in question remained loosely defined. Instead, Tamar explained that she wasn't 'mainstream'. She explained:

> There was a real sort of, the word we used at the time was townie. And that was, we weren't townie, we weren't understood by townies and didn't want to understand townies either so that was, yeah. It was the other if you like, we were the other.

Damon utilised similar linguistic touchstones in his interview, recalling:

> Basically I always wanted to not be in the mainstream ... I never really wanted to go down that route of buying things from Topman and all that, or those sort of places. I certainly had a kind of snobbish, an inverse snobbery about people who shopped in those places. I didn't like the idea of buying clothes from Topman I also didn't like the idea of going to those glitzy chrome and mirrors sort of nightclubs. So the Leadmill was really important. And there was also the Limit ... basically you were either a mainstream sort of person or you went to the Leadmill and the Limit.

When asked whether he identified with any particular scene as a teenager, Damon explained:

> Post-punk is quite a good term for it all, but I've only really heard that used for it quite recently. I don't particularly remember that at the time. That would have been quite handy. Oh yeah I'm a post-punk you know, that probably would have summed it up quite nicely. But I don't really actually remember having a label or a term that would have described what I was until communist.

Despite the narrative construction of bounded and discrete youth cultures, many of my interviewees did not place themselves firmly within one youth scene; instead, the emphasis was placed on not being the 'other'. Another interviewee, Adrian, said: 'It's like everyone belonged to a tribe. That tribalism. So I belonged to, it might not have been evident to look at me, but I was part of that tribe basically.' Adrian, Tamar, and Damon, who all grew up in Sheffield in the late 1980s and early 1990s, each viewed themselves as being part of an 'alternative' youth culture, but none used specific cultural markers to describe themselves. The narrative framing utilised in these testimonies speaks to Andy Bennett's concept of neo-tribes, in which 'groupings

Leisure, consumption, and identity

which have traditionally been theorised as coherent subcultures are better understood as a series of temporal gatherings characterised by fluid boundaries and floating memberships'.[33] At the end of the twentieth century, when the concept of highly visible and clearly demarcated youth styles were arguably in decline, such a theory may explain the broader use of oppositional framing utilised here.

However, this oppositional framing was also apparent in interviews conducted with people who grew up in the 1960s and 1970s. David said that in his youth he was 'basically against the mainstream people'. When asked what it was he didn't like about the 'mainstream', David replied: 'Boring clothes, rubbish music, they expected you to grow up by the time you were about twenty and start listening to Frank Sinatra and rubbish like that!' David's 'mainstream' consisted of a comment on clothing and music that reflected his own tastes more than any specific style or genre, alongside a wider comment on societal expectations of the 1960s. Across the board, interviewees gave a sense that their positioning of themselves as 'against' the mainstream did not correlate to a cohesive group identity. Trish recalled:

> As for identifying with them [alternative groups], I think it was acceptance. It was acceptance of everybody and anybody. You just went in and if you showed up often enough you were one of them ... but yeah, probably acceptance. Probably acceptance and a chip on my shoulder.

Both Trish and David pointed to an 'attitude' being the key difference between mainstream and alternative groups. Rather than the traditionally recognised cultural signifiers, music and clothing, my interviewees suggest that youth groupings were defined as much by attitude as anything else. While for some, such as David, this was seen to manifest itself in certain types of clothing or music, these interviews suggest that it was not necessarily the cultural products themselves that were eschewed, but the image they projected and what they were perceived to represent.

One iteration of this was narrated through the term 'townie'. Tamar recalled how she chose where to socialise on a night out in 1980s Sheffield:

> I think mainly for me it was about the music. So I don't know if – I mean the townie scene was very much erm, nightclubs and suits and completely sort of made up and handbags and jokes about not wearing coats and tights in winter and all that sort of thing.

While Tamar stated she liked the music played in her chosen venues, she also alluded to a wider avoidance of 'townie' nightclubs. Similarly, Sue recalled of the 1960s nightclub Shades:

190 *Youth, lived experience, and identity*

> And it was very good. It was just, it wasn't like the townie nightclubs in town which were very glitz and glitter and martinis and that sort of thing. It was more pints and, Joe Cocker used to play there every Wednesday ... I loved to dance. And I could dance at Shades at least two nights a week, so it was my, it was the thing that really made me buzz. It was my drug if you like, was dancing.

Like Tamar, Sue's identity as being part of an alternative scene influenced where she chose to socialise. However, Sue continued: 'Places I did occasionally go to in town were the Top Rank, and the Locarno but that was more for individual events rather than somewhere that I went regularly.' Although Sue made a clear distinction between what she considered to be mainstream and alternative venues, labelling certain venues as 'townie', she did engage with these venues on occasion. Sue and Tamar both considered music a central part of their night out, but their decision on where to socialise was also influenced by a wider cultural framework; their use of the word 'townie' denoted a cultural 'other' that they wished to avoid. For Jeff, who moved to Sheffield as a student in the mid-1980s, this term also indicated his status as an outsider in the city:

> At the weekend you'd get more of the townsfolk, townie people out, and me being that age and not having a clue. I looked down on people who had to go clubbing on Fridays and Saturdays when I had the time available to go during the week.[34]

These testimonies support Robert Hollands's call to take seriously the 'spatial separation among different consumption groupings'.[35] One such separation is indicated here by the label 'townie', which draws on longstanding cultural associations between dominant forms of nightlife and its patrons who, according to Hollands, could be 'identified by their particular dress styles and demeanour'.[36]

By the 1980s, the range of youth-oriented leisure spaces in Sheffield had diversified, providing a spatial dimension to the city's alternative scene. The use of oppositional framing to situate an 'other' became most apparent when my interviewees from this period were discussing the city's nightlife. Of those who considered themselves to be members of the city's alternative culture, all three were regular visitors to either the Leadmill or the Limit nightclubs, and Damon said 'apart from those two places really I'm hard pushed to think about where else I would have willingly gone'. Both were primarily live music and club night venues, with strong attachments to the city's burgeoning metal, post-punk, and new wave scenes.[37] In the mid-1970s, in the few years before the Limit and the Leadmill opened in 1978

Leisure, consumption, and identity

Figure 5.1 Entrance to the Limit, West Street, Sheffield, 1981. © Sheffield Newspapers Ltd and Picture Sheffield.

and 1980 respectively, 'you had to look hard in Sheffield … to find musical entertainment that wasn't mainstream or obvious'.[38] When she discussed the city's smaller nightclubs, Debbie explained:

> I think it was a different kind of crowd. Yeah, and so when I went it weren't as comfortable as the crowd that, because I was quite middle of the road and that's what the bigger nightclubs catered for.

By describing herself as 'middle of the road', Debbie gave the impression that she felt she did not fit in or belong at the city's smaller and more specialised nightclubs, and her statement that she felt more comfortable in larger nightclubs is significant. Debbie's interview suggests a perception of an 'other', more extreme, form of nightlife. More significantly, her interview reveals how that made her feel. By tempering her own experience as 'middle of the road', Debbie's interview demonstrated a sense of feeling outside of, or alienated from, certain forms of youth culture.

However, for Jeff, whose image was actively curated to set him apart from others, the type of venue he socialised in was a way of communicating his belonging to what he considered to be the 'right' scenes. He recalled:

192 *Youth, lived experience, and identity*

> Music was very important and yeah, gigs, live music very important. I think live music was more important in some ways than actual clubbing. Yeah, going clubbing was an opportunity to pose actually. I don't remember much dancing going on. It was just hang out and look cool, and be seen with the right people and talk to the right people ... I think it was an identity thing ... I hang around with cool people, therefore I must be a cool person.

As an adult, Jeff reflected on this as being caused by teenage concerns about his 'self-esteem', and his broader privileging of live music as more culturally significant seems to dismiss the relative importance he attached to the club scene. Yet, despite this, it is clear that the spaces Jeff moved through as a young adult were key to the narration of his youthful self: attendance at certain nightclubs was used to signify cultural capital in a quest for the unquantifiable element of 'cool'. Jeff's involvement in the city's alternative scene as a Black teenager was also an important way for him to socialise and network. He recalled what drew him to certain venues:

> It was kind of like a, a sort of subculture, with its own kind of ecosystem you know. There was music, there was clothes, there was a social scene. There was very much the in crowd, and the cool people. And erm, I found that when I started to dress in this kind of way, you know, looking trendy, then I found that people were actually more interested in talking to me as well.

He continued:

> Friendships drove it I think. Being a part of a little set of people, kind of a little gang of people, but not a, not really a gang that didn't get up to no good, it was just a crowd of people ... I was interested in, well the music that I liked, I also liked reggae – reggae dancehall I think we called it then – and again, there was a racial element there as well. You know, I'm not white and I'm going to express that by listening to this music.

Jeff prioritised venues and club nights that gave him access to his preferred music genres and social scenes, while also seeking status and recognition from his peers.

During their interviews, many people recalled attaching particular meaning to commercial leisure spaces, and in particular recalled how their presence in these spaces made them feel. For those involved in alternative cultures, the use of cultural 'othering' became more apparent when a physical space was there to embody it. The emergence of venues such as the Leadmill and the Limit in the late 1970s and early 1980s provided young people with a way to physically position themselves within the binary paradigm of alternative or mainstream, and provided a space for people to

Leisure, consumption, and identity   193

more clearly visualise and conceive of the cultural 'other'. In this way, place becomes a central way of narrating alternative cultures as individual venues provided a tangible and physical marking of cultural difference.

This section has demonstrated that a form of oppositional framing remains a critical way of both narrating and making sense of youthful experiences. The development and diversification of the night-time economy, and in particular the growth of spaces catering to alternative youth tastes, became an important way for young people to understand their position within a wider set of cultural frameworks. The spatial division of youth at a local level, then, was fundamental to how young people understood both their own and others' engagements with youth culture.

'You could be whoever you wanted to be, and it was wonderful': consuming youth culture

While the majority of this book has focused on the spaces of youth leisure, this final section turns towards the broader question of youth consumption. In doing so it considers how two key tenants of youthful consumption – the making and purchasing of clothes, and the consumption of music – were utilised by adults in the construction of narratives about the teenage self. It argues that working-class teenagers growing up in Sheffield negotiated a range of barriers, and in particular that of access to disposable income, in their engagement with the products of youth culture. It draws on Tracy Shildrick and Robert MacDonald's work to demonstrate that 'a closer appreciation of the ways in which young people's leisure and cultural lives intersect with wider aspects of their biographies' holds the potential to offer a fuller and more nuanced insight into young lives.[39] Music and clothing were important – but not total – indicators of cultural identity, and young people navigated the landscape of consumer products with expertise and agency.

For many young people, clothing was a significant economic and cultural investment. It allowed them to express their identity and, for many, was one of the first ways they were able to actively curate their own image. A large body of work exists on the role of fashion as a signifier of selfhood and identity, the social significance of shopping for clothing, and the relationship between fashion, gender, and class. Anne Boultwood and Robert Jerrard have argued that people's relationship with fashion can be understood as a conflict between a desire for social cohesion and wanting to 'fit in' and the desire to display an authentic and individual self. They note:

Alongside our need to belong is the equally powerful need to see ourselves as unique; this is the concept of differentiation. The feeling of being unique

194   *Youth, lived experience, and identity*

> supports our sense of self, and the fact that physically we are unique reinforces
> that feeling. Body awareness provides a focus for differentiation, and the need
> to maintain uniqueness translates into our feelings about clothes.[40]

In this way, the relationship between clothing and the individual can be
understood at an analytical level as representing the conflict between belonging and differentiation, as opposed to solely or necessarily representing a
wider reflection of that individual's cultural values. An individual's fashion
and clothing choices represent more than their allegiance to, interest in, or
indeed perceived lack of interest in certain forms of youth culture. This relationship was also affected by structural factors such as access to disposable
income, geographical distance to shops, and autonomy over one's clothing
choices.

The changing economic fortunes of young people through the post-war
period warrant considered attention. While many young people of the mid-
to-late twentieth century had considerably more financial freedom than the
generations before them, many also grew up in moments of significant and
considerable economic hardship. In Sheffield, as in many other areas of the
country, the effects of youth unemployment were felt harshly as were the
broader effects – both personal and financial – of instability in the job market. For working-class teenagers growing up in this period, then, accessing the products of youth culture often required a careful negotiation with
available resources. Yet, as Carolyn Steedman powerfully argues, there is
much to be gained from paying attention to the relationship between the
working-classes and 'aspirational' consumption.[41] Trish grew up in a working-class household in the 1960s, and through her school years she travelled
to the wealthier south west of the city to attend grammar school. As a result
she recalled feeling acutely aware of the financial constraints placed on her
access to the products of youth culture when compared with many of her
wealthier middle-class classmates, remembering 'I didn't even think there
were other people like me there'. In discussing her clothing purchases, Trish
recalled:

> I'd sort of save up and buy material and make clothes every now and again.
> Because of my size I couldn't buy ready-made, you know, I was too tall for
> anything to fit. Erm, so I'd perhaps spend it on some material and things like
> that. Yeah. I remember my first pair of Levis.

That Trish remembered her first pair of Levi jeans suggests both their cultural and economic importance. As somebody who made many of her own
clothes, and often felt excluded from parts of the mass clothing market

Leisure, consumption, and identity

available to her peers, Trish positioned her first pair of Levi jeans as a significant milestone. She continued:

> They were so stiff you could stand them up. You could stand them up on their own and they needed shrinking to fit – I'm sure other people have told you this. Get in the bath and shrink them to fit and then I shuffled round the concrete path round – my parents lived in a bungalow – shuffled round the concrete path on my bum to try and get a bit of fading going on the bum there and on my knees. And another pair, just after I passed my A-levels I went to stay in my sister's caravan with my friend, at Mablethorpe, big deal – a week in Mablethorpe. Erm, and I had a new pair then and I walked in the sea in them and then walked along the sand so they were sand washed, genuine sand washed jeans!

As a child from a working-class family, Trish outlined that she was not accustomed to regular holidays, and her strong memories of walking on the sand in her new jeans indicate their importance to her both at the time and retrospectively. The anecdote was incidental to her broader discussion about making her own clothes, but this narrative interjection signified the meaning that this particular piece of clothing held to her. For Trish, buying and customising a pair of Levi jeans was a substantial economic investment and her recollection of the process of customisation in the wider context of a significant holiday with a friend indicates the important position they continued to hold to her. Trish's interview also detailed how she was often unable to buy 'ready-made' clothing due to her height, thereby excluding her from many of the new products available to other girls her age. Furthermore, these clothes were, while being cheap and accessible for some, a significant economic investment for others. Trish's limited finances meant she learned to be both thrifty and resourceful. She recalled her eldest sister, who was 15 years older than her, helping her:

> One thing I did do, because my eldest sister used to help, she teases me that I'd walk in with a packet of material and throw it at her and say here, I'm wearing it tomorrow. But, yeah, made a, a full length, an ankle length coat once in the weekend.

Trish utilised the skills of her family members to enable her to engage with youth culture despite having a limited income. Making clothes thus became, for Trish, a key part of her youth cultural experience, something that gave her both pleasure and enabled her to 'keep up' with her peers. Her leisure time was spent curating her image, not just through shopping, but also through making items of clothing.[42]

196   *Youth, lived experience, and identity*

Damon, who grew up in the 1980s, recalled privileging records over clothing. However, he did reflect on his experiences of buying clothes as a teenager. He recalled:

> I didn't have a lot of disposable income anyway and to be honest I was more interested in buying records. There was, the plus side of buying scrimp army surplus in jumble sales was obviously you were paying pence, or a couple of quid, you weren't spending very much money on clothes. So although it was, it kind of mattered to me what I looked like, it didn't matter to the extent that I had to spend loads of cash on it.

Damon began buying clothes from army surplus stores as a teenager in the mid-1980s. When asked what his cultural influences were, Damon replied:

> I mean it certainly was coming from the music side of things. And other people, my friends who were into similar things. Certainly the idea of going to jumble sales and things like that, there was one particular kid in our school who, he suddenly started wearing – an important thing actually, I'm trying to put a date on, but probably around 1981 or 82 across Sheffield, school uniform was abolished … So suddenly you were able to come to school into all kinds of stuff … there was one particular kid who suddenly started wearing granddaddy looking shirts and kind of, with trousers that didn't quite fit and interesting jackets and stuff but looked dead good, and we said oh where do you get all this stuff and he said oh you just go to jumble sales and it's like five pence for a shirt and stuff so I started doing that.

By shopping at army surplus stores he was able to curate the image he wanted, but clothing was not a key priority for his disposable income. However, the impetus may have been on Damon to curate a stronger image for himself due to the abolition of school uniform in Sheffield during part of his time at school.[43] The use of second-hand clothing by Damon echoed a longer-standing use of 'vintage' or 'retro' clothing within an 'entrepreneurial infrastructure' of youth culture.[44] However, the growth of second-hand clothing took on particular importance in the recession of the 1980s and, in a city like Sheffield, where youth unemployment reached over 28 per cent in 1981, these practices enabled many young people to continue participating in youth fashion 'scenes'.[45]

Sue, who grew up in the 1960s, also used her clothing as a key way of expressing her sense of individuality. She recalled attending the local art college after an education at grammar school, saying:

> Sheffield Art College was then on Psalter Lane and was an annex on Union Road and if I could talk about it forever, I would. It was, it was very free and

Leisure, consumption, and identity

easy after a very strict grammar school. Erm, where you hadn't been taught to think for yourself which was the problem you were totally expected to think for yourself. Nobody else was going to do it for you. And I still don't know how to stretch a canvas! So that was a bit of a disaster. But socially it was like coming home. It was like everybody who didn't fit in anywhere else fitted at the art college. And you could be whoever you wanted to be, and it was wonderful.

For Sue, clothing was a large part of her identity creation during her years at the Sheffield School of Art. She explained:

I always loved clothes. I can remember some of my outfits now. Erm, when I was at college I'd already started buying from Oxfam but there was also, there was a Biba in town ... there was a Biba boutique upstairs and I liked to buy from there. Oh heck ... see I can remember the boutiques but I can't remember the names of them. But I wasn't averse to C&A either! I didn't buy posh. I was very, I liked to keep a little bit ahead. It was an obligation.

The growing marketplace of consumer goods provided important opportunities for young people to experiment with their image and identity. As Andy Bennett has argued, 'the increased spending power of the young facilitate[d] and encourage[d] experimentation with new, self-constructed forms of identity'.[46] However, much like Damon, Sue's use of charity shops was a cost-effective way of experimenting with style. In a period of emerging affluence, image curation still needed to be cost-effective for many working-class adolescents. These experiences act as a powerful reminder of the limits of affluence. For working class teenagers this affluence was often relative, and for young people like Sue their access to the products of youth culture were a balanced negotiation between consumption, thrift, and societal and familial expectations. Sue spoke explicitly about finances when she recalled her clothing purchase, saying:

I do specifically remember Biba, that was quite late on in the sixties I think erm, and was exceptional. I think it was financially exceptional. But I also wore a lot of, this isn't helpful to you, but my grandfather's wife ... died in the sixties. And when we went through her drawers, there were all these 1930s clothes, and twenties, that were really beautiful, beautifully cut, silk, and I used to wear a lot of those.

S: So were you quite into creating your own style?

Yeah. Especially around seventeen, eighteen. It was, they were just, they just felt so nice they just looked so nice and even better they were free! But at art college you were expected, if you like, to look different. I remember that there was the best part of a year where we didn't wear shoes. It was 1967. Or if you did you wore clogs. And I'm talking proper clogs, wooden clogs! Erm, I suppose we did try to draw attention to ourselves, but look like we weren't drawing attention to ourselves, which we were. And mark ourselves off as different.

The wider socio-cultural context of Sue's time at art school is important here. Historians have written at length about the cultural significance of art colleges to fashion and the countercultural movement in this period, and many art college students positioned themselves as overtly countercultural in their political beliefs and outward presentation in the mid-to-late 1960s.[47] As a student at the city's art college, where looking different was 'expected', Sue had to negotiate the desire to be seen as being culturally innovative on a limited budget. Further, her decision to dress in this way may well have been influenced by the behaviour of her peers and a perceived societal obligation to 'keep up', thereby navigating the boundaries between belonging and differentiation.[48]

Jeff, whose clothing choices and image were also part of a wider attempt to 'distinguish' himself from others, went to greater extremes to ensure that his image was perceived as individual. As a student, he recalled:

We would go to Manchester or Kensington Market or whatever and come back with these exotic creations and it would take a while to learn how to wear a hat. You couldn't just get a hat and wear it. It would probably take a day or two of wearing it in the house indoors to blend with it. I don't know. To work it out. There had to be a sort of jaunty angle or something which would make it work but er, yeah, probably look quite ridiculous really but I suppose the point was the more ridiculous the better really, to stand out.

Jeff explained that his desire to showcase his individuality in this way came from

Establishing an identity, there was a bit of rebellion. I think my identity was a bit rebellious so yeah, I wanted to make a statement. And it was creativity as well. Yeah, it was a, not being an artist or anything, not being able to draw or play music or anything but kind of thinking of new costumes to wear was a sort of outlet for that kind of creativity.

Jeff recalled that he'd been drawn to alternative cultures since his early teenage years, citing Shane Meadows's *This Is England* as charting his changing cultural tastes.[49] Jeff's relationship with fashion was an outlet for his personality and creativity, and his desire to 'make a statement' seemed to be the central draw to alternative culture. He reflected how this influenced his wider image, recalling:

Leisure, consumption, and identity

> [My friend] and I we were just partners in crime. Yeah, I think somebody had
> a name for us. Because we would, yeah to express our creativity, individuality
> and all the rest of it, we would wear, we had an impressive hat collection. We
> would wear different hats. So this DJ in Sheffield ... his nickname for us was
> Mr and Mrs Hat.

Jeff and his friend built a reputation for outlandish behaviour, which
informed future clothing choices and shopping behaviours. For Jeff, clothing was not just a way of denoting his personal taste, but a way of drawing
attention to himself.

For another interviewee, Jacqueline, clothing was very important. While
Jacqueline's love of clothes didn't manifest itself in a desire to 'make a statement', it was an important part of her wider youth cultural landscape.
Shopping and buying new clothes formed a significant part of her economic
and cultural experiences as a teenager. She recalled:

> I can't even remember my wages but I knew I'd like save it so I could go
> clothes shopping. But I was also lucky in the fact my mum gave me my fam-
> ily allowance so I had that. So I always had a lot of clothes ... I wasn't one
> of those who set to the clothes for all of the tide, but there were some people
> around who were like that. Like I said, if rah-rah skirts were in we were in a
> rah-rah skirt, but if Harrington jackets were in we'd do that. I think I was a
> more of a, what's in fashion, you know.

The wearing and displaying of clothing was, for many young people, a
critical part of their outward identity curation, 'yet the hours spent seeking them out on Saturday afternoons' were just as important.[50] However,
also important here is Jacqueline's statement indicating that identity creation fitted into a wider pattern of social meaning and expectation. By
noting that she 'wasn't one of those people who set their clothes for all
of the tide', Jacqueline simultaneously positioned her own experiences
directly against those of her peers. This extract also signifies an aware-
ness of the 'spectacular' other; Jacqueline tempered her own experience
against those that she perceived to be more committed to spectacular
youth styles.

Experiences like Jacqueline's have often been overlooked in favour of
more overtly 'spectacular' practices such as Jeff's.[51] However, by focusing
on the lives of young people more widely, it is possible to shed light on
the many different cultural practices of young people; Jacqueline shopped
in similar high-street stores to the more overtly 'alternative' Sue, and the
different levels with which Sue and Jeff, both 'alternative' in their outlook,
engaged with curating their image through clothing provides nuance to

more traditional models of subcultural youth that tie music, politics, and clothing neatly together.

For some young people, music was a driving factor in their clothing choices. Debbie explained how her love of Two-Tone and ska music heavily influenced her fashion choices as a teenager:

> I was really into the ska music at the time and I wore the black and white asymmetrical dresses and my boyfriend at the time he wore the Two-Tone suits and the pork pie hat ... I remember [us] really being into the ska music and all that style. And the little shoes and everything that went with it.

Similarly, Tamar's clothing choices were influenced by her wider interests. She explained that clothes were

> Massively important. But I couldn't afford them. So fashion was really important, but it was really sort of voyeuristic until I got a Saturday job and could afford them for myself. Yeah, loved all the sort of punk and new romantic stuff when I was really young, in the sort of, '83, '84. And then sort of moved on to I suppose the indie scene and Morrissey and all the sort of, grandad coats and all that sort of thing. And then you know, later, late teens, it was grunge and rave were the things that I went into.

She continued:

> Politics and music were big for me. A sort of feeling of despair if you like you know, the financials, and being bought up in a slightly left wing family then that whole ... against the yuppie thing that was on, that making money was not – so I didn't know how I was going to, what was I going to do when I grew up if you like, because this wasn't what I wanted to be yet there didn't seem to be any place for me, so I escaped through culture, through art, through music, through fashion, rather than going into the sort of that whole, I suppose what typified it would be Harry Enfield's Loadsamoney character.

Tamar's cultural identification encompassed her political beliefs, her musical tastes, and her clothing choices; by building her identity in opposition to the prevalent 'yuppie' culture of the late 1980s, Tamar's consumption habits were narrated clearly in line with her social and cultural values.[52] However, her identity creation and consumption practices did not necessarily correspond with a more authentic, or more committed, level of engagement with youth culture than her less easily categorised peers.

Young people's relationship with the products of youth culture could be complex, as were the meanings they attached to them. Through the 1960s, 1970s, and 1980s, young people growing up and going out in Sheffield

Leisure, consumption, and identity 201

navigated this in different ways. For a number of young people, clothing, traditionally the visible marker of youth cultural interests, was simply not a priority. For those young people who did engage with fashion, a variety of approaches were used, including traditional high-street shopping, buying from charity shops, and hand-making items of clothing, much of which also acted as a negotiation between the competing concerns of affordability and 'keeping up'. There was also the influence of the wider peer group and societal expectations, which undoubtedly contributed to the consumer decisions made by some young people. Focusing on clothing and music, this final section has demonstrated that many young people were managing competing priorities, often on a limited budget. By placing youth consumption within the wider landscape of the lived everyday, it has demonstrated the importance of decentring the visual markers of youth culture in favour of a biographically driven account of youth consumption that considers the meanings young people attached to the products of youth culture.

Conclusions

Oral history provides a way of accessing perspectives onto the past not usually afforded by other historical sources. It is the product of both the interviewer's approach and the interviewee's response, and as such it offers the opportunity to ask questions about culture, identity, and emotion in new ways. This chapter has shown how oral history can be utilised to explore the lived experiences of youth culture, arguing that the cultural frameworks placed on young people in post-war Britain rarely mapped out in practice. In answering broad and open-ended questions about their youthful experience, interviewees constructed a narrative that reflected their ongoing engagement with dominant cultural frameworks. As such, this chapter has explored how these cultural frameworks influenced my interviewees' perceptions of their youthful experience, and has provided evidence to support an approach to youth culture that recognises the fluidity and individual nature of young people's engagement with youth culture, whilst not overlooking the ongoing structural factors such as class and access to disposable income that may influence the extent to which a young person was able to engage with the products of youth culture in the second half of the twentieth century.

However, despite arguing for an approach to histories of youth culture that recognises the fluidity and individuality of young lives in the past, this chapter has not sought to argue that the established mainstream/alternative dichotomy had no bearing on young people's perceived sense of self. This chapter has shown that the identity politics of those who moved in alternative circles sought to uphold a separation between themselves and what they perceived to be the 'mainstream', while many others positioned themselves outside of a dominant culture that they perceived as exclusionary. By examining the language used by interviewees who considered themselves to be alternative, it is possible to see that this identity was bound in very loose terms, built against an imagined mainstream that represented an attitude as much as any stylistic or cultural traits.

This chapter has also shed light on the cultural practices of the supposedly unspectacular young people of post-war Britain. It argues that traditionally visible markers of youth cultural activity, such as clothing, do not necessarily correspond with how young people lived and experienced youth culture. A lack of interest in fashion, for example, should not be read as denoting a wider lack of engagement with other components of youth culture. Further, for those young people who did engage with fashion, this was often influenced by their wider social group. Studies that hold up of the products of youth culture as celebrated artefacts of creativity run the risk of detracting from the lived experience of young people in post-war Britain. As such, this chapter has argued that histories that engage directly with the lives of young people are needed to better understand the myriad of ways in which youth engaged with youth culture, and has demonstrated that the alternative/mainstream dichotomy highlighted by many scholars does not map clearly onto the lived experiences of young people.

Notes

1 Material from Sarah Kenny, '"Basically You Were Either a Mainstream Sort of Person or You Went to the Leadmill and the Limit"' in Kristine Moruzi, Nell Musgrove, and Carla Pascoe Leahy (eds), *Children's Voices from the Past: New Historical and Interdisciplinary Perspectives* (London: Palgrave Macmillan, 2019), 233–262. Reproduced with permission of SNSC.
2 van der Steen and Verburgh (eds), *Researching Subcultures*, 2.
3 Fuhg, *London's Working Class Youth*, 13; Harrison, *Dangerous Amusements*, 2.
4 Gildart, *Images of England*, 14.
5 Osgerby, *Youth in Britain*, 2.
6 Sociologists have considered that the 'modernisation' of society has contributed to a standardisation of the life course. For a cogent summary of this research, and the subsequent argument for 'individualisation' in the transition to adulthood, see Michael J. Shanahan, 'Pathways to Adulthood in Changing Societies: Variability and Mechanisms in Life Course Perspective', *Annual Review of Sociology*, 26:1 (2000), 667–692, https://doi.org/10.1146/annurev.soc.26.1 .667. See also Andy Furlong, 'Revisiting Transitional Metaphors: Reproducing

Inequalities under the Conditions of Late Modernity', *Journal of Education and Work*, 22:5 (2009), 343–353, https://doi.org/10.1080/13639080903453979.

7 Jeffrey Arnett, *Emerging Adulthood: The Winding Road from the Late Teens Through the Twenties* (2nd edn, New York: Oxford University Press, 2015), 8.

8 *Ibid.*, 8.

9 Langhamer, 'Love and Courtship', 188.

10 Claire Langhamer, *The English in Love: The Intimate Story of an Emotional Revolution* (Cambridge: Cambridge University Press, 2013), 5.

11 Office for National Statistics, 'Milestones: Journeying into Adulthood' (2019), via https://www.ons.gov.uk/peoplepopulationandcommunity/populationandmigration/populationestimates/articles/milestonesjourneyingintoadulthood/2019-02-18 [last accessed 10 April 2023].

12 *Ibid.*

13 On age see Brian Wilson, *Fight, Flight, or Chill: Subcultures, Youth, and Rave into the Twenty-First Century* (Montreal, QC: McGill Queen's University Press, 2006), 120. On rave and youth at the end of the twentieth century more broadly, see Steve Redhead, *Rave Off: Politics and Deviance in Contemporary Youth Culture* (Farnham: Ashgate, 1993); Steve Redhead, *End of the Century Party: Youth, Pop and the Rise of Madchester* (2nd edn, Manchester: Manchester University Press, 2020); George McKay (ed.), *DiY Culture: Party & Protest in Nineties Britain* (London: Verso, 1998); Maria Pini, *Club Cultures and Female Subjectivity: The Move from Home to House* (London: Palgrave Macmillan, 2001).

14 Hadfield, *Bar Wars*; Hollands and Chatterton, *Urban Nightscapes*.

15 Tara Brabazon, *From Revolution to Revelation: Generation X, Popular Memory and Cultural Studies* (London: Routledge, 2005), 2.

16 *Ibid.*, 13.

17 On the cultural significance of the cabaret club in 1960s Britain, see Russell, 'Glimpsing "*La Dolce Vita*"'.

18 Andy Bennett and Paul Hodgkinson, 'Introduction' in Andy Bennett and Paul Hodgkinson (eds), *Ageing and Youth Cultures: Music, Style and Identity* (London: Berg, 2012), 1. See also Andy Bennett, '"Speaking of Youth Culture": A Critical Analysis of Contemporary Youth Cultural Practice' in Dan Woodman and Andy Bennett (eds), *Youth Cultures, Transitions, and Generations: Bridging the Gap in Youth Research* (London: Palgrave Macmillan, 2015), 42–55.

19 Within popular music studies and cultural geography, the relationship between music and geography was given much greater attention by the 1990s, though much of this discussion revolved around music 'scenes' rather than the wider cultural landscape. For a summary of research in this area, see Roy Shuker, *Understanding Popular Music Culture* (5th edn, London: Routledge, 2016), 201–206.

20 See for example Vered Amit and Helena Wulff, *Youth Cultures: A Cross-Cultural Perspective* (2nd edn, London: Routledge, 2022).

204 *Youth, lived experience, and identity*

21 Frank Coffield, Carol Borrill, and Sarah Marshall, *Growing Up at the Margins: Young Adults in the North East* (Milton Keynes: Open University Press, 1986), 153.

22 Jephcott, *Rising Twenty*, 150.

23 Auriel Majumdar, Witness Oral History Project (2012).

24 Jon Savage, 'More Music', *The Observer*, 13 November 1988, 41.

25 Haslam, *Life After Dark*, 322.

26 Massey, *Space, Place, and Gender*, 4.

27 Dick Hebdige, *The Meaning of Style* (London: Routledge, 1979), 3.

28 John Clarke, 'Style' in Stuart Hall and Tony Jefferson (eds), *Resistance through Rituals: Youth Subcultures in Post-War Britain* (London: Routledge, 1993), 178.

29 The scholarship on this topic is extensive, but for a cogent summary of the key theoretical developments, see Blackman, 'Youth Subcultural Theory'; Osgerby, 'Subcultures, Popular Music and Social Change: Theories, Issues and Debates'.

30 Bennett and Kahn-Harris (eds), *After Subculture*, 11.

31 Sarah Baker, Andy Bennett, and Jodie Taylor (eds), *Redefining Mainstream Popular Music* (Abingdon: Routledge, 2013), ix.

32 J. P. Williams, 'Myth and Authenticity in Subculture Studies' in van der Steen and Verburgh (eds), *Researching Subcultures*, 36.

33 Andy Bennett, 'Subcultures or Neo-Tribes? Rethinking the Relationship Between Youth, Style, and Musical Taste', *Sociology*, 33:3 (1999), 600, https:// doi.org/10.1177/S0038038599000371. Bennett's concept of neo-tribes is drawn from Maffesoli's study of individualism. See Michel Maffesoli, *The Time of the Tribes: The Decline of Individualism in Mass Society* (London: Sage, 1996).

34 The development of Sheffield's student scene is charted by Matthew Cheeseman in 'On Going Out and the Experience of Students' in Jodie Burkett (ed.), *Students in Twentieth-Century Britain and Ireland* (London: Palgrave Macmillan, 2017), 15–44.

35 Hollands, 'Divisions in the Dark', 154.

36 *Ibid.*, 163.

37 For more on the Leadmill, see Kenny, 'A "Radical Project"'. On the Limit, see Neil Anderson, *Take It to the Limit: The Story of a Rock'n'Roll Legend* (Sheffield: ACM Retro, 2009).

38 Haslam, *Life After Dark*, 287.

39 Shildrick and MacDonald, 'In Defence of Subculture', 126.

40 Anne Boultwood and Robert Jerrard, 'Ambivalence, and Its Relation to Fashion and the Body', *Fashion Theory*, 4:3 (2000), 307, https://doi.org/10 .2752/136270400778995480.

41 Carolyn Steedman, *Landscape for a Good Woman* (London: Virago, 1986), 9.

42 Claire Langhamer outlines the importance of sewing and crafts to women's leisure time. See *Women's Leisure in England*, 178–179.

43 Patrick Seyd outlines that the abolition of school uniform was included alongside the abolition of corporal punishment in the 1981 election manifesto. The

Leisure, consumption, and identity 205

policy was unpopular, with 77 per cent of schools opposing removing uniforms, but was implemented regardless. Patrick Seyd, 'Radical Sheffield: From Socialism to Entrepreneurialism', *Political Studies*, 38:2 (1990), 342, https://doi.org/10.1111/j.1467-9248.1990.tb01498.x.

44 Angela McRobbie, 'Second-Hand Dresses and the Role of the Ragmarket' in Angela McRobbie (ed.), *Zoot Suits and Second Hand Dresses: An Anthology of Music and Fashion* (Basingstoke: Macmillan, 1989), 24.

45 SCA, SYCC PL/36/44, Economic Development Programme, Youth Unemployment Priority: The Case for South Yorkshire, 1981, 7; McRobbie, 'Second-Hand Dresses', 24.

46 Bennett, 'Subcultures or Neo-Tribes?', 602.

47 See for example Simon Frith and Howard Horne, *Art into Pop* (Abingdon: Routledge, 1987); Angela McRobbie, *British Fashion Design: Rag Trade or Image Industry* (London: Routledge, 1998); Donnelly, *Sixties Britain*, 91–103.

48 Boultwood and Jerrard, 'Ambivalence, and Its Relation to Fashion and the Body', 301.

49 On the representation of subcultural style in *This Is England*, see David Buckingham, *Youth on Screen: Representing Young People in Film and Television* (London: Polity Press, 2021), 119–137.

50 McRobbie, 'Second-Hand Dresses', 24.

51 For an interesting discussion of 'unspectacular' subculture and the everyday, see Keith Kahn-Harris, 'Unspectacular Subculture? Transgression and Mundanity in the Global Extreme Metal Scene' in Bennett and Kahn-Harris (eds), *After Subculture*, 107–118.

52 For more on the cultural power of 'Loadsamoney' and the emergence of the Yuppie, see Graham Stewart, *Bang! A History of the 1980s* (London: Atlantic Books, 2013), 247–248, 416–418.

Conclusion

> The industry has collapsed now. The name of the knife blade reads
> Korea or Singapore. The Little Mesters' workshops, where self-
> employed craftsmen applied the beauty and finish to cutlery blanks,
> have all closed. The terrifying buffer girls, cutlery polishers who – still
> wrapped like parcels in protective brown paper and string – marched
> arm-in-arm when work was done, are gone. The endless black steel-
> works, each an inferno of molten metal and noise, are demolished.
> Our industry was our identity, and now we have lost both.[1]

Writing for the *Guardian* in 1991, Richard Burns documented the post-
war decline of Sheffield's once powerful industry, describing with poetic
and devastating detail what this meant for the city. The city's history and its
civic culture had been driven by steel and cutlery, the landscape dominated
by fire and smoke; by the end of the twentieth century, large swathes of the
city were being reclaimed by nature as dereliction replaced industry. Out of
the ashes of this industrial decline, however, came the whisper of something
new. As the reverberations of metal tools at work quietened, the sound of
laughter and high heels on pavements grew louder. As the glow of furnaces
dimmed, flashing disco lights and taxi headlights took their place.

   This story, of urban transformation and change, is one that *Growing
Up and Going Out* has sought to explore. Yet, in many ways, the post-
war reimagining of the urban environment is only one half of the story.
This is also a study of the transformation of youth and, in particular, of
young people's changing relationship with the built environment. For young
people growing up and going out in the second half of the twentieth century, increased access to the products of a growing global consumer market
intersected in powerful ways with the emergence of new spaces in which
to consume them. Coffee bars materialised in the mid-1950s as places to
dance and listen to records, show off the latest outfits, and gossip over a hot
drink. Late-night beat clubs, a short-lived phenomenon through the 1950s
and 1960s made possible by creative exploitation of loopholes in the licensing system, extended the temporal possibilities of youthful sociability by
opening through the night and into the early hours. Ballrooms and dance
halls, which had for many decades retained semi-formal conventions for

Conclusion 207

social interaction, turned their attention towards static and group dancing, with many halls being swept up in the demand for late-night licensed youth leisure and repositioning themselves as nightclubs. Cinemas, similarly a well-entrenched space of youth leisure, were often remade in the image of post-war leisure demands, as ice rinks, ten-pin bowling lanes, and nightclubs.

Growing Up and Going Out has argued that locating youth within the lived and local environment is vital. The built environment through which young people moved was not static, nor was their relationship to it. Between the 1950s and the 1990s, many urban centres in Britain transformed in fundamental ways, being remade as sites of leisure, recreation, and consumerism. As such, the space that young people moved through was a 'fundamental and changing part of everyday life, one which was intimately connected to social rituals and approaches'.[2] Far from acting as a backdrop to days spent shopping with friends, first dates, or nights out dancing, the built environment was intricately woven into new patterns and forms of youthful sociability. The steamed-up windows of coffee bars offered glimpses of semi-privacy where gossip could be shared over hot espresso or soda. Pubs became meeting places for friends on route to the weekly dance at the local discotheque, where eyes might meet across the dance floor.

This book has charted the changing landscape of late-night leisure, and young people's relationship to it, at both a local and national level. The sweeping transformation of youth lifestyles and leisure was seen across Britain, yet this played out with markedly local ramifications, and the distinct spatial landscape of each town and city shaped the way that young people moved through it. In this sense, the use of Sheffield through the pages of this book has served as both illustrative and idiosyncratic. Young people who grew up, went out, and moved through the city's developing leisurescape were in many respects representative of wider trends in youth leisure across Britain. And yet the experiences of young people in this city were shaped by the particular dynamics of its recent history; from the policy of spatial regulation practised by the city's licensing magistrates, to its manufacturing decline and economic reorientation, the experiences of young people growing up and going out in Sheffield could not be directly replicated elsewhere. It has served to act as a reminder that a fuller understanding of how young people experienced their leisure time can only be gained by situating it firmly within the local and the everyday. The bus into town, the chosen route between different venues, and the reputation of individual clubs with authorities, parents, and young people themselves all played an important part in how young people experienced their local leisurescape.

The use of Sheffield as a way of locating youth in their built environment therefore allowed this book to chart, with a level of detail not afforded to national studies of youth culture, the relationship young people built with the world they moved through. This world, often unknown or unfamiliar to those outside of it, was built on an intricate network of knowledges that allowed young people to carve out spaces for themselves in an environment that was often, and increasingly, hostile to their presence. In particular, *Growing Up and Going Out* has paid attention to the intersection between the spatial and the temporal. It has argued that, as the urban centre at night was remade as a site of youth leisure, young people's experience of the city became increasingly separate from that of the wider population. That separation was both spatial – in the spaces they moved in and between – and temporal – in the way that the night was both feared and controlled. It is also this intersection that reveals more clearly how contemporaries understood and narrated post-war youth leisure, not only as driven by immediate gratification and hedonism but marked apart as both spatially and temporally distinct from the wider leisure landscape.

This has also been a history that requires us to take popular culture seriously, not as an entry-point into wider studies of social, cultural, and political change, nor as a vignette that sheds light on more serious or worthy topics of historical enquiry. It requires us to pay attention to popular culture, on its own terms, because it is a central part of how many people moved through and understood the world around them. For many young people, popular culture afforded opportunities for pleasure and excitement, and it was often formative in building an independent sense of self. Yet, as Lucy Robinson has powerfully argued, the factors that shape which forms of popular culture are accorded value and which are overlooked speak to deeply binary visions of what is considered socially and culturally significant.[3] Who, what, and how we remember has critical implications for the histories that we tell. Many of the spaces explored in this book were driven by the giants of commercial leisure provision, who poured millions of pounds into the British night-time economy to provide affordable glamour to the masses. While we can – and should – remain critical of the homogenising power of big business, it remains the case that these spaces, the hallowed grounds of Top 40 pop, of late-night kisses, and of dressing up and dancing round handbags, were a central and fundamental part of growing up for generations of young people in Britain.

Part I of *Growing Up and Going Out* considered how young people moved through and moulded the urban leisurescape. In particular, it argued for a greater recognition of the tangible ways that youthful leisure changed the urban environment. The purchasing power of young people, and the appetite of leisure providers to capitalise on this, had the potential to transform the urban centre after dark. Through a study of the post-war urban centre, it demonstrated clearly how youth lifestyles changed in the post-war period, becoming reoriented around the growing number of venues that sought to speak solely to their interests. These shifts in youth lifestyles and leisure, however, drew calls for regulation and control. These were, in many ways, a continuation of longstanding anxieties about commercial youth leisure, but also spoke to the particular fears attached to young people's movement through the city after dark.

Chapter 1 utilised both new and established forms of evening youth leisure to demonstrate how new patterns of youthful sociability were being woven into the fabric of the post-war built environment. Moving away from the metropole, it argued that provincial towns and cities were home to a growing number of leisure spaces that were designed predominantly or solely for young consumers. It situated the emergence of new spaces of youth leisure – the coffee bar and late-night jazz and beat club in particular – within a wider landscape of youth-oriented venues including ballrooms, dance halls, and youth clubs to argue that while the primary aims of youth leisure remained oriented around the chance to meet and socialise with friends, the opportunity to retreat into semi-private spaces away from the adult gaze was important to young people. This retreat, and the growing spatial separation between the leisure experiences of adults and young people, exposed significant intergenerational tensions. Longstanding anxieties about the threat of commercial leisure to young consumers clashed with a clear, if sometimes reluctant, recognition that existing provision for young people was inadequate. Youth clubs installed juke boxes and coffee bars, while dance halls were branded as a reputable and preferred alternative to the moral dangers posed by the all-night beat club.

Chapter 2 explored the commercial implications of an increasingly affluent and time-rich youthful demographic. Charting the diversification and expansion of two giants of the leisure industry, Mecca and the Rank Organisation, alongside the meteoric rise of the Bailey Organisation, Chapter 2 demonstrated the central role that commercial leisure organisations played in remaking the post-war landscape. From the transformation of existing leisure destinations such as cinemas and dance halls into nightclubs, and agreements with building corporations involved in city-centre redevelopment and New Town construction, to the creation of new leisure supercentres, the role of commercial enterprise in urban redevelopment was significant. This commercial investment also had a dramatic effect on the types of leisure spaces that young people had access to; as the numbers of youth-oriented venues in Britain became concentrated in the hands of a minority of companies, young people were simultaneously offered access to a fast-expanding variety of leisure spaces while being placed at the mercy of strategic business decisions. For young people in smaller towns, this had significant consequences as new and more lucrative markets were identified,

210   *Growing up and going out*

while many racially and sexually minoritised young people were subjected to discriminatory management practices.

Chapter 3 turned to the question of regulation, considering how the new spaces of youth-oriented leisure in post-war towns and cities were controlled. In particular, it argued that the desire to control access to late-night leisure was driven by longstanding associations between moral transgressions and the night; these anxieties were only further compounded in relation to adolescents and young adults, particularly young women, whose visible movement through the modern urban night was a cause of significant unease. The growth of licensed leisure venues for the young only served to further heighten this concern, as fears about the movement of youth through the urban night intersected with anxieties about intoxication and public drunkenness. Governments, local authorities, the media, and licensing magistrates all communicated the importance of maintaining strong control over how, when, and where young people were able to access spaces of commercial leisure. Despite meaningful and deep-seated changes to the leisure landscape across the second half of the twentieth century, the desire to regulate youthful leisure remained a constant. Licensing magistrates emerged as one key way of achieving this, and as such, the way that youth leisure was regulated played out with distinctly regional variations.

Part II of *Growing Up and Going Out* turned towards the experiences of young people themselves to ask what meanings they attached to their leisure experiences, how they moved through the urban environment, and how they constructed new patterns of sociability. The growth of new late-night leisure spaces offered the opportunity for new experiences, particularly for young women. The public house and late-night bar emerged as an acceptable and increasingly desirable leisure space, though women exercised discretion in the types of venues they socialised in. The consumption of alcohol became a growing, and far more visible, component of youth leisure as the night-time economy became ingrained as a youth-oriented leisure destination. Underage drinking was common for both young men and women, and over the course of the second half of the twentieth century, the entrenchment of alcohol in youth leisure spaces drove a distinct drinking culture that reflected the spatial separation of youth from the wider urban leisurescape. However, structural barriers – particularly those of gender and class – remained, and young people built clear strategies to navigate these.

Chapter 4 argued that the development of a distinct culture of youth drinking can be charted between the 1960s and 1990s. While much attention has been paid to the binge-drinking panics of the 1990s and early 2000s, Chapter 4 demonstrated how alcohol consumption was built into youthful sociability, for both men and women, across the post-war period. In particular, it demonstrated the ordinary spectacle of youth, in which forms of consumption that are generally considered unremarkable are rendered spectacular and extraordinary when practised by young people. While the majority of youthful drinking was often unremarkable in its nature, differing predominantly in the type of alcohol consumed and the location of its consumption, it was nonetheless tied to concerns about rising rates of violence and disorder which served to further entrench anxieties about young people socialising after dark. For young women, the changing drinking culture was most stark, and provides a productive way of charting the shifting nature of the expectations and restrictions placed on their free time across the post-war period.

Chapter 5 asked what these changes, to the built environment and to youth lifestyles, meant for young people themselves. It demonstrated that the built environment played a significant role in how young people felt about their cultural experiences and, in particular, the meanings that they attached to them. Individual venues and events were ascribed meaning by those who moved through the city at night, though these were porous and often reflected wider concerns with youth cultural frameworks. However, it argued that those established narrative frameworks, of an active and alternative culture in binary opposition to a passive mainstream, rarely mapped onto lived experience. Young people moved through the city in ways that prioritised sociability, choosing spaces that aligned with the desires of wider friendship groups, whether to drink, dance, flirt, gossip, or pose. Young people also valued spaces that they felt comfortable in, and this feeling of comfort was often constructed in relation to who else moved through those spaces; did they play music that was easy to dance to, did they dress 'up', or dress in ways that suggested 'insider' status, did they provide space for groups of women to socialise without ongoing harassment by men, or did they provide the opportunity for romantic or sexual encounters? These were all questions that shaped how youth engaged with late-night leisure spaces in their local environment. In short, young people built a powerful local knowledge of the late-night leisurescape and exercised this knowledge in ways that gave them agency over their cultural experiences. This local knowledge also extended to their consumption practices, in which decisions about record stores, clothing, and travel were often part of a balanced negotiation between affordability and the construction of desirable leisure experiences.

There is, of course, much more that can be said about the leisured lives of young people in post-war Britain, and it is hoped that *Growing Up and Going Out* has posed questions that others will take up in their own work. How, for example, did young people in rural areas and small towns navigate access to the commercial spaces of late-night leisure? How far did structural barriers such as public transport shape their experiences and opportunities,

212 *Growing up and going out*

and what meanings did they attach to their local leisure spaces?[4] Further consideration should also go to the shifting relationship between race, migration, and late-night leisure. How did young people of colour navigate and shape the leisure landscape, and how did young people from different cultural backgrounds, particularly those who did not drink, navigate the often disparate expectations of family, friends, and society?[5] There is also much to be said about the growing numbers of university students across this period. This book has touched on the experiences of students briefly, but a fuller discussion of their relationship to the towns and cities they lived in would be illuminating.[6] Finally, as we move into the twenty-first century, how did technology and access to new virtual spaces of youth culture shape young people's relationship with the built environment?

Growing Up and Going Out has asked us to take the everyday experiences of youth leisure seriously. In doing so, it has extended our knowledge of young lives in post-war Britain and shown how young people navigated the world around them. Everyday engagement with youth culture in Britain was played out at the level of street, high street, and city centre, and was founded on discrete and specialised knowledges. The built environment was central to new and continued patterns of sociability that prioritised friendship and social interaction, and it provides an essential way of understanding the meanings young people attached to their leisure time. Over the course of the post-war period, the 'night out' became embedded as a central cultural space for young men and women across Britain, one that offered escapism and pleasure as well as opportunities for self discovery and independent movement through the city. Pulp's Jarvis Cocker sang of Britain's 'common people', those who would go out to 'dance, and drink, and screw'.[7] *Growing Up and Going Out* is their history.

Notes

1 'Sheffield, the City of Craft and Graft', *Guardian*, 16 October 1991, 2.

2 Harrison, *Dangerous Amusements*, 216.

3 Lucy Robinson, 'How Hard Is It to Remember Bananarama? The Perennial Forgetting of Girls in Music', *Popular Music History*, 12:2 (2020), 152–173, https://doi.org/10.1558/pomh.40052.

4 On youth and rural life, see Edwards, *Youth Movements, Citizenship and the English Countryside*; Sian Edwards, '"A Richness That Is Lacking Now": Country Childhoods, Nostalgia and Rural Change in the Mass Observation Project', *History*, 104:363 (2019), 941–963, https://doi.org/10.1111/1468 -229X.12921; Laura Harrison, '"There Wasn't All That Much to Do … At Least Not Here": Memories of Growing Up in Rural South West England in

the Early Twentieth Century', *Rural History*, 31:2 (2020), 165–180, https://doi
.org/10.1017/S0956793320000199.
5 These themes are explored in Caspar Melville, *It's a London Thing: How Rare
Groove, Acid House and Jungle Remapped the City* (Manchester: Manchester
University Press, 2019).
6 Matthew Cheeseman's study of students in Sheffield explores the rise of 'student land', showing clearly how the city's student population helped transform
the leisurescape in the post-war period: Cheeseman, 'On Going Out'.
7 Pulp, 'Common People' on *Different Class* [CD], Island Records (1995).

Appendix

Brief biographical details of the men and women interviewed:

Notes:

i) Participants who have chosen to use a pseudonym are not distinguished from those participants who have used their real names for reasons of privacy.
ii) Participants were asked to briefly introduce themselves, rather than filling in a biographical questionnaire. Where a section is left blank, or information is brief, it is because this information did not arise during the interview process.
iii) Where an age rather than a date of birth is given, this is the age at the date of the interview.

Adrian

Born/age: 44 years old, born in Sheffield.
Education: Left school at 16, entered a Youth Training Scheme.
Career: Unknown.
Contact: Interview conducted by Sarah Kenny, 8 October 2015.

Ann

Born/age: 1942, born in Sheffield.
Education: Attended Abbeydale Grammar School, attended Commercial College and then entered Nurses' College aged 18.
Career: Nurse.
Contact: Interview conducted by Sarah Kenny, 29 September 2015.

216 *Growing up and going out*

Barbara

Born/age: 78 years old, born in Sheffield.
Education: Unknown.
Career: Before marriage she worked in a cutlery firm. After marriage, she was a full-time mother, and she began a playgroup for local children after her three children were born.
Contact: Interview conducted by Sarah Kenny, 24 September 2015.

Damon

Born/age: 48 years old, born in Sheffield.
Education: Attended local comprehensive school, completed a foundation course in Art and Design at Sheffield Polytechnic before attending Coventry Polytechnic to do a degree in Fine Art.
Career: Freelance writer.
Contact: Interview conducted by Sarah Kenny, 31 September 2015.

Darren

Born/age: 1967, born in Sheffield.
Education: Attended local comprehensive school, attended Richmond College before attending Huddersfield Polytechnic to do a degree in Accounting.
Career: Accountant.
Contact: Interview conducted by Sarah Kenny, 9 September 2015.

David

Born/age: 1952, born in Sheffield.
Education: Attended local comprehensive school, expelled during exams. Gained qualifications in metallurgy, photography, and computing as an adult.
Career: Worked as an analytical chemist after leaving school.
Interview date: 15 September 2015.

Appendix

Debbie

Born/age: 51 years old, born in Sheffield.
Education: Left school at 16 and joined the Police Cadets.
Career: Police Constable.
Contact: Interview conducted by Sarah Kenny, 6 November 2014.

Gillian

Born/age: 1961, born in Sheffield.
Education: Attended local comprehensive school, left during A-levels.
Career: Worked in insurance after leaving school.
Contact: Interview conducted by Sarah Kenny, 5 October 2015.

Helen H.

Born/age: 1960, born in Sheffield.
Education: Left school at 16 and completed a pre-nursing course at Granville
College before joining the Nursing College.
Career: Nurse.
Contact: Interview conducted by Sarah Kenny, 31 July 2015.

Helen M.

Born/age: 47 years old, born in the north-east but grew up in Cheshire.
Education: Attended the local comprehensive until the age of 18 before
attending university in Sheffield to do a degree in Accounting and Maths.
Career: Accountant.
Contact: Interview conducted by Sarah Kenny, 29 September 2015.

Jacqueline

Born/age: 1966, born in Sheffield.
Education: Completed qualifications at local comprehensive school before
attending Nottingham Polytechnic to do a degree in Teaching.
Career: Teacher.
Contact: Interview conducted by Sarah Kenny, 3 September 2015.

Jeff

Born/age: 49 years old, born in Kent.
Education: Educated in Kent, moved to Sheffield aged 19 to do a degree in Psychology, before completing an MSc in Software Engineering.
Career: Unknown.
Contact: Interview conducted by Sarah Kenny, 28 September 2015.

Juan

Born/age: Exact age unknown, likely born between 1962–1963. Went to university in 1981. Born in Sheffield.
Education: Attended local comprehensive school until the age of 18 before going to Wolverhampton Polytechnic to do a degree in Physics and Computing.
Career: IT services.
Contact: Interview conducted by Sarah Kenny, 27 January 2015.

Kevin

Born/age: 64 years old, born in Sheffield.
Education: Attended local Secondary Modern, before attending the Technical School aged 14. Failed A-levels and attended Richmond College of Further Engineering on day-release from work. Retrained as a teacher towards the end of the 1970s.
Career: Teacher.
Contact: Interview conducted by Sarah Kenny, 15 October 2015.

Marian

Born/age: 1954, born in Sheffield.
Education: Educated at Notre Dame Grammar School before attending Bradford University to do a degree in Human Purposes and Communication. She left the degree before graduating and came back to Sheffield.
Career: Unknown.
Contact: Interview conducted by Sarah Kenny, 23 September 2015.

Appendix

Mark

Born/age: 43 years old, born in Sheffield.
Education: Attended local comprehensive school, left with no qualifications before joining a Youth Training Scheme.
Career: Worked in the care industry; at time of interview was retraining in academia.
Contact: Interview conducted by Sarah Kenny, 18 September 2015.

Owen

Born/age: 52 years old, born in Sheffield.
Education: Attended local comprehensive school before completing O-Levels and CSEs. Left education at 16.
Career: Has worked in family business since leaving school.
Contact: Interview conducted by Sarah Kenny, 26 January 2015.

Pat

Born/age: 1953, born in Sheffield.
Education: Attended grammar school until the age of 18 before attending teacher training college.
Career: Teacher.
Contact: Interview conducted by Sarah Kenny, 25 September 2015.

Sue

Born/age: 1950, born in Sheffield.
Education: Attended Abbeydale Grammar School. Left at 16 to do an art foundation course at Sheffield School of Art before attending teacher training college.
Career: Teacher.
Contact: Interview conducted by Sarah Kenny, 28 September 2015.

Tamar

Born/age: 44 years old, moved to Sheffield aged 10.
Education: Attended local comprehensive school before completing A-levels at Richmond College. Completed a degree at Nottingham University.
Career: Works in the creative and cultural sector.
Contact: Interview conducted by Sarah Kenny, 22 September 2015.

Tony

Born/age: 59 years old, born in Sheffield.
Education: Left school at 17 and joined the army just before his 18th birthday.
Career: Following three years in the army, he joined a Sheffield tool firm, working in exports.
Contact: Interview conducted by Sarah Kenny, 4 November 2014.

Trish

Born/age: 1949, born in Sheffield.
Education: Attended grammar school before going to the University of Leicester to do a degree in Combined Studies. Following completion of her degree, she retrained as a teacher.
Career: Taught in mainstream schools before specialising as a teacher in Special Educational Needs schools.
Contact: Interview conducted by Sarah Kenny, 21 September 2015.

Bibliography

Primary sources

Archival collections

Sheffield City Archives

MC 20/1/1, Registers of licences, publicans
MC 20/1/2, Registers of licences, publicans
MC 20/2/1, Registers of licences, beer on or off the premises
MC 20/4/1, Registers of licences, music
MC 20/5/462, Licensing files for individual pubs, clubs, and on-licensed premises, Stone House
MC 20/5/471, Licensing files for individual pubs, clubs, and on-licensed premises, Roxy
MC 2008/146, Sheffield Corporation, Licensing Justices, Minutes
      Box 83, 10/11/1965–06/01/1970 and 10/02/1970–17/08/1971
      Box 82, 28/09/1971–23/10/1973 and 13/11/1973–09/12/1975
      Box 81, 13/01/1976–06/12/1977 and 10/01/1978–11/12/1979
      Box84,05/02/1980–17/12/1980,06/01/1981–16/12/1981,15/01/1985–8/12/1985
      Box85,18/01/1982–04/01/1983,08/02/1983–17/01/1984,07/02/1984–18/12/1984
      Box 87, 10/01/1986–02/12/1986, 09/01/1987–15/12/1987
      Box 86, 08/01/1988–08/11/1988, 06/01/1989–24/11/1989
CA 674/4/25, Town Clerk's files, Correspondence and reports relating to the Mojo Club
SYCC ADMIN/10/16/2 (SYCC/CB/1526), Leadmill Papers, 1983–86
SYCC ADMIN/10/16/1 (SYCC/CB/1527), Leadmill Papers, 1985–86
SYCC PL/36/44, Economic Development Programme, Youth Unemployment Priority: The Case for South Yorkshire, 1981
SYCC PL/36/50, Economic Development Programme, Trends in Youth Unemployment, 1980

Cadbury Research Library

MS 227/1/1/1/3, Council and AGM Minutes, 1948–67
MS 227/1/1/1/4, Council and AGM Minutes, 1967–84

222   *Bibliography*

MS 227/1/1/7/18, Youth Work Committee, 1973–76
MC 227/7/3/1, External and related items, books and pamphlets, 1939–2014

National Archives

BN 29/984, Reports on the Work of the Children's Department, Delinquency and the Courts, 1967–69
BN 29/1046, Committee on Social Services, Sub-committee on the Youth Service, 1969
BN 29/1684, Home Office and Department of Heath and Social Security: Children, Causes of Juvenile Delinquency, Undesirable Clubs, 1964–1965
CK 2/358, Commission for Racial Equality and Predecessors, Samantha's Club, 1975–1976
HO 295/118, Alcohol and Crime: Standing Conference on Crime Prevention, Working Group on Young People and Alcohol, 1986–1987
HO 287/4375, Home Office Standing Conference on Crime Prevention, Working Group on Young People and Alcohol, 1987
HO 287/4331, Home Office Standing Conference on Crime Prevention, Working Group on Young People and Alcohol, 1987

Oral history interviews

Interviews conducted by the author, 2014–2015. See Appendix for further details.
Witness Oral History Project, University of Sheffield
Interviews archived at https://witness.sites.sheffield.ac.uk/home [last accessed 02/03/2024]

Printed primary sources

Newspapers, magazines, and journals

Extensive use

Daily Mail
Daily Mirror
Financial Times
Justice of the Peace (also titled *Justice of the Peace and Local Government Review*)
The Guardian (Renamed from *Manchester Guardian* in 1959)
Star
The Economist
The Stage
The Times
Top Star Special

Occasional use

Aberdeen Evening Express

Bibliography

Acton Gazette
Bristol Evening Post
Birmingham Daily Post
Cambridge Evening News
Chester Chronicle
Coventry Evening Telegraph
Crewe Chronicle
Daily Herald
Daily Telegraph
Eastbourne Gazette
Eastbourne Herald
Hammersmith and Shepherds Bush Gazette
Harrow Observer
Kinematograph Weekly
Liverpool Echo
Melody Maker
Middlesex Country Times
Morning Telegraph
Newcastle Evening Chronicle
Newcastle Journal
Observer
Peterborough Advertiser
Petticoat
Sheffield Telegraph
Sunday Times
Wells Journal
Worthing Gazette

Books, pamphlets, and autobiographies

Blunkett, D., Green, G., *Building from the Bottom: The Sheffield Experience*, Fabian Society No. 491 (London: Fabian Society, 1983).

Coffield, F., Borrill, C., Marshall, S., *Growing Up at the Margins: Young Adults in the North East* (Milton Keynes: Open University Press, 1986).

Evans, W. M., *Young People in Society* (Oxford: Basil Blackwell, 1965).

Fairley, R., *Come Dancing Miss World* (London: Neamme, 1966).

Gosling, R., *Lady Albemarle's Boys* (London: The Fabian Society, 1961).

Hall, G. S., *Adolescence in Psychology and Its Relation to Physiology, Anthropology, Sociology, Sex, Crime, Religion, and Education: Vols I & II* (Englewood Cliffs, NJ: Prentice-Hall, 1904).

Hoggart, R., *The Uses of Literacy: Aspects of Working-Class Life* (6th edn, London: Penguin, 2009).

Jephcott, P., *A Troubled Area: Notes on Notting Hill* (London: Faber and Faber, 1964).

224   *Bibliography*

Jephcott, P., *Rising Twenty: Notes on Some Ordinary Girls* (London: Faber and Faber, 1948).
Jephcott, P., *Time of One's Own* (London: Oliver and Boyd, 1967).
Mays, J. B., *The Young Pretenders: A Study of Teenage Culture in Contemporary Society* (London: Schocken Books, 1966).
Schofield, M., *The Sexual Behaviour of Young People* (London: Longmans, 1965).
Steedman, C., *Landscape for a Good Woman* (London: Virago, 1986).
Willmott, P., *Adolescent Boys of East London* (2nd edn, London: Pelican, 1975).

Reports and surveys

Abrams, M., *The Teenage Consumer* (London: London Press Exchange, 1959).
Davies, J., Stacey, B., *Teenagers and Alcohol: A Developmental Study in Glasgow: Volume II* (London: HMSO, 1972).
Hawker, A., *Adolescents and Alcohol* (London: B. Edsall & Co Ltd, 1978).
Jahoda, G., Cramond, J., *Children and Alcohol: A Developmental Study in Glasgow: Volume I* (London: HMSO, 1972).
Mass Observation, FR 1837–7A, 'Juvenile Drinking', June 1947.
Ministry of Education, *The Youth Service in England and Wales* (London: HMSO, 1960).

Journal articles

Child, D., Paddon, M., 'Sheffield: Steelyard Blues', *Marxism Today* (July 1984), 18–22.
Cloyd, J., 'The Market-Place Bar: The Interrelation Between Sex, Situation, and Strategies in the Pairing Ritual of Homo Ludens', *Urban Life*, 5:3 (1976), 293–312.
Davies, J., Stacey, B., 'Drinking Behaviour in Childhood and Adolescence: An Evaluative Review', *Journal of Alcohol and Drug Education*, 17:3 (1972), 1–11.
Ghodsian, M., Power, C., 'Alcohol Consumption Between the Ages of 16 and 23 in Britain: A Longitudinal Study', *British Journal of Addiction*, 82 (1987), 175–180.
Gofton, L., 'On the Town: Drink and the "New Lawlessness"', *Youth and Policy*, 29 (1990), 33–39.
Lawless. P., Ramsden, P., 'Sheffield in the 1980s: From Radical Intervention to Partnership', *Cities*, 7:3 (1990), 202–210, https://doi.org/10.1016/0264 -2751(90)90048-C.
Measham, F., 'The "Big Bang" Approach to Sessional Drinking: Changing Patterns of Alcohol Consumption Amongst Young People in North West England', *Addiction Research*, 4:3 (1996), 283–299, https://doi.org/10.3109/16066359609005573.

Web sources

Blake, H., Collier, J., Polnay, L., Armstrong, S., 'Drinking Habits of 16 Year Olds: Secondary Analysis of the 1970 British Cohort Study', Short Accessible Report

Bibliography

May 2001, Academic Division of Child Health, University of Nottingham, via https://nottingham-repository.worktribe.com/index.php/preview/702962/AERC _FinalReport_0007.pdf [last accessed 9 April 2023].

'EMI Report: Report and Accounts, Chairman's Review' (1974), via https://web.archive.org/web/20170624071641/ttp://www.kronemyer.com/EMI/EMI%20Music%20AR%201974.pdf [last accessed 19 May 2023].

'EMI Report: Report and Accounts, Chairman's Review' (1978), via https://web.archive.org/web/20170624051043/http://www.kronemyer.com/EMI/EMI%20Music%20AR%201978.pdf [last accessed 19 May 2023].

Hansard, via https://hansard.parliament.uk/ [last accessed 19 September 2024].

'History and Heritage', via sheffield.ac.uk/about/history [last accessed 22 May 2023].

Hollands, R., *Friday Night, Saturday Night: Youth Cultural Identification In The Post-Industrial City* (Newcastle: Newcastle University, 1995), 1–90, via https://research.ncl.ac.uk/youthnightlife/hollands.pdf [last accessed 12 April 2023].

Office for National Statistics, 'Milestones: Journeying into Adulthood' (2019), via https://www.ons.gov.uk/peoplepopulationandcommunity/populationandmigration/populationestimates/articles/milestonesjourneyingintoadulthood/2019-02-18 [last accessed 10 April 2023].

Winkler, A., 'Sheffield City Report', *CASE Report* 45 (2007), via http://eprints.lse.ac.uk/5133/1/CASEreport45.pdf [last accessed 22 May 2023].

Media

The Long Journey [film], directed by Philip Donnellan (BBC, 1964).

Pulp, 'Common People' on Different Class [CD], Island Records (1995).

Sheffield: City on the Move [film], directed by Jim Coulthard (Sheffield City Council, 1972).

Secondary sources

Abra, A., *Dancing in the English Style: Consumption, Americanisation and National Identity in Britain, 1918–1950* (Manchester: Manchester University Press, 2017).

Abra, A., 'Doing the Lambeth Walk: Novelty Dances and the British Nation', *Twentieth Century British History*, 20:3 (2009), 346–369, https://doi.org/10.1093/tcbh/hwp035.

Abrams, L., *Oral History Theory* (London: Routledge, 2010).

Albiez, S., 'Know History!: John Lydon, Cultural Capital and the Prog/Punk Dialectic', *Popular Music*, 22:3 (2003), 357–374, https://doi.org/10.1017/S0261143003003234.

Aldridge, J., Measham, F., Williams, L., *Illegal Leisure Revisited: Changing Patterns of Alcohol and Drug Use in Adolescents and Young Adults* (London: Routledge, 2011).

Bibliography

Alexander, K., Sleight, S. (eds), *A Cultural History of Youth in the Modern Age* (London: Bloomsbury, 2022)

Allred, N., 'Mother Gin and the Bad Examples: Figuring a Drug Crisis, 1736–51', *Eighteenth Century Fiction*, 33:3 (2021), 369–392, https://doi.org/10.3138/ecf.33.3.369.

Amit, V., Wulff, H., *Youth Cultures: A Cross-Cultural Perspective* (2nd edn, London: Routledge, 2022).

Anderson, N., *Dirty Stop Out's Guide to 1960s Sheffield* (Sheffield: ACM Retro, 2011).

Anderson, N., *Take It to the Limit: The Story of a Rock'n'Roll Legend* (Sheffield: ACM Retro, 2009).

Andrews, A., Kefford, A., Warner, D., 'Community, Culture, Crisis: the Inner City in England, c. 1960–1990', *Urban History*, 50:2 (2023), 202–213, 10.1017/S0963926821000729.https://doi.org/

Arnett, J., *Emerging Adulthood: The Winding Road from the Late Teens Through the Twenties* (2nd edn, New York: Oxford University Press, 2015).

Bailey, P., *Leisure and Class in Victorian England: Rational Recreation and the Contest for Control, 1830–1885* (London: Routledge, 1978).

Bailey, P., 'The Politics and Poetics of Modern British Leisure: A Late Twentieth-Century Review', *Rethinking History*, 3:2 (1999), 131–175, https://doi.org/10.1080/13642529908596341.

Baker, S., Bennett, A., Taylor, J. (eds), *Redefining Mainstream Popular Music* (Abingdon: Routledge, 2013).

Baldwin, P., *In the Watches of the Night: Life in the Nocturnal City, 1820–1930* (Chicago, IL: University of Chicago Press, 2012).

Baldwin, P., '"Nocturnal Habits and Dark Wisdom": The American Response to Children in the Streets at Night, 1880–1930', *Journal of Social History*, 35:3 (2002), 593–611, https://doi.org/10.1353/jsh.2002.0002.

Baun, D., Pascoe Leahy, C., 'Spaces and Places' in Alexander, K., Sleight, S. (eds), *A Cultural History of Youth in the Modern Age* (London: Bloomsbury, 2022), 41–62.

Bean, J. P., *Singing from the Floor: A History of British Folk Clubs* (London: Faber and Faber, 2014, eBook edn).

Beaven, B., *Leisure, Citizenship and Working-Class Men in Britain, 1850–1945* (Manchester: Manchester University Press, 2005).

Beckingham, D., 'Gender, Space, and Drunkenness: Liverpool's Licensed Premises, 1860–1914' *Annals of the Association of American Geographers*, 102:3 (2012), 647–666, https://doi.org/10.1080/00045608.2011.652850.

Beckingham, D., *The Licensed City: Regulating Drink in Liverpool, 1830–1920* (Liverpool: Liverpool University Press, 2017).

Bennett, A., '"Speaking of Youth Culture": A Critical Analysis of Contemporary Youth Cultural Practice' in Woodman, D., Bennett, A. (eds), *Youth Cultures, Transitions, and Generations: Bridging the Gap in Youth Research* (London: Palgrave Macmillan, 2015), 42–55.

Bibliography

Bennett, A., 'Subcultures or Neo-Tribes? Rethinking the Relationship Between Youth, Style, and Musical Taste', *Sociology*, 33:3 (1999), 599–617, https://doi.org/10.1177/S0038038599000371.

Bennett, A., Hodgkinson, P. (eds), *Ageing and Youth Cultures: Music, Style and Identity* (London: Berg, 2012).

Bennett, A., Hodgkinson, P., 'Introduction' in Bennett, A., Hodgkinson, P. (eds), *Ageing and Youth Cultures: Music, Style and Identity* (London: Berg, 2012), 1–9.

Bennett, A., Kahn-Harris, K. (eds), *After Subculture: Critical Studies in Contemporary Youth Culture* (Basingstoke: Palgrave Macmillan, 2004).

Berridge, V., *Demons: Our Changing Attitudes to Alcohol, Tobacco, and Drugs* (Oxford: Oxford University Press, 2013).

Berridge, V., Herring, R., Thom, B., 'Binge Drinking: A Confused Concept and Its Contemporary History', *Social History of Medicine*, 22:3 (2009), 597–607, https://doi.org/10.1093/shm/hkp053.

Berridge, V., McGregor, J., 'Local and National Policy Making for Alcohol: Nottingham, UK, 1950–2007', *Social History of Alcohol and Drugs*, 25:1–2 (2011), 148–164, https://doi.org/10.1086/SHAD25010148.

Bianchini, F., 'Night Cultures, Night Economies', *Planning Practice & Research*, 10:2 (1995), 121–126, https://doi.org/10.1080/02697459550036667.

Blackman, S., 'Youth Subcultural Theory: A Critical Engagement with the Concept, Its Origins and Politics, from the Chicago School to Postmodernism', *Journal of Youth Studies*, 8:1 (2005), 1–20, https://doi.org/10.1080/13676260500063629.

Boultwood, A., Jerrard, R., 'Ambivalence, and Its Relation to Fashion and the Body', *Fashion Theory*, 4:3 (2000), 301–321, https://doi.org/10.2752/136270400778995480.

Boyd Whyte, I. (ed.), *Man-Made Future: Planning, Education and Design in Mid-Twentieth-Century Britain* (London: Routledge, 2007).

Brabazon, T., *From Revolution to Revelation: Generation X, Popular Memory and Cultural Studies* (London: Routledge, 2005).

Bradford, S., 'Managing the Spaces of Freedom: Mid-Twentieth-Century Youth Work' in Mills, S., Kraftl, P. (eds), *Informal Education, Childhood and Youth* (Basingstoke: Palgrave Macmillan, 2014), 184–196.

Bradley, K., 'Rational Recreation in the Age of Affluence: The Café and Working-Class Youth in London, c.1939–1965' in Rappaport, E., Trudgen Dawson, S., Crowley, M. J. (eds), *Consuming Behaviours: Identity, Politics and Pleasure in Twentieth-Century Britain* (London: Bloomsbury, 2015), 71–86.

Brocken, M., *The British Folk Revival: 1944–2002* (Aldershot: Ashgate, 2003).

Brown, C., *The Battle for Christian Britain: Sex, Humanists and Secularisation, 1945–1980* (Cambridge: Cambridge University Press, 2019).

Buckingham, D., *Youth on Screen: Representing Young People in Film and Television* (London: Polity Press, 2021).

Butler, S., Elmeland, K., Thom, B., Nicholls, J., *Alcohol, Power and Public Health: A Comparative Study of Alcohol Policy* (London: Routledge, 2017).

Campbell, L., 'Paper Dream City/Modern Monument: Donald Gibson and Coventry' in Boyd Whyte, I. (ed.), *Man-Made Future: Planning, Education and Design in Mid-Twentieth-Century Britain* (London: Routledge, 2007), 121–144.

Carder, T., *The Encyclopaedia of Brighton* (Brighton: Brighton and Hove Libraries, 1990).

Carr, N., 'Editorial: Positioning Alcohol in the Leisure Experience', *Annals of Leisure Research*, 11:3–4 (2008), 265–270, https://doi.org/10.1080/11745398.2008.9686797.

Carr, P., 'The Lost Musical Histories of Merthyr Tydfil', *Popular Music History*, 12:1 (2019), 112–40, https://doi.org/10.1558/pomh.v12i1.2775.

Carter, F., 'A Taste of Honey: Get-Ahead Femininity in 1960s Britain' in Ritchie, R., Hawkins, S., Phillips, N., Kleinberg, S. J. (eds), *Women in Magazines: Research, Representation, Production and Consumption* (London: Routledge, 2016), 183–197.

Caslin, S., *Save the Womanhood! Vice, Urban Immorality and Social Control in Liverpool, c.1900–1976* (Liverpool: Liverpool University Press, 2018).

Catterall, S., Gildart, K., *Keeping the Faith: A History of Northern Soul* (Manchester: Manchester University Press, 2020).

Chambers, E., 'The Jamaican 1970s and Its Influence on the Making of Black Britain', *Small Axe*, 23:1 (2019), 134–149, https://doi.org/10.1215/07990537-7374502.

Charnock, H., 'Teenage Girls, Female Friendship and the Making of the Sexual Revolution in England, 1950–1980', *Historical Journal*, 63:4 (2020), 1032–1053, https://doi.org/10.1017/S0018246X19000396.

Chatterton, P., Hollands, R., 'Changing Times for an Old Industrial City: Hard Times, Hedonism and Corporate Power in Newcastle's Nightlife', *City* 6:3 (2002), 291–315, https://doi.org/10.1080/1360481022000037742

Chatterton, P., Hollands, R., 'Theorising Urban Playscapes: Producing, Regulating and Consuming Youthful Nightlife City Spaces', *Urban Studies*, 39:1 (2002), 95–116, https://doi.org/10.1080/00420980220099096.

Chatterton, P., Hollands, R., *Urban Nightscapes: Youth Cultures, Pleasure Spaces and Corporate Power* (London: Routledge, 2003).

Cheeseman, M., 'On Going Out and the Experience of Students' in Burkett, J. (ed.), *Students in Twentieth-Century Britain and Ireland* (London: Palgrave Macmillan, 2017), 15–44.

Clarke, J., 'Style' in Hall, S., Jefferson, T. (eds), *Resistance through Rituals: Youth Subcultures in Post-War Britain* (London: Routledge, 1993), 175–191.

Clarke, J., Hall, S., Jefferson, T., Roberts, B., 'Subcultures, Cultures and Class: A Theoretical Overview' in Hall, S., and Jefferson, T. (eds), *Resistance Through Rituals* (London: Routledge, 1993), 9–74.

Clarkson, A., 'Virtual Heroes: Boys, Masculinity and Historical Memory in War Comics 1945–1995', *Boyhood Studies*, 2:2 (2008), 175–185, https://doi.org/10.3149/thy.0202.175.

Clements, C., 'Lady Albemarle's Youth Workers: Contested Professional Identities in English Youth Work 1958–1985', *History of Education*, 48:6 (2019), 819–836, https://doi.org/10.1080/0046760X.2019.1588395.

Bibliography

Cohen, S., *Folk Devils and Moral Panics* (3rd edn, Abingdon: Routledge, 2011).

Cohen, S., Young, J. (eds), *The Manufacture of News: A Reader* (Beverly Hills, CA: Sage, 1973).

Collin, M., *Altered State: The Story of Ecstasy Culture and Acid House* (London: Serpent's Tail, 1997).

Conekin, B., Mort, F., Waters C. (eds), *Moments of Modernity: Reconstructing Britain, 1945–1964* (London: Rivers Oram Press, 1999).

Connell, K., Hilton, M. (eds), *Cultural Studies 50 Years On: History, Practice and Politics* (London: Rowman and Littlefield, 2016).

Connell, K., Hilton, M., 'The Working Practices of Birmingham's Centre for Contemporary Cultural Studies', *Social History*, 40:3 (2013), 287–311, https://doi.org/10.1080/03071022.2015.1043191.

Cook, M., 'Local Matters: Queer Scenes in 1960s Manchester, Plymouth, and Brighton', *Journal of British Studies*, 59:1 (2020), 32–56, https://doi.org/10.1017/jbr.2019.244.

Coslett, T., Lury, C., Summerfield, P. (eds), *Feminism and Autobiography: Texts, Theories, Methods* (London: Routledge, 2000).

Cox, P., *Gender, Justice and Welfare in Britain, 1900–1950: Bad Girls in Britain, 1900–1950* (London: Palgrave, 2003).

Crowson, N., Hilton, M., and McKay, J. (eds), *NGOs in Contemporary Britain: Non-State Actors in Society and Politics Since 1945* (Basingstoke: Palgrave, 2009).

Cunningham, H., *Time, Work and Leisure: Life Changes in England Since 1700* (Manchester: Manchester University Press, 2014).

Daunton, M. (ed.), *The Cambridge Urban History of Britain: Volume III* (Cambridge: Cambridge University Press, 2001).

Davies, A., *Leisure, Gender and Poverty: Working-Class Culture in Salford and Manchester, 1900–39* (Milton Keynes: Open University Press, 1992).

Davies, B., *From Voluntaryism to Welfare State: A History of the Youth Service in England, Volume 1 1939–1979* (Leicester: Youth Work Press, 1999).

Davis, J., 'Central Government and the Towns' in Daunton, M. (ed.), *The Cambridge Urban History of Britain: Volume III* (Cambridge: Cambridge University Press, 2001), 259–286.

Donnelly, M., *Sixties Britain: Culture, Society and Politics* (Harlow: Pearson Education, 2005).

Dorn, N., *Alcohol, Youth and the State* (London: Croom Helm, 1983).

Downs, C., *A Social, Economic and Cultural History of Bingo (1906–2005): The Role of Gambling in the Lives of Working Women* (Berlin: VDM Verlag, 2009).

Downs, C., 'Mecca and the Birth of Commercial Bingo 1958–70: A Case Study', *Business History*, 52:7 (2010), 1086–1106, https://doi.org/10.1080/00076791.2010.523460.

Dunn, N., 'Place After Dark: Urban Peripheries as Alternative Futures' in Edensor, T., Kalandides, A., Kothari, U. (eds), *The Routledge Handbook of Place* (London: Routledge, 2020), 153–167.

Bibliography

Dyhouse, C., *Girl Trouble: Panic and Progress in the History of Young Women* (2nd edn, London: Zed Books, 2014).

Edensor, T., Kalandides, A., Kothari, U. (eds), *The Routledge Handbook of Place* (London: Routledge, 2020).

Edwards, S., '"A Richness That Is Lacking Now": Country Childhoods, Nostalgia and Rural Change in the Mass Observation Project', *History*, 104:363 (2019), 941–963, https://doi.org/10.1111/1468-229X.12921.

Edwards, S., *Youth Movements, Citizenship and the English Countryside: Creating Good Citizens, 1930–1960* (Basingstoke: Palgrave Macmillan, 2018).

Evans, K., Taylor, I., Fraser, P., *A Tale of Two Cities: Global Change, Local Feeling, and Everyday Life in the North of England* (London: Routledge, 2002).

Evans, T., 'Stopping the Poor Getting Poorer: The Establishment and Professionalisation of Poverty NGOs, 1945–95' in Crowson N., Hilton, M., McKay, J. (eds), *NGOs in Contemporary Britain* (Basingstoke: Palgrave, 2009), 147–163.

Eyles, A., *Odeon Cinemas: Oscar Deutsch Entertains Our Nation* (London: BFI Publishing, 2002).

Farmer, R., *Cinemas and Cinemagoing in Wartime Britain, 1939–1945: The Utility Dream Palace* (Manchester: Manchester University Press, 2016).

Feldman-Barrett, C., 'Back to the Future: Mapping a Historic Turn in Youth Studies', *Journal of Youth Studies*, 21:6 (2019), 733–746, https://doi.org/10.1080/13676261.2017.1420150.

Fenton, L., 'Practices of Learning, Earning and Intimacy in Women's Drinking Biographies' (Unpublished PhD, University of Manchester, 2017).

Fisher, T., 'Permissiveness and the Politics of Morality', *Contemporary Record*, 7:1 (1993), 149–195, https://doi.org/10.1080/13619469308581241.

Fitzgerald, R., *The Rise of the Global Company: Multinationals and the Making of the Modern World* (Cambridge: Cambridge University Press, 2016).

Flinn, C., '"The City of Our Dreams?" The Political and Economic Realities of Rebuilding Britain's Blitzed Cities, 1945–54', *Twentieth Century British History*, 23:2 (2012), 221–245.

Fogg, M., *Boutique: A '60s Cultural Icon* (London: Mitchell Beazley, 2003).

Fowler, D., *The First Teenagers: The Lifestyle of Young Wage-Earners in Interwar Britain* (London: Routledge, 1996).

Fowler, D., *Youth Culture in Modern Britain, c.1920–c.1970* (Basingstoke, Palgrave Macmillan, 2008).

Frith, S., *Sound Effects: Youth, Leisure, and the Politics of Rock 'n' Roll* (New York: Pantheon Books, 1981).

Frith, S., Horne, H., *Art into Pop* (Abingdon: Routledge, 1987).

Fuhg, F., 'Ambivalent Relationships: London's Youth Culture and the Making of the Multi-Racial Society in the 1960s', *Britain and the World*, 11:1 (2018), 4–26, https://doi.org/10.3366/brw.2018.0285.

Fuhg, F., *London's Working-Class Youth and the Making of Post-Victorian Britain, 1958–1971* (London: Palgrave Macmillan, 2021).

Bibliography

Furlong, A., 'Revisiting Transitional Metaphors: Reproducing Inequalities Under the Conditions of Late Modernity', *Journal of Education and Work*, 22:5 (2009), 343–353, https://doi.org/10.1080/13639080903453979.

Garland, J., Gildart, K., Gough-Yates, A., Hodkinson, P., Osgerby, B., Robinson, L., Street, J., Webb, P., Worley, M., 'Youth Culture, Popular Music and the End of "Consensus" in Post-War Britain', *Contemporary British History*, 26:3 (2012), 265–271, https://doi.org/10.1080/13619462.2012.703002.

Gensburger, S., 'Halbwachs' Studies in Collective Memory: A Founding Text for Contemporary "Memory Studies"?', *Journal of Classical Sociology*, 16:4 (2016), 396–413, https://doi.org/10.1177/1468795X16656268.

Gildart, K., '"The Antithesis of Humankind": Exploring Responses to the Sex Pistols' Anarchy UK Tour 1976', *Cultural and Social History*, 10:1 (2013), 129–149, https://doi.org/10.2752/147800413X13515292098313.

Gildart, K., *Images of England Through Popular Music: Class, Youth and Rock'n'Roll, 1955–1976* (Basingstoke: Palgrave Macmillan, 2013).

Gold, J. R., *The Practice of Modernism: Modern Architects and Urban Transformation, 1954–1972* (New York: Routledge, 2007).

Goodwin, J., O'Connor, H. (eds), 'Pearl Jephcott: Reflections, Resurgence and Replications', *Women's History Review*, 28:5 (2019), 711–813.

Green, J., *All Dressed Up: The Sixties and the Counterculture* (London: Random House, 1998).

Greenaway, J., *Drink and British Politics since 1830: A Study in Policy-Making* (Basingstoke: Palgrave Macmillan, 2003).

Greenhalgh, J., *Reconstructing Modernity: Space, Power and Governance in Mid-Twentieth Century British Cities* (Manchester: Manchester University Press, 2017).

Griffiths, J., '"Rivalling the Metropolis": Cultural Conflict between London and the Regions c.1967–1973', *Contemporary British History*, 33:4 (2019), 524–547, https://doi.org/10.1080/13619462.2018.1519434.

Gunn, S., *The Public Culture of the Victorian Middle Class* (Manchester: Manchester University Press, 2007).

Gunn, S., 'The Rise and Fall of British Urban Modernism: Planning Bradford 1945–1970', *Journal of British Studies*, 48:1 (2010), 849–869, https://doi.org/10.1086/654912.

Gutzke, D., *Pubs and Progressives: Reinventing the Public House in England, 1896–1960* (DeKalb, IL: Northern Illinois University Press, 2006).

Gutzke, D., *Women Drinking Out in Britain Since the Early Twentieth Century* (Manchester: Manchester University Press, 2014).

Hadfield, P., *Bar Wars: Contesting the Night in Contemporary British Cities* (Oxford: Oxford University Press, 2006).

Halbwachs, M., *On Collective Memory* (trans. L. A. Coser, Chicago, IL: University of Chicago Press, 1992).

Hall, L. A., *Sex, Gender and Social Change in Britain Since 1880* (London: Macmillan, 2000).

Hall, S., Critcher, C., Jefferson, T., Clarke, J., Roberts, B., *Policing the Crisis: Mugging, the State, and Law and Order* (2nd edn, Basingstoke: Palgrave Macmillan, 2013).

Hall, S., Jefferson, T. (eds), *Resistance through Rituals: Youth Subcultures in Post-War Britain* (London: Routledge, 1993).

Harrison, L., *Dangerous Amusements: Leisure, the Young Working Class and Urban Space in Britain, c. 1870–1939* (Manchester: Manchester University Press, 2022).

Harrison, L., '"The Streets Have Been Watched Regularly": The York Penitentiary Society, Young Working-Class Women, and the Regulation of Behaviour in the Public Spaces of York, c. 1845–1919', *Women's History Review*, 28:3 (2019), 457–478, https://doi.org/10.1080/09612025.2018.1477105.

Harrison, L., '"There Wasn't All That Much to Do ... At Least Not Here": Memories of Growing Up in Rural South West England in the Early Twentieth Century', *Rural History*, 31:2 (2020), 165–180, https://doi.org/10.1017/S0956793320000199.

Haslam, D., *Life After Dark: A History of British Nightclubs and Music Venues* (London: Simon and Schuster, 2016).

Hebdige, D., *The Meaning of Style* (London: Routledge, 1979).

Henry, W. 'L'., 'Reggae, Rasta and the Role of the Deejay in the Black British Experience', *Contemporary British History*, 23:3 (2012), 355–373, https://doi.org/10.1080/13619462.2012.703024.

Henry, W. 'L'., Back, L., 'Reggae Culture as Local Knowledge: Mapping the Beats on South East London Streets' in Henry, W. 'L'., Worley, M. (eds), *Narratives from Beyond the UK Reggae Bassline: The System Is Sound* (Basingstoke: Palgrave Macmillan, 2020), 29–57.

Henry, W. 'L'., Worley, M. (eds), *Narratives from Beyond the UK Reggae Bassline: The System Is Sound* (Basingstoke: Palgrave Macmillan, 2020).

Hesmondhalgh, D., 'Subcultures, Scenes or Tribes? None of the Above', *Journal of Youth Studies*, 8:1 (2005), 21–40, https://doi.org/10.1080/13676260500063652.

Hey, D., *A History of Sheffield* (3rd edn, Lancaster: Carnegie, 2010).

Hollands, R., 'Divisions in the Dark: Youth Cultures, Transitions and Segmented Consumption in the Night-Time Economy', *Journal of Youth Studies*, 5:2 (2002), 153–171, https://doi.org/10.1080/13676260220134421.

Hopkins, H., *The New Look: A Social History of the Forties and Fifties in Britain* (London: Secker and Warburg, 1963).

Horn, A., *Juke Box Britain: Americanisation and Youth Culture, 1946–60* (Manchester: Manchester University Press, 2009).

Houlbrook, M., *Queer London: Pleasures and Perils in the Sexual Metropolis, 1918–1957* (Chicago, IL: University of Chicago Press, 2005).

Hubbard, P., *Cities and Sexualities* (Abingdon: Routledge, 2001).

Hulme, T., *After the Shock City: Urban Culture and the Making of Modern Citizenship* (London: Bloomsbury, 2019).

Hutton, F., *Risky Pleasures: Club Cultures and Feminine Identities* (London: Routledge, 2006).

Jackson, C., Tinkler, P., '"Ladettes" and "Modern Girls": "Troublesome" Young Femininities', *The Sociological Review*, 55:2 (2007), 251–272, https://doi.org/10.1111/j.1467-954X.2007.00704.x.

Bibliography

Jackson, L., 'The Coffee Club Menace', *Cultural and Social History*, 5:3 (2015), 289–308, https://doi.org/10.2752/147800408X331407.

Jackson, L., *Palaces of Pleasure: From Music Halls to the Seaside to Football, How the Victorians Invented Mass Entertainment* (New Haven, CT: Yale University Press, 2019).

Jackson, L., Bartie, A., *Policing Youth: Britain, 1945–1970* (Manchester: Manchester University Press, 2014).

Jenks, C., *Childhood* (2nd edn, London: Routledge, 2005).

Jerram, L., *Streetlife: The Untold History of Europe's Twentieth Century* (Oxford: Oxford University Press, 2011).

Jones, R., Merriman, P., Mills, S., 'Youth Organizations and the Reproduction of Nationalism in Britain: The Role of Urdd Gobaith Cymru', *Social and Cultural Geography*, 175 (2016), 714–734, https://doi.org/10.1080/14649365.2016 .1139166.

Kahn-Harris, K., 'Unspectacular Subculture? Transgression and Mundanity in the Global Extreme Metal Scene' in Bennett, A., Kahn-Harris, K. (eds), *After Subculture: Critical Studies in Contemporary Youth Culture* (Basingstoke: Palgrave Macmillan, 2004), 107–118.

Kefford, A., 'The Arndale Property Company and the Transformation of Urban Britain, 1950–2000', *Journal of British Studies*, 61:3 (2022), 563–598, https:// doi.org/10.1017/jbr.2022.54.

Kefford, A., *The Life and Death of the Shopping City: Public Planning and Private Redevelopment in Britain since 1945* (Cambridge: Cambridge University Press, 2022).

Kenny, S., 'A "Radical Project": Youth Culture, Leisure, and Politics in 1980s Sheffield', *Twentieth Century British History*, 30:4 (2019), 557–584, https://doi .org/10.1093/tcbh/hwz006.

Kenny, S., '"Basically You Were Either a Mainstream Sort of Person or You Went to the Leadmill and the Limit"' in Moruzi, K., Musgrove, N., Pascoe Leahy, C. (eds), *Children's Voices from the Past: New Historical and Interdisciplinary Perspectives* (London: Palgrave Macmillan, 2019), 233–262.

Kenny, S., 'We Are No Longer Certain, Any of Us, What Is "Right" and What Is "Wrong": Honey, Petticoat, and the Construction of Young Women's Sexuality in 1960s Britain' in The Subcultures Network (eds), *Let's Spend the Night Together: Sex, Pop Music and British Youth Culture, 1950s–80s* (Manchester: Manchester University Press, 2023), 75–94.

King, L., 'Future Citizens: Cultural and Political Conceptions of Children in Britain, 1930s–1950s', *Twentieth Century British History*, Vol. 27:3 (2016), 389–411, https://doi.org/10.1093/tcbh/hww025.

Kneale, J., 'The Place of Drink: Temperance and the Public, 1856–1914', *Social & Cultural Geography*, 2:1 (2001), 43–59, https://doi.org/10.1080 /14649360020028267.

Kuhlman, M., *The Sound With the Pound: An Anthology of the 60s Merseybeat Sound* (Liverpool: Bluecoat Press, 2009).

Langhamer, C., *The English in Love: The Intimate Story of an Emotional Revolution* (Cambridge: Cambridge University Press, 2013).

Langhamer, C., 'Love and Courtship in Mid-Twentieth Century England', *The Historical Journal*, 50:1 (2007), 173–196, https://doi.org/10.1017/S0018246X06005966.

Langhamer, C., '"A Public House Is for All Classes, Men and Women Alike": Women, Leisure and Drink in Second World War England', *Women's History Review*, 12:3 (2003), 423–444, https://doi.org/10.1080/09612020300200367.

Langhamer, C., *Women's Leisure in England 1920–60* (Manchester: Manchester University Press, 2000).

Latham, E., 'The Liverpool Boys' Association and the Liverpool Union of Youth Clubs: Youth Organisations and Gender, 1940–1970', *Journal of Contemporary History*, 35:3 (2000), 423–437, https://doi.org/10.1177/002200940003500306.

Leeworthy, D., 'Singing Elton's Song: Queer Sexualities and Youth Cultures in England and Wales, 1967–85' in The Subcultures Network (eds), *Let's Spend the Night Together: Sex, Pop Music and British Youth Culture, 1950s–80s* (Manchester: Manchester University Press, 2023), 152–169.

Lefebvre, H., *The Production of Space* (trans. D. Nicholson-Smith, Oxford: Blackwell, 1991).

Leigh, S., *Twist and Shout: Merseybeat, The Cavern, The Star Club and The Beatles* (Liverpool: Nirvana Books, 2004).

Lister Sharp, D., 'Underage Drinking in the United Kingdom since 1970: Public Policy, the Law and Adolescent Drinking Behaviour', *Alcohol and Alcoholism*, 29:5 (1994), 555–563, https://doi.org/10.1093/oxfordjournals.alcalc.a045584.

Long, P., 'British Radio and the Politics of Culture in Post-war Britain: The Work of Charles Parker', *The Radio Journal*, 2:3 (2004), 131–152, https://doi.org/10.1386/rajo.2.3.131/1.

Lovatt, A., O'Connor, J., 'Cities and the Night-Time Economy', *Planning Practice & Research*, 10:2 (1995), 127–134, https://doi.org/10.1080/02697459550036676.

Lovett, L., 'Age: A Useful Category of Analysis', *Journal of the History of Childhood and Youth*, 1:1 (2008), 114–124, https://doi.org/10.1353/hcy.2008.0015.

Lynch, C., 'Moral Panic in the Industrial Town: Teenage "Deviancy" and Religious Crisis in Central Scotland, c.1968–9', *Twentieth Century British History*, 32:3 (2021), 371–391, https://doi.org/10.1093/tcbh/hwaa017.

Macnab, G., *J. Arthur Rank and the British Film Industry* (London: Routledge, 1994).

Maffesoli, M., *The Time of the Tribes: The Decline of Individualism in Mass Society* (London: Sage, 1996).

Malbon, B., *Clubbing: Dancing, Ecstasy and Vitality* (London: Routledge, 1999).

Mandler, P., 'New Towns for Old: The Fate of the Town Centre' in Conekin, B., Mort, F., Waters, C. (eds), *Moments of Modernity: Reconstructing Britain, 1945–1964* (London: Rivers Oram Press, 1999), 208–227.

Manning, S., *Cinemas and Cinema-Going in the United Kingdom: Decades of Decline, 1945–65* (London: Royal Historical Society, The Boydell Press, 2020).

Bibliography

Martinic, M., Measham, F. (eds), *Swimming with Crocodiles: The Culture of Extreme Drinking* (London: Routledge, 2008).

Marwick, A., *British Society Since 1945* (4th edn, London: Penguin, 2003).

Marwick, A., *The Sixties: Cultural Revolution in Britain, France, Italy, and the United States, c.1958–c.1974* (Oxford: Oxford University Press, 1998).

Massey, D., *Space, Place, and Gender* (Oxford: Polity Press, 1994).

Massey, D., 'The Spatial Construction of Youth Cultures' in Skelton, T., Valentine, G. (eds), *Cool Places: Geographies of Youth Cultures* (London: Routledge, 1998), 121–130.

Maynes, M. J., 'Age as a Category of Historical Analysis: History, Agency, and Narratives of Childhood', *Journal of the History of Childhood and Youth*, 1:1 (2008), 114–124, https://doi.org/10.1353/hcy.2008.0001.

McAllister, A., '"Giant Alcohol": A Worthy Opponent for the Children of the Band of Hope', *Drugs: Education, Prevention and Policy*, 22:2 (2014), 103–110, https://doi.org/10.3109/09687637.2014.977227.

McKay, G. (ed.), *DiY Culture: Party & Protest in Nineties Britain* (London: Verso, 1998).

McRobbie, A., *British Fashion Design: Rag Trade or Image Industry* (London: Routledge, 1998).

McRobbie, A., *Feminism and Youth Culture: From Jackie to Just Seventeen* (Basingstoke: Palgrave Macmillan, 1991).

McRobbie, A., 'Second-Hand Dresses and the Role of the Ragmarket' in McRobbie, A. (ed.), *Zoot Suits and Second Hand Dresses: An Anthology of Music and Fashion* (Basingstoke: Macmillan, 1989), 23–49.

McRobbie, A. (ed.), *Zoot Suits and Second Hand Dresses: An Anthology of Music and Fashion* (Basingstoke: Macmillan, 1989).

Melville, C., *It's a London Thing: How Rare Groove, Acid House and Jungle Remapped the City* (Manchester: Manchester University Press, 2019).

Milcoy, K., *When The Girls Come Out to Play: Teenage Working-Class Girls' Leisure Between the Wars* (London: Bloomsbury, 2017).

Milestone, K., 'Swinging Regions: Young Women and Club Culture in 1960s Manchester', *Film, Fashion, and Consumption*, 7:2 (2018), 179–194, https://doi.org/10.1386/ffc.7.2.179_1.

Mills, H., 'Using the Personal to Critique the Popular: Women's Memories of 1960s Youth', *Contemporary British History*, 30:4 (2016), 463–483, https://doi.org/10.1080/13619462.2016.1206822.

Mills, S., Kraftl, P. (eds), *Informal Education, Childhood and Youth* (Basingstoke: Palgrave Macmillan, 2014).

Mitchell, G. A. M., 'Reassessing "the Generation Gap": Bill Haley's 1957 Tour of Britain, Inter-Generational Relations and Attitudes to Rock 'n' Roll in the Late 1950s', *Twentieth Century British History*, 24:4 (2013), 573–605, https://doi.org/10.1093/tcbh/hwt01.3

Mold, A., '"Everybody Likes a Drink. Nobody Likes a Drunk." Alcohol, Health Education and the Public in 1970s Britain', *Social History of Medicine*, 30:3 (2017), 612–636, https://doi.org/10.1093/shm/hkw094.

Mold, A., 'From the Alcoholic to the Sensible Drinker: Alcohol Health Education Campaigns in England' in Jackson, M., Moore, M. D. (eds), *Balancing the Self: Medicine, Politics and the Regulation of Health in the Twentieth Century* (Manchester: Manchester University Press, 2020), 64–94.

Moran, J., 'Milk Bars, Starbucks and the Uses of History', *Cultural History*, 20:6 (2006), 552–573, https://doi.org/10.1080/09502380600973911.

Mort, F., *Cultures of Consumption: Masculinities and Social Space in Late-Twentieth Century Britain* (London: Routledge, 1996).

Moss, S., '"A Grave Question": The Children Act and Public House Regulation, c. 1908–1939', *Crimes and Misdemeanours: Deviance and the Law in Historical Perspective*, 3:2 (2009), 98–117.

Moss, S., '"Continental Connotations": European Wine Consumption in 1970s Britain', *Contemporary European History*, 29:4 (2020), 431–450, https://doi.org/10.1017/S0960777320000417.

Munting, R., *A Social and Economic History of Gambling in Britain and the USA* (Manchester: Manchester University Press, 1996).

Munting, R., 'Betting and Business: The Commercialisation of Gambling in Britain', *Business History*, 31:4 (1989), 67–85, https://doi.org/10.1080/00076798900000085.

Nicholls, J., 'Alcohol Licensing in Scotland: A Historical Overview', *Addiction*, 107:8 (2012), 1397–1403, https://doi.org/10.1111/j.1360-0443.2012.03799.x.

Nicholls, J., *The Politics of Alcohol: A History of the Drink Question in England* (Manchester: Manchester University Press, 2011).

Nott, J., 'Dance Halls: Towards an Architectural and Spatial History, c. 1918–65', *Architectural History*, 61 (2018), 205–233, https://doi.org/10.1017/arh.2018.8.

Nott, J., *Going to the Palais: A Social and Cultural History of Dancing and Dance Halls in Britain* (Oxford: Oxford University Press, 2015).

Nott, J., 'Contesting Popular Dancing and Dance Music in Britain During the 1920s', *Cultural and Social History*, 10:3 (2013), 439–456, https://doi.org/10.2752/147800413X13661166397300.

Nott, J., *Music for the People: Popular Music and Dance in Interwar Britain* (Oxford: Oxford University Press, 2002).

Oatley, N., Mackie, C., 'Sheffield's Cultural Industries Quarter', *Local Economy*, 11:2 (1996), 172–179, https://doi.org/10.1080/02690949608726324.

Ortolano, G., 'Planning the Urban Future', *The Historical Journal*, 54:2 (2011), 477–507, https://doi.org/10.1017/S0018246X11000100.

Osgerby, B., 'Subcultures, Popular Music and Social Change: Theories, Issues and Debates' in The Subcultures Network (eds), *Subcultures, Popular Music and Social Change* (Cambridge: Cambridge Scholars Publishing, 2014), 1–46.

Osgerby, B., '"Well It's Saturday Night an' I Just Got Paid": Youth, Consumerism and Hegemony in Post-War Britain', *Contemporary Record*, 6:2 (1992), 287–305, https://doi.org/10.1080/13619469208581212.

Osgerby, B., *Youth in Britain Since 1945* (Oxford: Blackwell, 1998).

Osgerby, B., *Youth Media* (London: Routledge, 2004).

Payling, D., *Socialist Republic: Remaking the British Left in 1980s Sheffield* (Manchester: Manchester University Press, 2023).

Bibliography

237

Perks, R., Thomson, A. (eds), *The Oral History Reader* (London: Routledge, 1997).

Peter, B., 'The Impact of the Talkies on Scottish Cinema Architecture', *Visual Culture in Britain*, 20:3 (2019), 202–220, https://doi.org/10.1080/14714787.2019.1686415.

Phillips, D., 'The Press and Pop Festivals: Stereotypes of Youthful Leisure' in Cohen, S., Young, J. (eds), *The Manufacture of News: A Reader* (Beverly Hills, CA: Sage, 1973), 323–334.

Pini, M., *Club Cultures and Female Subjectivity: The Move from Home to House* (London: Palgrave Macmillan, 2001).

Plant, M., Plant, M., *Risk Takers: Alcohol, Drugs, Sex and Youth* (London: Routledge, 1992).

Portelli, A., 'What Makes Oral History Different' in Perks, R., Thomson, A. (eds), *The Oral History Reader* (London: Routledge, 1997), 63–74.

Pugh, M., *'We Danced All Night': A Social History of Britain Between the Wars* (London: Vintage Books, 2009).

Qvortrup, J., Corsaro, W. A., Honig, M. S. (eds), *The Palgrave Handbook of Childhood Studies* (London: Palgrave Macmillan, 2009).

Ramamurthy, A., *Black Star: Britain's Asian Youth Movements* (London: Pluto Press, 2013).

Rappaport, E., Trudgen Dawson, S., Crowley, M. J. (eds), *Consuming Behaviours: Identity, Politics and Pleasure in Twentieth-Century Britain* (London: Bloomsbury, 2015).

Redhead, S., *End of the Century Party: Youth, Pop and the Rise of Madchester* (2nd edn, Manchester: Manchester University Press, 2020).

Redhead, S., *Rave Off: Politics and Deviance in Contemporary Youth Culture* (Farnham: Ashgate, 1993).

Redhead, S., Wynne, D., O'Connor, J. (eds), *The Clubcultures Reader: Readings in Popular Cultural Studies* (Oxford: Blackwell, 1997).

Richards, J., *The Age of the Dream Palace: Cinema and Society in 1930s Britain* (3rd edn, London: I.B. Tauris, 2010).

Ritchie, D., *The Oxford Handbook of Oral History* (Oxford: Oxford University Press, 2010).

Ritchie, R., Hawkins, S., Phillips, N., Kleinberg, S. J. (eds), *Women in Magazines: Research, Representation, Production and Consumption* (London: Routledge, 2016).

Roberts, M., Eldridge. A., *Planning the Night-Time City* (Abingdon: Routledge, 2009).

Robinson, L., 'How Hard Is It to Remember Bananarama? The Perennial Forgetting of Girls in Music', *Popular Music History*, 12:2 (2020), 152–173, https://doi.org/10.1558/pomh.40052.

Russell, D., 'Glimpsing *"La Dolce Vita"*: Cultural Change and Modernity in the 1960s English Cabaret Club', *Journal of Social History*, 47:2 (2013), 297–318, https://doi.org/10.1093/jsh/sht083.

Rusterholz, C., *Responsible Pleasure: The Brook Advisory Centres and Youth Sexuality in Postwar Britain* (Oxford: Oxford University Press, 2024).

Bibliography

Sandbrook, D., *Never Had It So Good: A History of Britain from Suez to the Beatles* (London: Abacus, 2006).

Sandbrook, D., *White Heat: A History of Britain in the Swinging Sixties* (London: Abacus, 2007).

Sauerteig, L. D. H., Davidson, R. (eds), *Shaping Sexual Knowledge: A Cultural History of Sex Education in Twentieth Century Europe* (London: Routledge, 2009).

Saumarez Smith, O., *Boom Cities: Architect Planners and the Politics of Radical Urban Renewal in 1960s Britain* (Oxford: Oxford University Press, 2019).

Saumarez Smith, O., 'Central Government and Town-Centre Redevelopment in Britain, 1959–1966', *The Historical Journal*, 58:1 (2015), 217–244, https://doi.org/10.1017/S0018246X14000077.

Saumarez Smith, O., 'The Lost World of the British Leisure Centre', *History Workshop Journal*, 88:1 (2019), 180–203, https://doi.org/10.1093/hwj/dbz007.

Savage, J., *Teenage: The Creation of Youth: 1875–1945* (London: Pimlico, 2007).

Schivelbusch, W., *Disenchanted Night: Industrialization of Light in the Nineteenth Century* (Oakland, CA: University of California Press, 1998).

Schofield, C., 'In Defence of White Freedom: Working Men's Clubs and the Politics of Sociability in Late Industrial England', *Twentieth Century British History*, 34:3 (2023), 515–551, https://doi.org/10.1093/tcbh/hwad038.

Searle, K., *From Farms to Foundries: An Arab Community in Industrial Britain* (Oxford: Peter Lang, 2010).

Seyd, P., 'Radical Sheffield: From Socialism to Entrepreneurialism', *Political Studies*, 38:2 (1990), 335–344, https://doi.org/10.1111/j.1467-9248.1990.tb01498.x.

Shanahan, M. J., 'Pathways to Adulthood in Changing Societies: Variability and Mechanisms in Life Course Perspective', *Annual Review of Sociology*, 26:1 (2000), 667–692, https://doi.org/10.1146/annurev.soc.26.1.667.

Shapely, P., 'Civic Pride and Redevelopment in the Post-War British City', *Urban History*, 39:2 (2012), 310–328, https://doi.org/10.1017/S0963926812000077.

Shildrick, T., MacDonald, R., 'In Defence of Subculture: Young People, Leisure and Social Divisions', *Journal of Youth Studies*, 9:2 (2006), 125–140, https://doi.org/10.1080/13676260600635599.

Shuker, R., *Understanding Popular Music Culture* (5th edn, London: Routledge, 2016).

Skelton, T., Valentine, G. (eds), *Cool Places: Geographies of Youth Cultures* (London: Routledge, 1998).

Sleight, S., 'Rites of Passage: Youthful Walking and the Rhythms of the City, c.1850–1914' in Bryant, C., Burns, A., Readman, P. (eds), *Walking Histories, 1800–1914* (London: Palgrave Macmillan, 2016), 87–112.

Sleight, S., *Young People and the Shaping of Public Space in Melbourne, 1870–1914* (Abingdon: Routledge, 2013).

Snape, R., 'The New Leisure, Voluntarism and Social Reconstruction in Inter-War Britain', *Contemporary British History*, 29:1 (2015), 51–83, https://doi.org/10.1080/13619462.2014.963060.

Bibliography

Snape, R., Pussard, H., 'Theorisations of Leisure in Inter-War Britain', *Leisure Studies*, 32:1 (2013), 1–18, https://doi.org/10.1080/02614367.2011.629371.

Sneeringer, J., *A Social History of Early Rock'n'Roll in Germany: Hamburg from Burlesque to the Beatles, 1956–69* (London: Bloomsbury, 2018).

Springhall, J., *Youth, Popular Culture and Moral Panics: Penny Gaffs to Gangsta Rap, 1830–1996* (London: Palgrave Macmillan, 1998).

Stewart, G., *Bang! A History of the 1980s* (London: Atlantic Books, 2013).

Stratton, J., 'Disco Before Disco: Dancing and Popular Music in the 1960s and 1970s in England', *Journal of Popular Music Studies*, 33:1 (2021), 50–69, https://doi.org/10.1525/jpms.2021.33.1.50.

Stratton, J., *Spectacle, Fashion and the Dancing Experience in Britain, 1960–1990* (London: Palgrave Macmillan, 2022).

The Subcultures Network (eds), *Let's Spend the Night Together: Sex, Pop Music and British Youth Culture, 1950s–80s* (Manchester: Manchester University Press, 2023).

Summerfield, P., Peniston-Bird, C., 'Women in the Firing Line: The Home Guard and the Defence of Gender Boundaries in Britain in the Second World War', *Women's History Review*, 9:2 (2000), 231–255, https://doi.org/10.1080/09612020000200250.

Takayanagi, M., 'Astor the Fairy Godmother: The Intoxicating Liquor Act 1923', *Open Library of Medical Humanities*, 6:2 (2020), 13, https://doi.org/10.16995/olh.567.

Tebbutt, M., *Being Boys: Youth, Leisure and Identity in the Inter-War Years* (Manchester: Manchester University Press, 2014).

Tebbutt, M., *Making Youth: A History of Youth in Modern Britain* (London: Bloomsbury, 2016).

Thom, B., *Dealing with Drink: Alcohol and Social Policy in Contemporary England* (London: Free Association Books, 1999).

Thompson, P., *The Voice of the Past: Oral History* (3rd edn, Oxford: Oxford University Press, 2000).

Thomson, A., 'Memory and Remembering in Oral History' in Ritchie, D. (ed.), *The Oxford Handbook of Oral History* (Oxford: Oxford University Press, 2010), 77–91.

Thornton, S., *Club Cultures: Music, Media and Subcultural Capital* (Cambridge: Polity Press, 1995).

Tinkler, P., 'An All-Round Education: The Board of Education's Policy for the Leisure Time Training of Girls', *History of Education*, 23:4 (1994), 384–403, https://doi.org/10.1080/0046760940230404.

Tinkler, P., '"Are You Really Living?" If Not, "Get With It!"', *Cultural and Social History*, 11:4 (2014), 597–619, https://doi.org/10.2752/147800414X14056862572186.

Tinkler, P., 'Cause for Concern: Young Women and Leisure, 1930–50', *Women's History Review*, 12:2 (2003), 233–262, https://doi.org/10.1080/09612020300200359.

Tinkler, P., *Constructing Girlhood: Popular Magazines for Girls Growing Up in England, 1920–1950* (London: Routledge, 1995).

Tisdall, L., 'Education, Parenting and Concepts of Childhood in England, c. 1945 to c. 1979', *Contemporary British History*, 31:1 (2017), 24–46, https://doi.org/10.1080/13619462.2016.1226808.

Todd, S., 'Phoenix Rising: Working-Class Life and Urban Reconstruction, c. 1945–1967', *Journal of British Studies*, 54:3 (2015), 679–702, https://doi.org/10.1017/jbr.2015.55.

Todd, S., Young, H., 'Baby-Boomers to "Beanstalkers": Making the Modern Teenager in Post-War Britain', *Cultural and Social History*, 9:3 (2012), 451–467, https://doi.org/10.2752/147800412X13347542916747.

Valentine, G., *Public Space and the Culture of Childhood* (London: Routledge, 2004).

Valentine, G., Holloway, S., Jayne, M., 'Generational Patterns of Alcohol Consumption: Continuity and Change', *Health and Place*, 16:5 (2010), 916–925, https://doi.org/10.1016/j.healthplace.2010.05.003.

Valverde, M., *Diseases of the Will: Alcohol and the Dilemmas of Freedom* (Cambridge: Cambridge University Press, 1998).

Valverde, M., *Law's Dream of a Common Knowledge* (Princeton, NJ: Princeton University Press, 2003).

van der Steen, B., Verburgh, T. (eds), *Researching Subcultures, Myth and Memory* (London: Palgrave Macmillan, 2020).

Vickers, J. E., *A Popular History of Sheffield* (Wakefield: EP Publishing, 1978).

Walkowitz, J., *Nights Out: Life in Cosmopolitan London* (New Haven, CT: Yale University Press, 2012).

Wetherell, S., *Foundations: How the Built Environment Made Twentieth-Century Britain* (Princeton, NJ: Princeton University Press, 2020).

Wetherell, S., 'Painting the Crisis: Community Arts and the Search for the "Ordinary" in 1970s and '80s London', *History Workshop Journal*, 76:1 (2013), 235–249, https://doi.org/10.1093/hwj/dbt008.

Widdicombe, S., Wooffitt, R., '"Being" Versus "Doing" Punk: On Achieving Authenticity as a Member', *Journal of Language and Social Psychology*, 9:4 (1990), 257–277, https://doi.org/10.1177/0261927X9094003.

Wildman, C., *Urban Redevelopment and Modernity in Liverpool and Manchester, 1918–1939* (London: Bloomsbury, 2016).

Williams, J. P., 'Myth and Authenticity in Subculture Studies' in van der Steen, B., Verburgh, T. (eds), *Researching Subcultures, Myth and Memory* (London: Palgrave Macmillan, 2020), 35–54.

Williams, R., 'Night Spaces: Darkness, Deterritorialization, and Social Control', *Space and Culture*, 11:4 (2008), 514–532, https://doi.org/10.1177/1206331208320117.

Wilson, B., *Fight, Flight, or Chill: Subcultures, Youth, and Rave into the Twenty-First Century* (Montreal, QC: McGill Queen's University Press, 2006).

Withers, C. W. J., 'Place and the "Spatial Turn" in Geography and in History', *Journal of the History of Ideas*, 40:4 (2009), 637–658, https://doi.org/10.1353/jhi.0.0054.

Bibliography

Woodman, D., Bennett, A. (eds), *Youth Cultures, Transitions, and Generations: Bridging the Gap in Youth Research* (London: Palgrave Macmillan, 2015).

Woolley, E., *The Golden Years of Merseybeat* (Liverpool: Bluecoat Press, 2008).

Worley, M., *No Future: Punk, Politics, and British Youth Culture, 1976–1984* (Cambridge, Cambridge University Press, 2017).

Worley, M., 'Past! Future! In Extreme!: Looking for Meaning in the "New Romantics", 1978–82', *Journal of British Studies* (2024, advanced online access), 1–26, https://doi.org/10.1017/jbr.2024.57.

Yeomans, H., *Alcohol and Moral Regulation: Public Attitudes, Spirited Measures and Victorian Hangovers* (Bristol: Policy Press, 2014).

Yokoe, R., *Alcohol and Liver Cirrhosis in Twentieth-Century Britain* (London: Palgrave Macmillan, 2023).

Zeleny Bishop, S., 'Inner-City Possibilities: Using Place and Space to Facilitate Inter-Ethnic Dating and Romance in 1960s–1980s Leicester', *Urban History*, 50:2 (2023), 232–247, https://doi.org/10.1017/S0963926821000742.

Index

Note: Published works are indexed under the author's name. 'n.' after a page reference indicates the number of a note on that page.

19 162

Aberdeen 44
Abra, Allison 12, 68, 71
Abrams, Mark 7, 39
acid house *see* rave
Albemarle Report 6
Albiez, Sean 10
alcohol 74, 96, 105–107, 112–114,
  115–127, 137–168 *passim*, 181,
  184, 210–211
  gender 100, 137–138, 142–144, 146,
    149, 156–160
  off-licences 109, 145–146
  regulation 74, 105, 108, 112, 115,
    117–127, 140
  research 106–107, 141–145,
    147–148
  temperance 56, 105, 119, 139–
    141, 167
  underage drinking 6, 19, 106–107,
    110, 112–113, 120, 122, 128,
    137–138, 140–146, 157, 170n.33,
    210–211
Ale Houses Act (1551) 108
Arnett, Jeffrey 177

Back, Les 46
Bailey, Peter 11
Bailey Organisation 81–84, 88–89, 209
Baldwin, Peter 97, 99
Band of Hope 139
Bartie, Angela 11, 139
Baun, Dylan 14
BBC 31, 60n.14
Bean, J. P. 150

beat clubs 1, 3, 11, 20, 31–32, 49–58
  passim, 74, 101–104, 112, 149,
  159, 206, 209
  licensing 52–56, 112
  membership 49–50, 53, 101
  opening hours 49–50, 53, 89, 102
  public attitudes 31, 53–54, 56–57,
    102, 104, 159, 209
  regulation 49, 54, 101–103, 112
Beckingham, David 108
Bennett, Andy 10, 180, 188, 197
Birkenhead 45, 70
Birmingham 1, 36, 45, 50, 74, 75, 100
Blackburn 35
Blackpool 48
Blackpool Tower Company 48, 84
Blunkett, David 115
Boultwood, Anne 193
Boys' Brigade 43
Brabazon, Tara 180
Bradford 45
Bradley, Kate 40, 42, 45
Brighton 70, 79, 101, 103
Bristol 37, 71–72, 76, 83
British Cohort Study (1970) 144
Brocken, Michael 151
Brooke, Henry (1903–1984), Home
  Secretary (1962–1964) 102
Brown, Callum 56
Brownies 43
Butler, Shane 109

cabaret 1, 16, 33, 69, 73, 74, 83,
  88–90, 111, 180
Cambridge 85, 86
Caslin, Samantha 100

Index

243

Centre for Contemporary Cultural
 Studies *see* subculture, theory
Charnock, Hannah 18, 162–163, 167
Chatterton, Paul 13, 25n.44, 69,
 163, 165
Chester 79, 141
Chicago, IL 102
Children Act (1908) 140
cinemas 5, 12, 35, 37, 47, 66, 69, 70,
 77–80, 91n.9, 98, 104, 115
 popularity 39, 42, 44, 67–68, 77, 79
 redevelopment 48, 79, 81, 84, 88,
 112, 207, 209
Clarke, John 9
Clements, Charlotte 44
clothing 10, 34, 68–69, 174, 188–189,
 192–202 *passim*
Cloyd, Jerald 163
Coalville 75
Cocker, Jarvis 212
coffee bars 1, 11, 13, 16, 20, 32, 38–47
 passim, 49, 57, 58, 78, 100–102,
 104–105, 158, 206, 209
 appeal 32, 38–40, 42–45, 57,
 89, 207
 moral panics 32–33, 38, 40–41, 53,
 98, 100–101, 103
Coffield, Frank 182
Cohen, Stanley 7
Coslett, Tess 18
courting 8, 10, 12, 73, 105, 152, 156,
 159, 161, 163, 166, 200, 207
 sexual encounters 83, 162–167
 passim
Coventry 35, 48
Crewe 70, 85
Criminal Justice Act (1982) 96

Daily Herald 40
Daily Mail 104, 106, 141
Daily Mirror 36, 84, 100, 105, 141
dance floors 6, 21, 32, 53, 58, 65, 73,
 113–114, 124–127, 164–166, 168,
 177, 183, 206
 changing uses 47–48, 54, 71, 73–75,
 84, 88, 90, 112–113, 124–125,
 127, 164, 168, 207
 sexual encounters 73, 83, 98,
 104–105, 161, 162–168 *passim*,
 173n.103, 207
dance halls 1, 12, 32–33, 37, 39, 42,
 44, 46–47, 58, 63n.81, 68, 69,

 73–74, 78, 80–81, 88, 91n.13,
 103–105, 142–144, 157, 184,
 206, 209
 door policies 16, 76, 86–87, 90, 105
 redevelopment 12, 47, 65, 73–75,
 77, 79, 82, 84, 88, 90, 112,
 128, 209
 regulation 48, 74, 86, 96, 103–104
Darwen 75
dating *see* courting
Davies, John 142–143
Davis, John 108
Downs, Carolyn 75
Dunn, Nick 99

Eastbourne 44
Edinburgh 75
education *see* school
Education Act (1944) 7
Electric and Music Industries (EMI) 20,
 66, 81–85, 89, 185
Erroll Committee 109–110, 119

Falkirk 101
family *see* parental regulations
fashion *see* clothing
Feldman-Barrett, Christine 9
Fenton, Laura 156
First World War 11, 68, 97, 156
Fogg, Marnie 37
folk music 150–151
Fowler, David 7
friendship 1–3, 8, 10–11, 21, 46,
 58, 83, 142, 149–155 *passim*,
 159–160, 164–166, 168, 176–178,
 181–186 *passim*, 192, 195–196,
 199, 207, 209, 211–212
Frith, Simon 10
Fuhg, Felix 14, 33, 87, 175

Gaumont-British 77
Gildart, Keith 3, 40, 175
Girl Guides *see* Brownies
Glasgow 39, 79, 142
Gloucester 37
Guardian 44, 206
Gutzke, David 146, 156–157

Hadfield, Phil 157, 163
Halbwachs, Maurice 18
Hall, Granville Stanley 6
Hall, Lesley 162

244 *Index*

Hall, Stuart 9, 104, 187
Hamburg 13
Harrison, Laura 8, 14, 19, 98, 175
Haslam, Dave 185
Hawker, Ann 143–145
Hebdige, Dick 187
Henry, William 'Lez' 46
Hesmondhalgh, David 17
Hogarth, William (1697–1764),
    Artist 139
Hoggart, Richard 6, 9, 38, 39
Hollands, Robert 13, 25n.44, 69, 160,
    163, 165, 190
Horn, Adrian 40
Houlbrook, Matt 99
House of Commons 96
House of Lords 96, 103, 137
Hull 70, 83
Hurd, Douglas (b. 1930), Home
    Secretary (1985–1989) 107, 147

ice rinks 37, 65, 71, 80, 84, 87–89, 207
Intoxicating Liquor Act (1923) 140

Jackson, Lee 67
Jackson, Louise 11, 40, 49, 56, 139
Jefferson, Tony 9, 187
Jenks, Chris 15
Jephcott, Pearl 6, 7, 39, 41, 61n.34,
    104, 157, 184
Jerrard, Robert 193
Justice of the Peace 110, 119

Kahn-Harris, Keith 10
Kefford, Alistair 66
King, Laura 6

Langhamer, Claire 162, 177
Latham, Emma 43
Leeds 35, 139
Leeworthy, Daryl 164
Lefebvre, Henri 14
Leicester 70, 81, 84, 86
leisure
    access to 2, 15, 33–38 passim, 42,
        68–69, 74, 85, 104, 155–156,
        193–198 passim, 212
    class 11, 36, 51, 176, 179, 193–202
        passim, 210
    gender 15, 56, 63n.93, 69, 99, 101,
        105, 156–167 passim, 173n.103,
        179, 181, 184, 210–211

industry 66–69, 71–75, 79–81,
    83–87 passim, 97, 124–127, 146,
    163, 208
marker of cultural identity 180–193
    passim
race 16–17, 41, 45–46, 86–87, 90,
    179, 181, 184–185, 192, 212
region 3, 8, 11, 14–15, 39, 74–77,
    85–86, 97, 153, 175, 182, 193,
    207–208, 212
regulation 15, 49–58 passim,
    97–102, 111, 113–127
licensing 16–17, 19, 41, 49–58 passim,
    86, 88–89, 96–103, 105, 108–129
    passim, 140, 145, 207, 210
    alcohol 48, 51, 55, 74, 101, 105–
        106, 108–110, 112–129
    capacity 88, 113, 122–123, 125–127
    local policy 74, 96, 97, 112–128, 207
    music 41, 88, 103, 112, 125
    regulatory tool 48–49, 54–57,
        96–97, 103, 108–129 passim,
        131n.64, 210
    Special Hours Certificate 104–105,
        109, 113, 124
Licensing Act (1961) 109, 145
Licensing Act (1964) 103, 109
Licensing Act (1988) 109
Licensing Act (2003) 110, 146
live music 3, 32, 45–56 passim, 58,
    65, 70, 73–74, 81, 83–84, 88, 90,
    112, 115, 125, 150, 152, 183,
    190, 192
Liverpool 36, 43, 48–50, 81, 84, 85,
    100, 179
Liverpool Echo 44
Local Government Act (1974) 155
London 1, 4, 11–14 passim, 19, 31, 33,
    36, 38–40, 46, 48, 49, 68, 78, 84,
    85, 99–105 passim, 109, 114, 143,
    147, 175
    Greater London Council 105, 114, 166
Lury, Celia 18
Luton 79
Lynch, Charlie 101

Mablethorpe 195
MacDonald, Robert 10, 193
Macnab, Geoffrey 78
mainstream, idea of 16, 19, 21, 66,
    166, 175, 181, 187–193, 199,
    201–202, 211

Index

Manchester 34, 36, 40, 46, 49, 50, 56, 101, 186, 198
Manning, Sam 78
Margate 32
marriage 1, 152, 156, 158, 167, 177–180
Marwick, Arthur 109
Masham Report *see* Working Group on Young People and Alcohol
Massey, Doreen 14, 186
Mass Observation 70–71, 140
Mays, John Barron 39
Mecca 17, 20, 65–66, 70–77, 79, 81–82, 84, 86, 89, 98, 124–127, 163, 185, 209
  dance halls 71–77 *passim*, 81, 85, 88, 124, 163
  Fairley, Alan 70–71, 74
  Heimann, Carl 70–71
  inter-war success 69–71
  nightclubs 74–77, 87–90, 96, 124–127, 163, 185
Melbourne 13
Milestone, Katie 40
Mills, Helena 8, 18, 158–159
mods 7, 11, 16, 55, 96
Mold, Alex 142
Moran, Joe 39, 40
Morse, Mary 43
Muggleton, David 10

National Association of Mixed Clubs and Girls Clubs (NAMGC) 43
National Child Development Survey (1958) 144
Newcastle 50, 75–76
New Towns Act (1946) 34
Nicholls, James 109, 118
nightclubs 1–2, 6, 11–13, 48, 58, 65, 73, 75, 82–84, 86–88, 90, 111, 115–127 *passim*, 149, 154–156, 163–167, 180, 185, 190–193, 207, 211
  door policies 86–87, 90, 164–166, 184–185
  marker of identity 83, 181–193
  moral panics 100, 104–105, 122
  regulation 86–87, 116–118, 120–127, 164
night-time economy 3, 6, 12–13, 49, 58, 66–67, 69, 74–76, 81–84, 89–90, 97, 99–105 *passim*, 107–108,

114, 127, 147, 153–156, 159–160, 163, 180–181, 184–185, 193, 208, 210
  post-war redevelopment 1–2, 58, 69, 79–81, 111, 209
  regulation 6, 54, 74, 96–97, 99, 103, 113–114, 120–127 *passim*, 184–185
Noise Abatement Act (1960) 54
northern soul 87
Norwich 76
Nott, James 12, 48, 71, 86
Nottingham 119

Odeon 77, 91n.9
Oldham 79
Osgerby, Bill 7, 9, 35, 177

parental regulations 41, 153, 157–159, 207
parenting 177–180
Pascoe Leahy, Carla 14
Payling, Daisy 5, 46
Peterborough Advertiser 40
Petticoat 141
Phillips, Damien 100
Plant, Martin 144
Plant, Moira 144
Plymouth 79, 85
police 17, 32, 49, 53, 56, 74, 98, 100–103, 106, 113, 120–121, 123, 147, 149
Portelli, Allesandro 18
Portsmouth 79
Preston 79
Private Places of Entertainment (Licensing) Act (1967) 49, 55, 56, 63–64n.94, 74, 103, 104
Public Health Act (1936) 54
public houses 3, 11, 16, 38, 41, 49, 55, 58, 74, 81, 84, 86, 106, 110, 112–113, 123, 128, 137–144 *passim*, 149–153, 168, 177, 207
  attendance at 140, 142–144, 149–153, 157–160, 186
  avoidance of 41–42, 51, 55, 74, 156–159
  live music 44–45, 112–113, 128, 144, 150–152
  redevelopment and redesign 81, 84, 110, 146, 152, 157, 165, 168, 179
  regulation 101, 109–110, 112–113, 140

Index

public transport 34, 37, 41, 51, 153–156, 172n.69, 207, 211
punk 8, 11, 12, 16, 86, 104, 188, 190, 200

Rank Organisation 17, 20, 66, 70, 72, 74, 76–82, 84–86, 88, 90, 103, 185, 209
  dance halls 78–79, 85–86
  financial strategy 78–81
  nightclubs 81, 89–90, 152, 158, 183, 185, 190
  Rank, J. Arthur 77, 79
  Xerox 78
rave 11, 179, 186, 200, 203n.13
Redhead, Steve 10
Richards, Jeffrey 77
Robinson, Lucy 208
rockers *see* mods
Rotherham 68
Russell, Dave 16, 83

Saumarez Smith, Otto 35
Savage, Jon 7, 185
Schofield, Camilla 16
Schofield, Michael 162
school 5, 19, 42–43, 45, 77, 116, 148, 152–153, 194, 196–197
  friends *see* friendship
  uniform 153, 196, 204–205n.43
Scouts 43
Second World War 4, 6, 34, 48, 68, 140n.171
sexual encounters *see* courting; dance floors
sexual encounters, unwanted 165–166, 168
Sheffield 1, 3–4, 17, 31, 41, 44, 46, 48, 50–58 *passim*, 65, 75, 82, 88–89, 96, 111–129 *passim*, 138, 147, 149–160 *passim*, 164–168, 176, 181, 185, 188, 190, 194, 197, 200, 207
  city centre 35–36, 40, 88, 121, 154–156, 185, 190
  city council 1, 54, 114–116
  demographics 4–5, 46, 182
  economy 4, 116, 156, 194, 196, 206–207
  local politics 5, 111, 114–116, 155, 196
  post-war redevelopment 4–5, 35–36, 111, 206–207

suburbs 19, 40, 42, 48, 53, 55, 112–114, 118, 153
Shildrick, Tracy 10, 193
shopping 3, 34–38, 40, 57, 66, 75, 111, 188, 193, 196–199, 201
  boutiques 37, 57, 68, 89, 197
  charity shops and second hand 196–198, 201
  leisure activity 37–38, 89, 195, 197–199, 207
  records 37, 196
skinheads 11, 16
Sleight, Simon 13
Sneeringer, Julia 13
Stacey, Barrie 142–143
Stage, The 1, 17, 73, 84
Star 31, 44, 48, 53, 55, 115, 165
Steedman, Carolyn 194
Stevenage 85
Stockport 68
Stratton, Jon 163, 165
Stringfellow, Geoff 50–55 *passim*, 57
Stringfellow, Peter 50–55 *passim*, 57
students 7, 46, 58, 150–151, 153–154, 171n.67, 190, 196–198, 204n.34, 212
subculture 9–10, 15–19 *passim*, 87, 174, 181, 186–193 *passim*, 198, 200, 205n.49
  theory 9–10, 23n.28, 186–187, 204n.29
Summerfield, Penny 18
Sunday Entertainments Act (1932) 78
Sunday Mirror 85
Sunday Times 103
Swindon 73

Tebbutt, Melanie 7, 8, 12
teddy boys 32, 41, 48, 103
ten-pin bowling 37, 69, 70, 78–81, 84, 88, 90, 207
Thatcher, Margaret (1925–2013), Prime Minister (1979–1990) 106, 109, 147
Thornton, Sarah 10
Thornton, Terry 31, 48, 50–53
Tinkler, Penny 43, 97
Todd, Selina 14, 36
Top Rank *see* Rank Organisation
Top Star Special 48, 50–53, 65
townie *see* mainstream, idea of
Trusthouse Forte 84–85
two-tone 19, 200

Index

unemployment 4–5, 114–116, 147, 155, 194, 196
urban space
  deindustrialisation, effects of 47, 111–112, 156
  night 2, 21n.3, 53, 55, 58, 88–89, 96–99, 100–101, 103–107, 111, 120–121, 127–128, 137–138, 146–147, 153–158 *passim*, 181, 206, 208, 211
  post-war redevelopment 2, 33–38, 58, 60n.10, 66, 79–81, 88, 98, 111–115 *passim*, 117–122 *passim*, 206–207, 209
  regulation 2, 50–56, 96–97, 99–102, 111–124 *passim*

Valentine, Gill 98, 149, 158
Valverde, Mariana 108–109
van der Steen, Bart 174
Verburgh, Thierry 174

wages 21, 34, 37, 68, 147, 152, 154, 159, 177–178, 194, 199–200
Wakefield 76
Weinzierl, Rupert 10
Welwyn Garden City 40
Whitbread 81
Williams, J. P. 187
Willmott, Peter 39
Withers, Charles W. J. 14

Working Group on Young People and Alcohol 27n.72, 106–107, 137, 143, 145, 147–148
Working Party on Juvenile Jazz and Dance Clubs in the West End of London 101–103
Worley, Matthew 8
Worthing 48

York 14
youth
  attitudes to 8, 32, 97–98, 100, 107, 122, 141, 146–147, 158, 210
  definition of 3, 15, 17, 19–20, 22n.12, 146, 177–180
  leisure and consumption patterns 20, 44, 49, 57–58, 68, 78, 90, 103, 106, 111, 113, 137, 141–147 *passim*, 149–167 *passim*, 174, 176, 181–186, 208–210
  reflections on 18–19, 175–176
  research into 6–7, 9–10, 17, 39, 106–107, 141, 162, 187
  transitions out of 15, 177–180
youth clubs 5, 33, 37, 38, 42–47, 57, 58, 62n.56, 78, 106, 182, 209
  religion 44–47, 52
  role of 43, 45–46, 52

Zeleny Bishop, Sue 86

EU authorised representative for GPSR:
Easy Access System Europe, Mustamäe tee 50,
10621 Tallinn, Estonia
gpsr.requests@easproject.com